Work in Progress

Occupational Therapy in Work Programs

Edited by

Sarah Hertfelder and Carol Gwin

American Occupational Therapy Association

American Occupational Therapy Association
1383 Piccard Drive
P. O. Box 1725
Rockville, MD 20850-0822

© 1989 by the American Occupational Therapy Association, Inc.
All rights reserved. Published 1989
Printed in the United States of America

Editing and text design by Edelfelt Johnson, Chapel Hill, North Carolina
Cover design by Robert Sacheli

ISBN 0-910317-54-2

Contents

Foreword		*ix*
Acknowledgments		*xi*
About the Authors		*xiii*
Introduction		***1***
Sarah Hertfelder and Carol Gwin		

1 *Work Is a Four-Letter Word! A Historical Perspective* — **3**
Robert K. Bing

Evolution of the Work Ethic	5
The Grecians and the Hebrews	5
Early Christians	7
The Reformation	8
The American Transformation	10
The Usefulness Doctrine	10
The Industrial Work Ethic	12
The Postindustrial Age	14
Functions of Work	16
Contemporary Meanings of the Work Ethic	17
Definition of Work	19

2 *Use of Department of Labor References and Job Analysis* — **23**
Karen Jacobs and Joane Wyrick

History of the *Dictionary of Occupational Titles*	24
Descriptions of Specific Occupational References	25
Guide for Occupational Exploration	26
Dictionary of Occupational Titles	28

Selected Characteristics of Occupations Defined in the "Dictionary of Occupational Titles"	33
Classification of Jobs According to Worker Trait Factors	35
Guide to Job Analysis	38
Application of the References	40
Computerized Systems	41
Job Analysis	43
Purpose of Job Analysis	43
Typical Content of Job Analysis	44
Work Performed and Worker Characteristics	44
Criteria for Assessing Physical Demands	45
Methods of Job Analysis	45
Preparation	45
Suggested Equipment for an On-Site Job Analysis	46
Summary	46
Glossaries	47
Abbreviations	47
Terms	47
Appendix 2-A, Job Analysis Schedule	52
Appendix 2-B, Occupational Therapy Job Analysis	56

3   *Work Hardening*   67
Melanie T. Ellexson

Workers' Compensation Laws	69
Program Development	70
Market Analysis	70
Elements for Site Location	71
Staffing Patterns and Ratios	71
Space Requirements	72
Equipment	74
Milieu	76
Structure	78
Program Design	82
Scheduling	82
Evaluation	82
Content	84
Documentation	85
Reimbursement	86
Marketing and Public Relations	87
Summary	89
Case Study: Doug Ramm	91
Glossary	96
Appendix 3-A, Resources: Work Hardening	101
Appendix 3-B, Occupational Therapy Physical Capacities Evaluation	103

	Appendix 3-C, Work Performance Evaluation	114
	Appendix 3-D, Work Activity Record Program Samples	121
	Appendix 3-E, Work Activity Records: Doug Ramm	124

4   *Ergonomics and the Occupational Therapist*   127
Ellen Rader Smith

Introduction to Ergonomics	128
Historical Background	129
Anthropometrics	131
Biomechanics and Work Load Factors	131
Job Analysis	132
Job Station Design	134
Adapting Seated Work	137
Adapting Standing Workplaces	140
Musculoskeletal Injury Prevention	141
Cumulative Trauma Disorders	141
Manual Material Handling Injuries	142
Tools	144
Ergonomic Principles	146
Information-Processing and Environmental Issues	146
Implementing an Ergonomics Program	148
Summary	149
Glossary	150
Appendix 4-A, Resources: Tool Manufacturers	156

5   *The Transition from School to Adult Life*   157
Karen Spencer

The Transition Initiative	158
Transition: An Interdisciplinary and Interagency Process	160
Occupational Therapy and the Transition Process	161
Assessment	161
Program Planning	162
Program Implementation	165
Summary	165
Glossary	166
Appendix 5-A, Transition-Planning Time Line	169
Appendix 5-B, Current Levels of Functioning/Needs	171
Appendix 5-C, Transition-Planning Areas	172
Appendix 5-D, Transition Plan	176

6   *Overview of Supported Employment*   181
Karen Spencer

Supported Employment: A National Priority	181
Characteristics of Supported Employment Service	183

	Occupational Therapy and Supported Employment	184
	Assessment	184
	Individualized Program Planning	185
	Program Implementation	186
	Supported Employment Approaches in Common Use	186
	Individual Job Placement	187
	Enclave	187
	Mobile Work Crew	188
	Summary	189
	Glossary	190
	Appendix 6-A, Job Analysis Terminology and Forms	192

7   *Intervention in Traumatic Head Injury: Learning Style Assessment*   *197*

Carol J. Wheatley and Judy J. Rein

Learning Style Assessment	197
Determining the Optimal Method of Presentation	198
Identifying the Best Retention Strategies	199
Ascertaining the Optimal Environment	200
Assessing Metacognitive Capacity	200
Conducting a Learning Style Assessment	200
Applying the Findings from a Learning Style Assessment	202
Management Strategies	202
Environmental Restructuring	203
Vocational Rehabilitation	205
Alternatives to Traditional Vocational Rehabilitation	206
Summary	208
Glossary	208

8   *Prevention*   *213*

Joy White Danches

Definitions of Prevention, Health Promotion, and Wellness	213
Prevention	213
Health Promotion and Wellness	215
Prevention Providers	216
Rationale for the Occupational Therapist as a Prevention Provider	217
Industrial Injury Prevention	218
Job Site Redesign	218
Preplacement Screening	219
Training Programs for Industrial Injury Prevention	221

	Health Promotion	227
	FMC Health Promotion	227
	AT&T Health Promotion	228
	Health and Religion Project	228
	Massachusetts Department of Public Health	228
	Design of Injury Prevention and Health Promotion Programs	229
	Health-Risk Appraisals	229
	National Health Surveys	229
	Injury Statistics	230
	Socioeconomic Considerations Relating to Employees	231
	Marketing	231
	Future Work Force Trends and Opportunities	232
	Summary	235
	Glossary	235
	Appendix 8-A, Participant Survey	244
	Appendix 8-B, Trainer's Posttest	246

9   *The Occupational Therapist as an Expert Witness*   249
Doris J. Shriver

Rules Governing Evidence	249
Qualifications of an Expert Witness	251
General Application	251
Qualifying the Occupational Therapist as an Expert	252
Evidence	254
General Application	254
Evidence Provided by the Occupational Therapist	255
Testimony	256
Cross-Examination	258
Depositions and Interrogatories	260
Testimony from the Occupational Therapist	261
Do's and Don'ts of Expert Testimony	262
Summary	269
Glossary	270

Appendixes   *275*

A	*Resources*	275
B	*Work Hardening Guidelines*	277
C	*The Role of Occupational Therapy in the Vocational Rehabilitation Process*	281
D	*Occupational Therapy Services in Work Programs*	285
E	*Occupational Therapy Services in Work Hardening*	287
F	*Significant Legislation Related to Work*	289

Foreword

Occupational therapy's beginnings in the world of work can be traced to the founders and the early leaders of the profession. The writings of Herbert J. Hall, William Rush Dunton, Jr., George Edward Barton, and Thomas B. Kidner all addressed the importance of work as part of occupational therapy's focus and purpose. The profession's first educational standards, established in 1923, included the intent for occupational therapists to be engaged in work activities.

The importance of work testing in a "reality situation or work sample method" was the focus of Lilian Wegg's 1959 Eleanor Clarke Slagle Lecture. She used terms such as *work capacities, work tolerance, work habits,* and *work aptitudes* to explain essentials of a work evaluation program in occupational therapy.

This book continues the efforts of occupational therapy's founders and leaders to describe the profession's role in work programs. More directly it builds on the success of such AOTA efforts as a 1982 grant from the Office of Special Education and Rehabilitative Services that resulted in a continuing education curriculum entitled *Planning and Implementing Vocational Readiness in Occupational Therapy* (PIVOT) and a series of workshops based on the curriculum; the May 1985 issue of the *American Journal of Occupational Therapy* (AJOT), which was devoted entirely to work evaluation; the establishment of a Work Programs Special Interest Section in 1985; and passage by the Representative Assembly in 1986 of *Work Hardening Guidelines.*

External forces also gave impetus to this book. Recent legislation in rehabilitation, transition, and supported employment has led to many new programs focused on employing people with disabilities. The Commission on Accreditation of

Rehabilitation Facilities has for the first time published standards for work hardening.

For occupational therapy all of this is indeed "work in progress."

Jeanette Bair, Executive Director
American Occupational Therapy Association

Acknowledgments

Many people contributed to the production of this book, and we want to acknowledge them. Melanie Ellexson and Karen Jacobs not only wrote chapters but also acted as project advisers. The following people reviewed the content at various stages of manuscript development:

Susan Bachner	Frances Palmer
Carolyn Baum	Lillian Hoyle Parent
Jane Bear-Lehman	Sharon Rask
Teresa H. Bryan	Kathlyn L. Reed
Florence S. Cromwell	Sue Rhomberg
Rosemarie Cristelli	Kathleen A. Rickert
Julie DeBacker	Barbara Schell
Virginia Dickie	Kathy Schuster
Mary Ann Empson	James Scussel
Geri Harrand	Kristin Seidner
Betty Hasselkus	Betsy Slavik
Lois Hickman	Susan L. Smith
Dora M. Hutchens	L. Randy Strickland
Anne M. Laband	Sallie Taylor
Milana Lock	Karen Verbeke
Edwinna Marshall	Shirley Vulpe
Louise Montague	Marilyn Colvin Wright
Terrie Nolinske	Joane Wyrick
Linda Ogden-Niemeyer	

We also thank Margo Johnson, who edited the manuscript; AOTA's Publications Division, which supervised production;

and Wendy Schoen, secretary in the Practice Division, whose organizational abilities and attention to detail kept us on track from the beginning to the end of the project.

Sarah Hertfelder, Director

Carol Gwin, Assistant Director and Technology Program Manager

Practice Division
American Occupational Therapy Association

About the Authors

Robert K. Bing, EdD, OTR, FAOTA, is retired and living in Galveston, Texas, after nearly four decades as a clinician, administrator, and professor. He is a fellow of the American Occupational Therapy Association (AOTA); the 1981 Eleanor Clarke Slagle lecturer; a recipient of the AOTA Award of Merit; and a former AOTA president (1983–1986). Through his interests in the philosophy and the history of occupational therapy, he has written a play, *Point of Departure*. Currently he is working on a biographical novel about Eleanor Clarke Slagle.

Joy White Danches (formerly Joy White Randolph), MOT, OTR, CIRS, serves as marketing director of Health Enhancement Learning Programs (HELP), Inc., a medical and health promotion software company. She is also a health care consultant to Ortho Rehab Associates, mediating reimbursement, legislative, and clinical issues for this private practice in orthopedics and therapy. Previously she was vice president of Back Systems, Inc., a specialty risk management firm that contracted with industry to provide back injury prevention services and with insurance companies to provide cost containment services. Ms. Randolph has served on the Board of Directors of the Texas Occupational Therapy Association for five years as chair of the Council on Development and the Marketing Task Force. She received her undergraduate degree in human services from the University of Tennessee and her master's degree from Texas Woman's University.

Melanie T. Ellexson, OTR/L, is the director of Schwab Rehabilitation Center's STEPS Industrial Injury Clinics in Chicago, Illinois. She currently serves as chair of AOTA's Work Programs Special Interest Section. Ms. Ellexson has contributed extensively to industrial rehabilitation and work hardening through workshops, lectures, and articles. Her earlier work with the railroad industry and as a consultant to several major industries in the Midwest has provided the background to develop work hardening concepts and models of practice. Most recently Ms. Ellexson served on the Commission on Accreditation of Rehabilitation Facilities' National Advisory Committee to develop standards of practice for work hardening.

Karen Jacobs, MS, OTR/L, FAOTA, is adjunct clinical instructor in the Occupational Therapy Department at Boston University. She is also a private practitioner in greater Boston. She has contributed extensively to work programming through various publications, lectures, and workshops. Ms. Jacobs has been the president of the Massachusetts Association for Occupational Therapy for five years, in addition to chairing the state's annual conference. She was a member of the first standing committee of the Work Programs Special Interest Section and currently serves as liaison representative.

Judy J. Rein, MS, OTR/L, is a technology specialist at the Technology Resource Office of the Maryland Rehabilitation Center, Division of Vocational Rehabilitation, Maryland State Department of Education, Baltimore. Her experience includes general practice in pediatrics and specialization in applications of microcomputers as assistive devices in vocational rehabilitation. People with traumatic brain injury are a growing segment of her current client population. Her degrees include a basic master's from Virginia Commonwealth University and a master's in technology for the handicapped at The Johns Hopkins University.

Doris J. Shriver, OTR, CVE, is owner and director of O.T. Resources, Inc., in Denver, Colorado. She holds a Bachelor of Science in occupational therapy from Colorado State University, and she is certified as a vocational evaluator. During her 15 years in private practice, she has evaluated, treated, and provided consultation in pediatrics, mental health, gerontology, and physical disabilities. She has served as the Colorado representative to AOTA, as a member of the AOTA Commission on Practice, and as a member of other professional committees. The current focus of her practice is disability evaluation, case management, and expert testimony for plaintiffs, defendants, and judges.

Ellen Rader Smith, MA, OTR, is a private practitioner in occupational therapy and ergonomics. She received a Bachelor of Science in occupational therapy from the University of Pennsylvania in 1976 and a Master of Arts in occupational biomechanics and ergonomics from New York University in 1982. Since 1982 she has worked in a variety of consulting positions. She is now actively involved in ergonomics consulting and is working in the area of video display terminals, offering services to private industry, government agencies, and vocational rehabilitation facilities. For many years she has also provided disability and functional capacity assessment to the legal and insurance communities. Before 1982 Ms. Smith was senior therapist at the Hospital for Special Surgery in New York City. She is a member of the Human Factors Society, the American Society of Safety Engineers, and the local chapter of the American Industrial Hygiene Association.

Karen Spencer, MA, OTR, is coordinator of the Office of Transition Services, Department of Occupational Therapy, Colorado State University. She also holds a faculty position at the university. Ms. Spencer's office has been the recipient of numerous federal, state, and local grants to improve secondary education and postsecondary outcomes for people with significant disabilities. These outcomes include community-integrated employment, living, and recreation. Ms. Spencer has served on AOTA's standing committee for the Developmental Disabilities Special Interest Section and on AOTA's Commission on Practice. She received her undergraduate degree in occupational therapy from the University of New Hampshire and her master's degree in education from the University of Colorado.

Carol J. Wheatley, MS, OTR/L, is assistant supervisor of occupational therapy at the Maryland Rehabilitation Center, Division of Vocational Rehabilitation, Maryland State Department of Education, Baltimore. As part of the Pathways Project at the Maryland Rehabilitation Center, she has assisted in the expansion of occupational therapy services in support of return-to-work efforts for people with traumatic brain injury. In 1986 she served on the Maryland Division of Vocational Rehabilitation's Task Force for Services for the Traumatic Head Injured. Ms. Wheatley is a graduate of Virginia Commonwealth University's School of Occupational Therapy and has a Master of Science in education from The Johns Hopkins University. Since 1981 she has chaired the Cognitive/Visual Perceptual Special Interest Section of the Maryland Occupational Therapy Association.

Joane M. Wyrick, MA, OTR, FAOTA, is a graduate of the University of Kansas. She was formerly chair of the occupational therapy curriculum at the University of Kansas and is currently on the faculty of the University of Kansas Medical Center. She has served as a member and as chair of many national professional councils and is now on the Steering Committee of the AOTA Work Programs Special Interest Section. For over six years she has been engaged in private practice in personal injury evaluation.

Introduction

Carol Gwin, OTR
Sarah Hertfelder, MEd, MOT, OTR

The reader may wonder what the editors' message is in titling this book *Work in Progress:* Do they intend to convey the common, general interpretation that efforts are under way but not complete? —the idea that a particular practice area in occupational therapy is enjoying renewed attention? —the idea that purposeful activity contributes to advancement in habilitation and rehabilitation? The fact is that they intend all of these meanings.

Work in Progress is an attempt to capture and disseminate current thinking about an area of practice that has deep, strong roots in the profession, but is clearly undergoing a growth spurt. The book is offered as an aid to practitioners already engaged in work programming and an assist to specialists in other areas who are considering alternatives.

It is not intended to be all-inclusive. Rather it is an overview of the many aspects of occupational therapy in work programs.

In the opening chapter, "Work Is a Four-Letter Word!," Robert Bing offers a broad historical perspective on the phenomenon of work, with particular attention to the work ethic. Looking well beyond the bounds of this country and this century, he tracks work philosophies back to preindustrial times among the Grecians and the Hebrews. Other important contributions in this chapter are a definition of work and a delineation of its functions.

In the next three chapters Karen Jacobs and Joane Wyrick, Melanie Ellexson, and Ellen Rader Smith describe three aspects of practice in work programming. Occupational therapists helping clients find jobs suited to their skills and physical capacities will be greatly aided by Jacobs and Wyrick's discussion, "Use of Department of Labor References and Job Analysis." The two authors provide clear explanations of the purposes and the uses of the numerous occupational reference books published by the Department of Labor. They also decode the acronyms that abound in this realm—DOT, GOE, COJ, and more.

Professionals offering therapy to many types of clients, but particularly to workers who have sustained industrial injuries, will be drawn to Ellexson's contribution, "Work Hardening." This chapter not only explains work hardening as a phase of industrial rehabilitation but offers advice on developing and marketing a program.

Smith completes the picture in "Ergonomics and the Occupational Therapist." She characterizes the focus of ergonomics as the interaction between the worker and the workplace, and she describes its complementary relationship to occupational therapy.

Chapters 5, 6, and 7 discuss work programming with particular client populations. In the first two of these chapters, "The Transition from School to Adult Life" and "Overview of Supported Employment," Karen Spencer describes two recent federal initiatives, transition and supported employment, that have given considerable impetus to work programming with people who have developmental disabilities. Her chapters include some useful planning tools. In the next chapter, "Intervention in Traumatic Head Injury: Learning Style Assessment," Carol Wheatley and Judy Rein describe a promising approach to intervention with clients who have suffered head trauma. Basically their strategy is to identify and capitalize on a client's preferred styles of learning.

In Chapter 8, "Prevention," Joy White Danches shifts the focus from treatment to prevention, that is, from action after a problem occurs to action before it arises. She draws on the available literature and her personal experience to describe programs to prevent disease and injury, and programs to promote health and wellness.

In Chapter 9, "The Occupational Therapist as an Expert Witness," Doris Shriver primes the reader on a component of practice that occurs with unusually high frequency in work programming because of its heavy subsidization by workers' compensation and other disability benefit programs. Her chapter serves as a fitting close to the book, for any occupational therapist in work programming may at some point be called on to testify on behalf of a worker seeking benefits or an employer disputing a worker's eligibility for compensation.

Most chapters contain glossaries and suggested readings. Appended to some chapters are protocols and forms that will be useful in practice. Appendixes at the end of the book contain information and resources of general interest to occupational therapists in work programming.

1

Work Is a Four-Letter Word! A Historical Perspective

Robert K. Bing, EdD, OTR, FAOTA

Labor omnia vincit.
"Work conquers all."
—Virgil (70–19 B.C.)

In seeking the foundations of occupational therapy, any cultural anthropologist worthy of the credential would early discern the direct relationship of work to the form of treatment that employs its elements in social, physical, and emotional rehabilitation. The term *occupational therapy* has existed for about 75 years; however, its antecedents are clearly seen in moral treatment, an outcome of the dawning of the Age of Enlightenment or Reason in Europe more than 200 years ago. Moral treatment emerged from the prevailing attitudes of that day: a set of principles governing all of humanity; a faith declaring that man could reason; and a belief system placing the individual in an active and supreme position on Earth.

As becomes evident later in this chapter, work 200 years ago was everyone's responsibility, a direct, positive effort to better one's lot in life and to improve the collective society. Along came two quite different individuals with the same set of thoughts and a similar approach to employing work in the relief of suffering due to mental illness: Philippe Pinel, a French physician, and William Tuke, an English philanthropist. Pinel thought the loss of reason was the most calamitous of human afflictions. His approach to its restoration was to help the insane person gain insight into the delusional nature of the illness. Moral management included maintaining a continuity in approach, a predictable routine, and a gentle, but firm, method. These principles were incorporated into elements of work and introduced to the patient as soon as they could be tolerated, primarily to give the patient feelings of security and responsibility and a respect for authority. Work, along with other forms of activity, was designed and intended to reach man at his best, to help him become once again a responsible, rational, productive individual.

William Tuke, a devout English Quaker, helped found an institution for the insane under the direction of the Quakers in York. He became its superintendent and established his version of moral treatment, which included elements of labor. Work, along with a social environment resembling that of a family, was viewed as the preferred way for a patient to gain and maintain control over a mental disorder. The habit of attention to the details of work was stressed. Various practical exercises, such as mathematical problems of everyday living, were used to help the patient gain ascendancy over faulty habits of thinking and attention.

These early efforts at a "work cure" arrived in America as part of the Quakers' intellectual and religious luggage. Their ideals, closely akin to the Protestant ethic, served very well in establishing their social order. When they created institutions for the insane, they activated the beliefs and the practices of Tuke. Work-related activities held the seeds for recovery and return to a happy, useful, successful, and spiritual life.

Moral treatment declined almost to the point of extinction during and following the U.S. Civil War. It reemerged in the early decades of the 20th century as occupational therapy. Three quite different individuals figured prominently in defining a contemporary construct of a work cure: George Barton, William Rush Dunton, and Eleanor Clarke Slagle. Barton, an architect by profession who was debilitated by tuberculosis, founded an early prototype of a rehabilitation center. He was concerned that too many patients were being discharged from hospitals devoid of the proficiencies needed to return to home and to work. His Consolation House in Clifton Springs, New York, provided patients with elaborate medical and social history reviews and an evaluation of intellect, interests, and experiences that could be used in finding some form of gainful occupation.

Dunton, a psychiatrist, heavily depended upon his understanding of moral treatment to establish a set of principles by which work became a judicious regimen of activity for mentally ill patients. His various work centers, which he called occupational therapy shops, included a wide variety of labor-related tasks, such as farming, printing, repairing electric dynamos—nearly any kind of work that captured the attention and the interest of patients and could serve as antecedents to earning a living upon release from the hospital.

Eleanor Clarke Slagle also relied upon past successes of moral treatment in her efforts to normalize the lives of mentally ill people. She is particularly remembered for developing "habit training," a 24-hour schedule of reeducation in the habits of occupation, exercise, play, and rest. As these habits became manifest, patients were progressively moved from ward activities to advanced activity classes and ultimately to "occupational centers." There they enjoyed comparative freedom, performed actual responsibilities in productive work, and worked for themselves—all essential ingredients in an optimal existence after hospitalization.

As has been seen, the roots of contemporary occupational therapy have always existed in the subsoil of the society's work ethic. The ideas, the ideals, and the practices of the proponents of moral treatment, later of occupational therapy, spring from a simple belief that people who are sick or disabled can regain, retain, and attain some semblance of human function through the acts of making or doing—a paradigm of all human activity. The seeds of human activity contain the essential elements for recuperation and rehabilitation. The ethic of activity is synonymous with the ethic of work: to prepare the individual for a useful, happy, productive life within any limits imposed by the human organism or the condition of one's health.

Evolution of the Work Ethic

The typical historian's tendency is to take readers back to the beginning and bring them up-to-date. William Rush Dunton, Jr., one of occupational therapy's founders, insisted that the earliest form of work was Eve's crocheting of fig leaves for herself and Adam. This history will not go back that far. Rather, it will begin with the Grecians and the Hebrews.

The Grecians and the Hebrews

By the time of the Grecians' emerging importance, work had been fused with the basic need for survival through food and protection. Communal organizations had formed. Men and women worked equally hard at their tasks, men foraging for raw materials, women, largely because of their childbearing responsibilities, preserving and fashioning the materials for consumption and bartering. Their activities included agriculture, pottery, textiles, basketry, and crafting of essential tools from metals. This basic organization of work developed and remained relatively unchanged until the onset of industrialization, approximately 250 years ago.

Later the Grecians brought the class stratification of work to a fine point. To them, work was the gods' curse upon humankind, the excruciating price the gods extracted for the goods of life. No dignity, no value, was inherent in work; it was merely a means of escaping hunger and extinction or of reaching a prosperous level at which goodness, virtue, and independence might prevail. Further, the mechanical arts brutalized the mind. Craftsmen and artists were little better than slaves. They, along with peasants, were assigned the work of gathering, fashioning, and preserving the goods for survival and status. In the middle, between the slaves on the one hand and the nobility and the priests on the other hand, were the merchants and the traders, who distributed and exchanged the goods produced by others.

From this somewhat simplistic organizational structure, the Grecians sustained certain beliefs about work that greatly outlasted their civilization. Remnants may be found lying about yet today. There were those who were born to toil, and there were those who were born to live a life of leisure. The master and the nobleman either were born to that status or, through the right kinds of work and great luck, attained the position of being able to indulge in the luxuries of life, such as teaching, discovering, thinking, or composing music. So long as one was involved in the necessary toil of living, farming, or crafting objects, one could not hope to have leisure.

Socrates held an interesting viewpoint that eventually got him into trouble. "'Work is no disgrace, but idleness is,'" he often declaimed as he wandered in and out of shops, visiting artisans and artists who were performing nonessential tasks. To those who were experiencing difficulties or were bored with their tasks, he offered this prescription: "'Try a little work; it won't hurt you as much as you suspect, and a little of it may solve your problem.'" Socrates never took any large or small doses of his own medicine; he just talked about it. He was thought to be the self-appointed gadfly to the Athenians. Eventually he was chastised severely for meddling and disrupting the well-organized work structure of his day (Tilgher, 1962, pp. 9-12).

A few years later Aristotle took on the onerous task of trying to make distinctions between work, play, rest, and leisure. From his position that well-being was not the pursuit of pleasure, but the pursuit of the contemplative life, he employed his principles of explanation to identify the differences. He said nature required that humans be able to work well and to use leisure well. To him leisure was the first principle of all action; therefore it was better than work and was its own end. Play and rest (i.e., sleep) were for the sake of work, so work in turn was for the sake of leisure (deGrazia, 1962). This sat well with the Grecians, for they valued the contemplative life over other forms of nonstrenuous activity.

The Hebrews had different viewpoints. Here this account does need to go back to the beginning for just a moment. In Genesis the Lord laid down a fundamental principle because of Adam and Eve's transgression. Labor was to be the human's curse from that moment on: "Cursed is the ground because of you; in toil you shall eat of it all the days of your life. . . . In the sweat of your face you shall eat bread till you return to the ground" (Gen. 3:17–19). Thereafter, work was a painful existence for survival.

The Hebrews too held a reverence for work and the contemplative life. The Talmud states:

> The sincerest reverer of heaven is he who eateth the labor of his hand; such a man yet employing his spare time to acquire knowledge is far above him who entirely devotes himself to the study of God's word, but depends on others for his dependence. (as quoted in Rapaport, 1910, p. 91)

In another location the Talmud declares:

> Labor is a holy occupation, so that one who has no need to work for his daily bread is not absolved from doing some work. If he has an estate, let him do some labor on his field. Idleness causes untimely death. (as quoted in Rapaport, 1910, p. 223)

The Hebrews believed that labor was the way of expiating original sin. It was also a way to regain spiritual dignity. Workers in the fields were greeted and blessed by passersby. Hebrew literature subscribed to the view that the Kingdom of God would eventually arise in the world because of good will among people and the toil of humans in brotherly relationships. As Tilgher (1962) wrote,

> To work is to cooperate with God in the great purpose of the world's salvation. Man's labor tends to approach somewhat to that of God. The labor of man continues and prolongs the divine energy which overflowed in the act of creation. (p. 13)

Early Christians

Early Christians followed Hebrew thinking that work was God's punishment for original sin. In time, work took on some positive values. The bodily and spiritual health of the human was maintained through labor, particularly to the extent that it crowded out idleness and sloth, which were forms of evil. There was no intrinsic value to work; its spiritual worth came as a means to a worthwhile end—ultimate salvation.

In the early centuries of Catholicism, work was fostered as a way of delaying or avoiding despair. It was a preferred method of purification, of charity, of expiation of sin. An intrinsic value of labor had not yet been recognized. As the centuries unfolded, newer meanings took hold. Various sects arose and they defined work on the most fundamental level, as a painful, humiliating activity that counteracted sinful pride. Harsh labor in the fields was the antidote for pride and wantonness of the flesh.

Thomas Aquinas, in the 13th century, adopted Aristotelian logic for categorizing work in terms of value to society. Farming was first, handcrafts were second, commercial activities were last. Financial enterprises were not included because Aquinas believed that interest earned was not work. Rather, he insisted that profit was earned only through work or inheritance. Work was a necessity of nature. He proposed the division of society into guilds because he thought they were part of a providential plan.

As one might expect, some people worked harder than others or got lucky, and the issue of wealth, sin, and salvation reared its head. Before long, the prevailing belief system took care of that issue. If a person had the financial means not to work, that was fine; however, the person was expected to spend time in contemplation. Miserly greed made a person very unpopular with the church authorities and the neighbors. Whether wealth was good or evil depended upon how it was used for the benefit of others.

The Reformation

The thinking of Martin Luther came to bear in the very early years of the 16th century. As an innovator, he went well beyond the prevalent precepts of work. He did subscribe to the belief that work was natural, a way out of the dilemma of original sin. It was a punishment, but it was also educational in character, he thought. None of that was new. However, Luther surprised his supporters and detractors by declaring that everyone who could work should do so. Idleness, living off interest, and begging were all unnatural, in his view. Charity should be extended only to those who could not work because of infirmities or age. Everybody should earn enough for living—no more. Further, earnings should be within the boundaries imposed by the kind of work involved. In Luther's day most people were born to a trade or an occupation and were expected to stay within the confines of that sort of labor.

Luther also believed that work and serving God were synonymous. The best way to serve God was to do the very best job possible. Superiority of one kind of work over another was wiped away through the beliefs that work was related to obedience to God, that one should love one's neighbors, and that all work had its own kind of dignity. There is little wonder that the idea of work's being a calling came into vogue. One was called to one's work. Luther asserted that all activity was divinely inspired; therefore, no distinctions existed between everyday work and service to God. Thus the Protestant ethic took hold.

About a century later, as part of the Reformation, a Frenchman, John Calvin, added to some of the prevailing beliefs and practices related to work. Unlike Luther, who had desired a return to the simplicity of work, Calvin accepted the new ideas of capitalism, encouraged trade and production, and called for making a profit. Whatever profit was realized should be used to finance new work, to invest in expanded work, ad infinitum. Contemporary business practices may be traced back to the ascetic, though imaginative, ideas of Calvin. Dedication to one's calling was very important to him. Intermittent, casual effort simply would not do; work had to be disciplined, rigorous, methodical, rational, and therefore specialized. A religious duty was inherent in determining one's calling and then following it with all one's soul and one's might. There was no room for idleness, luxury, or any activity that softened the soul. If one disliked the work to which one was called, a bad decision obviously had been made. The contemplative life was not acceptable. Calvin believed that God was not in the habit of revealing himself to humans through thinking. Neither could humans influence their way of life or salvation through contemplation.

Puritanism evolved from Calvin's notion of capitalism. A person was expected to extract the greatest good from work, including profit. Success in work was demonstrated by wealth, which was to be used, in part, to care for the less fortunate. There was no honor in being poor; in fact, one was doing a disservice to God in accepting poverty as a way of life. Calvin saw no virtue in remaining in a dissatisfying occupation; it was everyone's responsibility to find work that offered the best results for self and society. The commandment was, Be successful, become wealthy, and thus glorify God!

This became the framework for the American work ethic: Work for the sake of work; prosper, save; avoid pleasures that distract from work; and rest only to prepare for more work. DeGrazia (1962) has summed up Calvin's period thus: "Once, man worked for a livelihood, to be able to live. Now he worked for something beyond his daily bread. He worked because somehow it was the right or moral thing to do" (p. 45).

The American Transformation

The work ethic, or the gospel of work as it often was called, arrived in America with few modifications in principles or practices. On this continent, however, it underwent a transformation largely due to the Industrial Revolution, which lasted nearly 100 years, from about 1750 to 1850. The Agrarian Age was reluctantly and dramatically left behind. Work began to center outside the home, away from one's property. With the introduction of power machinery, factories, and mass production, societies and their values markedly shifted. Left intact were standard ideas that all who could work, must; that idleness was the devil's workshop; that time away from work was work not done. Work as a cure for loss, loneliness, and pain remained, but a new locus for work and a compatible philosophy emerged. The Industrial Age is thought to have been the golden age of ideas about work. Tilgher (1962) has written, "It saw the acceptance of universal conscription in the army of labor; the spectacle of the whole race toiling" (p. 20).

The Usefulness Doctrine

The secular doctrine of usefulness replaced the notion of calling, which faded from everyday conversation. So much needed to be done that the work ethic became something more than the Puritan ethic with a new coat of paint. Benjamin Franklin's tireless aphorisms in *Poor Richard's Almanack* ("Early to bed and early to rise . . . .") were constantly updated, serving as rallying cries of the Industrial Revolution, as axioms of a working culture. This was the country of "self-made men," the country where from humble beginnings one could rise to lofty economic peaks. But that would take long hours, lots of them. Work kept the individual from "the despicable sinkhole of idleness." In 1884, in a particularly colorful description of the idle mind, the preacher Henry Ward Beecher told young men it was like an eerie, abandoned castle:

> Its gates sag and fall; . . . its windows give entrance to birds and reptiles; and its stately halls are covered with spiders' tapestry and feebly echo with mimic shrieks of the bat . . . The indolent mind is not empty, but full of vermin. (as quoted in Rodgers, 1978, p. 11)

That left a lasting impression!

Youngsters received undiluted dosages of the work ethic through *McGuffey's Eclectic Readers:* "Work while you work. /

Play while you play. / One thing each time; / That is the way" (*McGuffey's Eclectic Primer*, 1881, p. 53). In *McGuffey's Fourth Eclectic Reader* (1879) George Jones did not tend to his lessons and fell into idleness. When it came time to recite, he could not do so. Eventually he was expelled from school and became a poor wanderer, without money or friends. "Such are the wages of idleness," readers were admonished (pp. 110–112). In the very next lesson a classmate of George's, Charles Bullard, was not of a superior mind, but he studied hard, played hard, and excelled academically and athletically. Eventually he received good recommendations for entering college, did very well there, and graduated with great approval from his family. "Many situations of usefulness and profit were opened to him . . . He is still a useful and a happy man. He has a cheerful home, and is esteemed by all who know him" (pp. 113–114). That is heady stuff!

A quite different kind of usefulness was the lot of children and women. The early textile factories employed them for 14-hour work days—usually sunup to sundown. Because women were unskilled, their wages were low; because they were considered inferior, they could receive no training. A prevailing medical opinion was that specialized training would weaken the woman's mind and she would fall victim to men's diseases, such as nervous breakdowns and alcoholism. It took women one week to make as much as men made in one day (Flexner, 1972; Stephenson, 1986). Historians attribute this to the outcomes of the American and Industrial revolutions. Women's rights were never seriously considered because of what were thought to be more critical issues. In a famous letter to her husband John, who was away helping write the U.S. Constitution, Abigail Adams pleaded,

> By the way, in the Code of Laws which I suppose it will be necessary for you to make I desire you would Remember the Ladies, and be more generous and favorable to them. . . . If particular care and attention is not paid to the Ladies, we are determined to foment a Rebellion, and will not hold ourselves bound by any laws in which we have no voice or Representation. (as quoted in Hecht, Berbich, Healey, & Cooper, 1973, pp. 63–64)

John Adams paid no attention to his wife; perhaps he never received the letter. The "Ladies" were never mentioned in the Constitution.

More than a half-century later, women began to give voice to their irritation at being excluded from the full privileges of the work ethic's usefulness doctrine. In 1848 Elizabeth Cady Stanton, a reformer and a leader of the women's suffrage movement, devised a clever approach: She paraphrased the

Declaration of Independence. Instead of citing King George's tyrannies over the colonies, she enumerated various tyrannies of men over women. This document became the Seneca Falls Declaration of Sentiments and Resolution, July 19, 1848. In part she proclaimed:

> He has monopolized nearly all employments and from those she is permitted to follow, she receives but a scanty remuneration. He closes against her all avenues to wealth and distinction which he considers most honorable to himself.... He has denied her the facilities for obtaining a thorough education, all colleges being closed against her.... He has taken from her all rights in property, even to the wages she earns. (as quoted in Hecht, 1973, pp. 65–68)

Some progress was made within the next few years, such as women receiving their own wages, but the Civil War soon intervened.

The Industrial Work Ethic

As the Industrial Age droned on, complexities grew exponentially. More goods became available, in greater variety, and sharper distinctions between kinds of work appeared. Work increasingly became the center of people's lives and influenced all other aspects of living, such as where they resided in the community, what kind of social relations they enjoyed, and what long-range plans they might make.

Ugliness also was evident. The typical workplace lacked many comforts believed necessary for accomplishing "good work." Relationships between laborers and employers progressively deteriorated. Unionism took root, flourished, and attempted to right so many wrongs.

The Agrarian Age had indeed given way to the Industrial Age, yet there were troubling uncertainties. In the United States frenzied political changes, coupled with restless explorations and expansion into unclaimed or disputed territories, brought forth a religious revival of fundamentalism. Certain beliefs were reexamined and restated as truths to govern all aspects of living. Beliefs about work were among them. Religious leaders, poets, writers, philosophers, joined in a mighty chorus extolling the fundamental virtues of work as the rules by which one lived. Everyone needed something to hang on to in the turbulent times. There was no wish to debate anything. The preachments of Luther and Calvin became the bases for sermons and speeches to excitable crowds. Essayists were also in demand.

One recurring theme was that through work, man could influence the material world and, in turn, influence himself.

Ralph Waldo Emerson (n.d.) wrote, "Labor: a man coins himself into his labor; turns his day, his strength, his thoughts, his affection into some product which remains a visible sign of his power" (p. 297). In a letter to Thomas Carlyle, the Scottish historian and sociological writer, Emerson observed,

> Whoso cuts a straight path to his own bread, by the help of God in the sun & rain & sprouting of the grain, seems to me an *universal* workman. He solves the problem of life not for one but for all men of sound body. (as quoted in Slater, 1964, p. 261)

Carlyle, on the other hand, wrote a passionate, indignant book advocating the replacement of the landed aristocracy with a *real* aristocracy—"captains of industry, not the captains of idleness," as he phrased it. In *Past and Present* (1843) he intoned, "All work is noble; . . . the latest Gospel in this world is Know thy work and do it." He rejected the axiom, "Know thyself," as a source of torment and a useless venture. Rather, he wrote, "Know what thou canst work at; and work at it like a Hercules! That will be [a] better plan." Further, he declared, "Blessed is he who has found his work; let him ask no other blessedness; he has a work, a life-purpose . . ." (pp. 236-243).

More than one poet romanticized the worker, particularly the artist and the artisan. Craft traditions, which were legacies of the Agrarian Age, now were thought to lift work to a higher plane than sheer drudgery. Augustine Duganne (1855) deified the artisan in a popular poem: "God's high priest positioned midway / Between earth and heaven, all things sway / To thy high-working mind" (p. 111). What kept work from being drudgery, so the poets claimed, was the engagement of the mind. Those tragic creatures, the peasants and the slaves, often somberly depicted in paintings and poems, were thought not to be able to use their mental faculties for creative work. Workers who were allowed to employ the spirit and the mind transformed muscle labor into acts of skill and creation. "To become an artist in dealing with tools and materials is not a matter of choice . . . [but] a *moral* necessity," wrote Hamilton Mabie (1898). "Work is sacred . . . not only because it is the fruit of self-denial, patience, and toil, but because it uncovers the soul of the worker" (p. 116).

An interesting note: Centuries before, the work of the artisan—making pots, weaving fabrics, etc.—had been seen as the work of the slave and had been considered distasteful, brutalizing the mind. With this new age, work from the past age became an art form. It now engaged the mind, freed the soul. From at least one perspective it became therapeutic. To writer and artist William Morris (1884/1985) work was still necessary and right to perform, and all people had to have tasks to complete. However, certain conditions should prevail: "First, Work worth doing; second, Work of itself pleasant to do; third, Work done under conditions as would make it neither over-wearisome nor over-anxious" (p. 302).

The renamed American work ethic broadened its scope with the rapidly expanding size and complexity of labor. Nevertheless the underlying beliefs did not materially alter. Even under severe testing, the ethic held fast and proved a lifesaver to those savaged by the Great Depression of the 1930s. Studs Terkel (1970) poignantly depicts those times this way:

> The suddenly idle hands blamed themselves, rather than society . . . millions experienced a private kind of shame when the pink slip came; . . . the inner voice whispered, "I am a failure!" . . . Failure became, at times, violence, and violence turned inward. . . . It was a personal guilt. (pp. 19–20)

Work songs reflected the despair and the ultimate hope that the American work ethic would be restored as an act of patriotism. The "Soup Song," to the tune of "My Bonnie Lies Over the Ocean," said in part, "I fell on my knees to my Maker; / I prayed every night to the Lord. / I swore to be faithful forever, / And now I've received my reward. / Soo-ooop, soo-ooop, / They give me a bowl of soup."[1]

Along came Franklin Roosevelt's New Deal and the songs gradually changed, many extolling the virtues of unions as the saver of the American work ethic. By the end of World War II the previous set of work beliefs had been restored, and hope returned through work songs, even though remnants of unemployment still existed. An example was Woody Guthrie's popular "This Land Is Your Land": "In the shadow of the steeple I saw my people, / By the relief office I seen my people; / As they stood there hungry, I stood there asking / Is this land made for you and me? / This land is your land, this land is my land."[2]

The Postindustrial Age

The present era or age, variously known as "Information," "Postindustrial," or just plain "New," caught nearly everyone by surprise. Giving it a name took a while. Ferguson (1980)

---

[1] As quoted in *Carry It On! A History in Song and Picture of the Working Men and Women of America* (pp. 130–131) by P. Seeger & B. Reiser, 1985, Poole, Dorset, UK: Blandford Press. Words by Maurice Sugar. Reprinted by permission of Ernest Goodman.
[2] © Copyright 1956 (renewed), 1958 (renewed), 1970 Ludlow Music, Inc., New York, NY. Used by permission.

was an early detector of this movement without a name that was growing out of the social ferment of the 1960s and the consciousness-raising of the 1970s. She called it a "social transformation resulting from personal transformation—change from the inside out" (p. 18), and she characterized it as

> fluid organizations reluctant to create hierarchical structures, averse to dogma. It operates on the principle that change can only be facilitated, not decreed. It seems to speak to something very old. And perhaps by integrating magic and science, art and technology, it will succeed where all the king's horses and all the king's men failed. (p. 18)

Naisbitt (1982) popularized the transformation by claiming that Western society was reluctantly leaving behind the Industrial Age and entering the "Information Age," in which the new wealth was know-how. He declared, "The occupational history of the United States tells a lot about us. For example, in 1979, the number-one occupation became clerk, succeeding laborer, succeeding farmer. Farmer, laborer, clerk—that is a brief history of the United States" (p. 14). After clerks the second largest classification is professionals, who are almost all information workers, doctors, teachers, nurses, social workers, and presumably occupational therapy personnel.

Louv (1983), a journalist, prefers "Postindustrial Age" to describe this period, in which he sees two conflicting cultures, like quarreling parents and children. Traditionalists are trapped in the present and highly distrustful of the new technologies. Others, almost adolescent in exuberance, see a transformation "into something new and fresh: [they] perceive the future as a new technological frontier to be conquered and won" (p. xii).

Of very recent vintage is "New Age." As Otto (1987) states, "So here we are in the New Age, a combination of spirituality and superstition, fad and farce about which the only certainty is that it is not new" (p. 62). It is hard to define because it includes rituals, fads, and beliefs and is being employed in religious, spiritual, health, and work practices. Largely from a spiritual perspective, the New Age has entered the world of commerce, particularly motivation and management training, through various exercises to clear the mind, to maximize intuition, and to release creativity. The assumption is that these characteristics are essential to a successful work career. The U.S. Army employs various techniques to help personnel visualize combat tasks and to cope effectively with stressful isolation over long periods.

There is substantial agreement that whatever one calls the present time, the work ethic is in considerable flux. The old ethic, imported and improved upon more than 200 years ago, is in the process of being scrapped or so markedly altered that it is barely recognizable. One development seems certain: Technology, the "is" of things, has taken center stage, and the belief system, the "why" of things, is under attack. Yet while technological change continues unabated, there is this curious phenomenon, a recurring need to explain work from a philosophical framework as the central focus of life.

Historians indicate that this road has been traveled before. When the Agrarian Age gave way to the Industrial Revolution, social turbulence was pronounced. Religious revivalism came about, with a rebirth of former, well-tested beliefs. The explanation is that during turbulent times people tend to turn to structure for stability. In the present the knowledge-driven technology is but shifting sand, changing too rapidly for people to base their assurances upon it. They are looking to older beliefs, a workable ethic, from which they can make decisions about why and how they will work. As one observer has stated in commenting on the New Age, "People look at all this and say, 'If this is the Establishment, then I don't want this. I want something else, something I can trust.' It's people latching on to a belief system to get certainty where there is no certainty" (Otto, 1987, p. 72).

This examination of the evolution of the work ethic encourages a consideration of the functions and the meanings of work today and an effort to arrive at a suggested definition.

Functions of Work

As the Industrial Age was fading during the consciousness-raising 1970s, the American work ethic was under scrutiny and review. A federal task force cited several functions of contemporary work (*Work in America,* 1973). The most obvious one is economic. From work, people "obtain gratification of transient wants, physical assets for enduring satisfactions, and liquid assets for deferable [sic] gratifications . . . [This] is paramount" (p. 4).

The *social* functions of work include its offering the workplace as a spot for people to congregate, talk, and form various degrees of friendship; often the workplace is the germination site of male-male and female-female bonding. Further, the locus of work and the types of tasks performed significantly influence the social status of the worker and his or her family: what class they are, where the family lives, where the children go to school, and with whom the family associates. From a two-year study of unemployed people, Maurer (1979) concludes that "work, if the longing of the unemployed is any indication, remains a fundamental human need. . . . It provides not simply a livelihood, but an essential passage into the human community. It makes us less alone" (p. 1).

The *emotional* function of work is its contribution to self-esteem. This occurs in at least two ways: First, "through the inescapable awareness of one's efficacy and competence in dealing with the objects of work, a person acquires a sense of mastery over both himself and his environment." Second, "engaging in activities that produce something valued by other people" daily tells the individual that he or she has something to offer. The self-proclaimed message is, not to have a job is not to have something that is valued by one's fellow human beings (*Work in America,* 1973, pp. 4-5).

The workplace functions as the worker's personal laboratory, where behavioral experiments take place and personal evaluations occur. The worker continuously asks, Am I succeeding, am I making the grade? Success or failure at work is translated into personal worth, into being valued and valuable or being worthless. As Fromm (1971) states, "Since modern man experiences himself both as the seller and as the commodity to be sold on the market, his self-esteem depends on conditions beyond his control. If he is successful, he is valuable; if he is not, he is worthless" (p. 26).

Contemporary Meanings of the Work Ethic

Most social observers agree that the Protestant-Puritan-industrial ethic is extant, but may well be fading or undergoing remarkable changes. Psychologist Daniel Yankelovitch (1981), who spends much of his time measuring the changing of work and social values, states, "Indeed, so central is the work ethic to American culture that if its meaning shifts, the character of our society will shift along with it" (pp. 33–34).

One significant shift under way is the feminization of the workplace. In an extensive review of the emerging trend of more women working outside the home, Basia Hellwig (1986) cites U.S. Department of Labor statistics indicating that in 1970, about one-half of all women between 25 and 54 had jobs. Sixteen years later nearly three out of four women worked away from home. By 1995, Hellwig continues, "81 percent of all women 25 to 34 are expected to be in the labor force" (pp. 129–130). This dramatic shift coincides with the move from the Industrial to the Information-Postindustrial Age. The rigid distinction between women's work and men's work has blurred significantly, and one of every two professional positions in the United States is now held by a woman.

The result, according to Hellwig, is

> a sweeping social revolution [that] has altered the very foundations of our economy. Women flooded into the work force for diverse reasons—economic necessity, self-fulfillment; but once there they became indispensable, integral parts of the complex economic machinery... By entering the system, women changed the system itself. It's adapting by fits and starts—and sometimes leaps—but there is no going back. (p. 132)

When women become corporate immigrants, they bring with them their own standards, ethics, and ideals, and to a considerable extent they have effectively merged these with the corporate culture. "'The organizational culture... is an extremely strong socializer,'" says Mary Anne Devanna of Columbia University's Management Institute. "Regardless of the values you bring to a corporation, if you want to rise in the ranks, you... adapt your behavior to what is expected of you'" (as quoted in Hellwig, 1986, p. 142). While adapting, women have been responsible for humanizing policies critical to their needs, such as child-care assistance, parental leaves with job-return guarantees, flexible work schedules, and company-directed relocations.

According to a study by Barnett, Baruch, and Rivess cited by Hellwig (1986), the restructuring of work and home to accommodate the working woman has already shown that she is happiest when she has both a sense of mastery from her job and pleasure from her home and family life. Restructuring has not become a women-only activity. Home management roles, for instance, have blurred too. Hellwig points out,

> "Job" descriptions for tasks around the house tend to be based more on demonstrated competencies and inclination than on some assumed innate ability and implicit duty. She's good at balancing the checkbook, and he loves to cook. Great, so she handles the family finances and he prepares supper. (p. 137)

The feminization of the work ethic is not complete and may be more fragile than one might suspect. Friedan (1986) warns that basic work values cannot change solely through women's efforts and "it can't be done *for* women alone either. It's only going to be done if it's done for women and men both." She calls for new caucuses made up of people from both sexes "who are going to demand the new structures for women and men in the child-rearing years, the new structures of work that are needed" (p. 154).

Yankelovitch (1981), who recently reported his study of basic American values, observes that there are four fundamental themes to the current work ethic. "These link work with peoples' life values and form essential parts of what we mean by the American work ethic" (p. 34):

- The **good provider theme**: The breadwinner who provides for the family is the *real* man or woman.
- The **independence theme**: By standing on one's own two feet, one avoids dependence upon others; work is equated with autonomy.
- The **success theme**: The ageless adage, "Hard work always pays off," is alive and well; the payoff comes in the form of home ownership in a select neighborhood, a rising standard of living, conspicuous consumption of leisure, and a secure retirement.
- The **self-respect theme**: People can feel good about themselves if they keep faith with the precept, "Work hard at something and do it well"; hard work, whether menial or exalted, has dignity.

Yankelovitch (1981) concludes that the significance of moral issues in people's lives is undervalued, that "more attention [is given] to the practical and pleasure-seeking sides of life. But most lives are immersed in a sea of morality, as fish are immersed in water: morality surrounds us. It is the element we breathe" (p. 34). The social scientist Arnold Mitchell (1983) echoes this conclusion in his study of American life-styles: "More than anything else, we are what we believe, what we dream, what we value." To a great extent, he thinks, we fashion our lives to underscore our beliefs and realize our dreams.

> And in our attempts to reach our goals, we test ourselves again and again in diverse ways and in doing so we grow. With this growth comes change, so that new goals emerge, and in support of these new goals come new beliefs, new dreams, and new constellations of values. (p. 3)

Such is the nature of the contemporary American work ethic.

Definition of Work

The rich, complex phenomenon called work cannot be reduced to a one-dimensional definition. Numerous interchangeable words are at our disposal—*job, employment, occupation, profession, vocation, labor, trade,* and *remunerated activity,* to cite just a few. The variety of contexts in which people speak of work attest to the belief that this form of human activity is truly a central institution in their lives: The child grows and develops in the surroundings of work-related objects and activities; the adolescent selects an occupation and prepares for work; the adult indulges major portions of his or her energy and time in a vocation or a profession; the retiree consumes benefits from past work.

Arguably there is one multidimensional definition that will appeal to occupational therapy personnel: "an activity that produces something of value for other people" (O'Toole, 1981, p. 14). This definition implies a meaning, a purpose to work. Pay or nonpay does not become an issue. One can be a volunteer or stay at home with chores and children and still be "at work." A social context is strongly suggested, the idea that even though one may work alone, such as in a cottage industry, the outcome, the product, is of value to someone else. Within the sense of this definition, one could make a compelling case for leisure as "an activity that produces something of value for oneself."

The philosopher Mortimer Adler (1981) has studied historical issues of work. In his view there are many kinds of activity along a continuum from drudgery to work that one might do even if pay is not involved. At the latter end, distinctions between work and leisure become ill defined. To Adler, leisure and *good* work are creative activities and are unlike adult playing or inactivity, which help kill time. In an ideal existence, Adler believes, people would be educated to spend their energies and time using their talents in good, creative work and leisure, leaving drudgery to machines.

In attempting to define work as distinct from leisure, Adler (1981) suggests four questions to differentiate among forms or categories of human activity:

1. Is the activity compulsory or optional? It is compulsory if necessary for staying alive, for living, if not living well.
2. If the activity is optional, is it morally desirable, morally obligatory, not just for living, but living well?
3. What purpose does the activity serve; what goals or values does it achieve for ourselves, others, or for society?
4. How is the activity related to the results it achieves and to the agent producing the results; . . . is the result intrinsic or inherent in the activity, or is it a consequence of the activity? (pp. 18–19)

Ann Landers, quoting from another source, is allowed the last word:[3]

---

[3]From the *Ohio Mason,* as quoted in "Ann Landers" [column], 1988, October 9, *Houston Chronicle,* p. 5L. © by The Ohio Mason Printing Company. Reprinted by permission.

I am the foundation of all business and the fount of all prosperity.

I am the parent of genius.

I have laid the groundwork for every fortune in America.

I must be loved before I can bestow my greatest blessings and achieve my greatest ends. Loved, I make life purposeful and fruitful.

I can do more to advance a youth than his own parents, no matter how rich they are.

Fools hate me. Wise men love me.

I am the mother of democracy. All progress springs from me.

Who am I? I am *Work*.

References

Adler, M. (1981). Work, education and leisure. In J. O'Toole, J. L. Scheiber, & L. C. Wood (Eds.), *Working: Changes and choices* (pp. 18–24). New York: Human Sciences Press.

Carlyle, T. (1843). *Past and present*. New York: Charles Scribner's Sons.

deGrazia, S. (1962). *Of time, work and leisure*. New York: Twentieth Century Fund.

Duganne, A. (1855). *The poetical works of Augustine Duganne*. Philadelphia: Parry and McMillan.

Emerson, R. W. (n.d.). *The complete works of Ralph Waldo Emerson, centenary edition* (Vol. 11). Boston: Houghton Mifflin.

Ferguson, M. (1980). *The aquarian conspiracy: Personal and social transformation in the 1980s*. Los Angeles: Jeremy P. Tarcher.

Flexner, E. (1972). *Century of struggle*. New York: Atheneum.

Friedan, B. (1986, November). Where do we go from here? The next step for today's working women—and men. *Working Woman*, pp. 152–156.

Fromm, E. (1971). *Revolution of hope*. New York: Bantam Books.

Hecht, M., Berbich, J. D., Healey, S., & Cooper, C. (1973). *The women, yes*. New York: Rinehart & Winston.

Hellwig, B. (1986, November). How working women have changed America. *Working Woman*, pp. 129–151.

Louv, R. (1983). *America II*. Los Angeles: Jeremy P. Tarcher.

Mabie, H. W. (1901). *Essays on work and culture*. New York: Dodd, Mead.

Maurer, H. (1979). *Not working: An oral history of the unemployed*. New York: Holt, Rinehart & Winston.

McGuffey's eclectic primer. (1881). New York: American Book.

McGuffey's fourth eclectic reader. (1879). New York: American Book.

Mitchell, A. (1983). *Nine American lifestyles: Who we are and where we are going.* New York: Macmillan.

Morris, W. (1985). Lecture to the Secular Society of Leicester. In G. Seldes (Ed.), *The great thoughts* (p. 302). New York: Ballantine Books. (Original work published 1884).

Naisbitt, J. (1982) *Megatrends: Ten new directions transforming our lives.* New York: Warner Books.

O'Toole, J. (1981). Work in America. In J. O'Toole, J. L. Scheiber, & L. C. Wood (Eds.), *Working: Changes and choices* (pp. 12–17). New York: Human Sciences Press.

Otto, F. (1987, December 7). New Age harmonies. *Time,* pp. 62–72.

Rapaport, S. (1910). *Tales and maxims from "The Talmud."* London: George Routledge & Sons.

Rodgers, D. T. (1978). *The work ethic in industrial America: 1850–1920.* Chicago: University of Chicago Press.

Slater, J. (1964). *The correspondence of Emerson and Carlyle.* New York: Columbia University Press.

Stephenson, J. (1986). *Women's roots: Status and achievements in western civilization.* Napa, CA: Diemer, Smith.

Terkel, S. (1970). *Hard times: An oral history of the great depression.* New York: Washington Square Press.

Tilgher, A. (1962). Work through the ages. In S. Nosow & W. H. Form (Eds.), *Man, work, and society: A reader in the sociology of occupation* (pp. 11–24). New York: Basic Books.

Work in America: Report of a special task force to the Secretary of Health, Education, and Welfare. (1973). Cambridge, MA: MIT Press.

Yankelovitch, D. (1981). The meaning of work. In J. O'Toole, J. L. Scheiber, & L. C. Wood (Eds.), *Working: Changes and choices* (pp. 33-43). New York: Human Sciences Press.

2

Use of Department of Labor References and Job Analysis

Karen Jacobs, MS, OTR/L, FAOTA
Joane Wyrick, MA, OTR, FAOTA

DOT, GOE, OOH, COJ. Although sounding more like the ingredients for alphabet soup, these acronyms are in actuality the abbreviations for terms that constitute a second language for occupational therapists providing work programming. As noted by Taylor (1988),

> Occupational therapy practice in an industrial rehabilitation framework demands that the practitioner communicate in nomenclature familiar in business and industry. The "language" of this market has been established by the U.S. Department of Labor and differs from the medical terminology in which occupational therapists have been schooled. The occupational therapist needs to become "bilingual" in a very real sense. Information regarding a client's performance may be reported to the referring physician in one way and to the insurance carriers, attorneys, Social Security administrative law judges and employers in different phraseology in order to provide the clearest meaning to the reader. (p. 300)

Developing an understanding of this terminology is applicable not only to occupational therapists whose clients have sustained industrial injuries, but also to those whose clients evidence various dysfunctions, such as developmental disabilities, psychiatric disorders, and disabilities across the age span, if work programming is the goal.

The *Dictionary of Occupational Titles* (DOT) and its companion publications, *Selected Characteristics of Occupations Defined in the "Dictionary of Occupational Titles,"* the *Guide*

The authors acknowledge Teresa Bryan, MS, OTR/L, chief of occupational therapy, and Alfred Walker, MS, CVE, senior vocational evaluator, both from the J. Leonard Camera Industrial Rehabilitation Center, Columbus, Ohio, for their assistance in the completion of this chapter.

for Occupational Exploration (GOE), and the *Occupational Outlook Handbook* (OOH), all developed by the U.S. Department of Labor (USDOL, 1977, 1981, 1979, and 1988, respectively), can assist therapists in developing this second language. These volumes provide orderly access to a systematized collection and classification of occupational information.

Most materials in the four publications are in the public domain and may be reproduced fully or partially without the permission of the federal government. Source credit is requested, but not required. Permission is necessary only to reproduce copyrighted photographs and other copyrighted items.

A publication that provides cross-references to the codes in the four Department of Labor publications is the *Classification of Jobs According to Worker Trait Factors* (COJ) (Field & Field, 1988). This was revised in 1988 and is published in two volumes by Elliot and Fitzpatrick Publishing Company in Athens, Georgia. It is copyrighted.

A Guide to Job Analysis, published in 1982 by the Department of Labor and distributed by the Materials Development Center, Stout Vocational Rehabilitation Institute, University of Wisconsin–Stout, is another excellent reference. It fully defines all worker trait factors and physical demand characteristics that are used in the Department of Labor publications. *A Guide to Job Analysis* replaces the *Handbook for Analyzing Jobs* (1972) and is a much more comprehensive version.

History of the "Dictionary of Occupational Titles"

In 1933 the first public program of occupational research began with the purpose of providing to public employment offices information that could be used to guide the placement of large numbers of unemployed workers. The information was originally published in separate volumes according to industries in which the occupations were found.

Based on the data gathered in this research, the first single edition of the DOT appeared in 1939. It summarized the information from earlier works, added data on occupations not previously studied, and used a system of numbers as an occupational code. There were 17,500 concise job definitions presented alphabetically by title. They were based on 550 occupational groups of skilled, semiskilled, and unskilled jobs. Jobs were given a five- or six-digit code. The DOT was primarily used by staff in public employment offices and required considerable practice for effective use.

In 1949 the second edition appeared. Information on occupations derived from World War II manpower research was included. For example, occupations in television and the new plastics industry appeared for the first time. There were 6,100 new occupations and a new coding for rating an individual's readiness and preferences (interests) for various types of jobs.

A considerably expanded (over 20,000 titles) and revised third edition was published in 1965. This edition introduced a new system called *worker functions,* which further facilitated the matching of individuals to job classifications. The occupational code was revised and made more readily understandable. A new system of classifying occupations, called *worker trait group* arrangement, was added, which made it possible for one to determine the degree to which aptitudes, interests, education, physical capacities, etc., were required for average successful job performance. The third edition was extensively modified so that it could be used in high school courses in occupational exploration and career decision making. During field testing it was also used with groups of disabled people. Like its predecessors, the third edition of the DOT had to be supplemented periodically (Robinson, 1979).

The fourth edition of the DOT was published in 1977 and updated in supplement form in 1982 and 1986. It is 2-1/2 inches thick and weighs almost 6 lbs. More than 75,000 on-site job analyses were performed to prepare the material; 2,100 new occupations have been added, in areas such as high technology, space defense, and water and air pollution control; and 3,500 jobs have been deleted. If one includes overlapping job titles, it contains 20,000 jobs—1,800 fewer than the third edition. The reduction is due in part to the elimination of age and sex references in both definitions and job titles.

Descriptions of Specific Occupational References

The DOT and its companion publications can be conceptualized in terms of Ginzberg's (1957) model of occupational choice (see Table 2-1). Using this framework, a therapist can guide an individual through the developmental periods of fantasy, tentative choice, and realistic choice. With the *Guide for Occupational Exploration,* the client can explore individual interests, capacities, and values related to job performance. When the client reaches the realistic choice period, the therapist can turn back to the DOT for descriptions of specific jobs that best fit the client's established interests and values. Next the therapist can go to either *Selected Characteristics of Occupations Defined in the "Dictionary of Occupational Titles"* or the *Classification of Jobs According to Worker Trait Factors* to ascertain the abilities and the training required for the selected jobs. At this point the client can be tested for abilities compared with the job requirements. Finally the *Occupa-*

Table 2-1
Model of the Classic Vocational References Based on the Occupational Choice Process

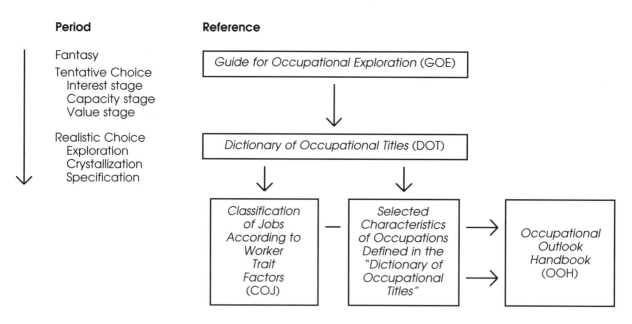

Note. Periods and stages in the occupational choice process from *Occupational Choice: An Approach to a General Theory* by E. Ginzberg, 1957, New York: Columbia University Press.

tional Outlook Handbook can be used to obtain information on the projected job opportunities to assist in a realistic assessment of the potential job market. The following sections explain some of these references so that an occupational therapist helping clients sort out job potentials can knowledgeably employ resources that match functional capabilities to job demands.

"Guide for Occupational Exploration"

In 1979 the USDOL's Employment and Training Administration released the *Guide for Occupational Exploration* (GOE). The GOE groups thousands of occupations by interests and by traits (values) required for successful performance. It provides a convenient crossover from occupational information about the individual's interests and values to potentially suitable occupational groups.

The GOE clusters jobs by interest areas, then by work groups and subgroups. Some general information is provided at the beginning of each work group. Each interest area has been assigned a number code, 01 through 12. Table 2-2 lists the 12 interest areas as delineated in the GOE. Performing Arts, for example, bears the interest code 01. To this interest code is attached a work-group number code. Dance, a work

Table 2-2
Twelve Interest Areas of the *Guide for Occupational Exploration*

01	Artistic	07	Business Detail
02	Scientific	08	Selling
03	Plants and Animals	09	Accommodating
04	Protective	10	Humanitarian
05	Mechanical	11	Leading-Influencing
06	Industrial	12	Physical Performing

Note. From *Guide for Occupational Exploration* (p. 8) by U.S. Department of Labor, 1979, Washington, DC: U.S. Government Printing Office.

---

group under Performing Arts, is assigned the number code 01.05. Within that code a subgroup number code, 01.05.09, is used for Instructing and Choreography. Thus a six-digit code identifies 1 of 12 major interest areas, 1 of 66 worker-trait groups, and 1 of 348 subgroups into which a job falls.

Using the interest areas as a base, the therapist would search the GOE's summary list for types of work that appear appropriate for a client's expressed or major interests. These become very specific according to work groups and subgroups. For example, occupational therapy is classified under interest area 10, Humanitarian, and then more specifically under work group 10.02, Nursing, Therapy and Specialized Teaching Services. This category describes workers who "care for, treat, or train people to improve their physical and emotional well being" (USDOL, 1979, p. 278).

Specific questions and some possible answers are used to help guide the individual in career exploration. Some of the questions that the individual is asked in the GOE are as follows:

- "What kind of work would you do?"
- "What skills and abilities do you need for this kind of work?"
- "How do you know if you would like or could learn to do this kind of work?"
- "How can you prepare for and enter this kind of work?"
- "What else should you consider about these jobs?"

In addition, the GOE provides specific job titles related to the DOT. An occupational therapist who is engaged in career exploration should be familiar with a variety of references and systems that are useful in matching a client's abilities with specific job tasks. Further vocational exploration is possible using the U.S. Employment Service (USES) Interest Inventory and Interest Checklist and the General Aptitude Test Battery (GATB). The results of the GATB can be translated and compared with a set of Occupational Aptitude Patterns (OAP) based on work groups in the GOE. Finally the GOE can be used independently for occupational exploration.

Information available in the GOE can easily be integrated into occupational therapy programming. In a school system, for example, an occupational therapist might be working with a 12-year-old male student with learning disabilities who has indicated an interest in cooking. By exploring information under the GOE interest area 09, Accommodating, the therapist can devise functional activities that incorporate both the student's interest in cooking and his treatment goals in a realistic, work-oriented environment.

The GOE can be used in a similar manner by occupational therapists working with psychiatric populations. In this context it can also serve as a vehicle to explore the appropriateness of previous employment. The GOE's concrete interest inventory can assist the therapist in collecting data on the work-role history of a client with psychiatric problems and can nonintrusively provide valuable information about his or her previous performance.

"Dictionary of Occupational Titles"

Continuing with the occupational choice model, the therapist and the client would next turn to the DOT. "The DOT is based on the premise that all jobs in our economy are slightly different from each other but that there are many similar" occupations in terms of interests, abilities, values, and requirements (Reynolds-Lynch, 1985b, p. 315). The information provided in the DOT is of a general nature, however, so one cannot expect a specific job to be exactly as described and defined there. For example, an actual job in a work setting may be a combination of two or more jobs reported in the DOT, with varying tasks. Therefore, one should not depend solely on the DOT. Whenever possible, if a client is employed, an analysis of his or her actual job should be performed to provide a better understanding of the tasks that compose the job.

The DOT has two major functions:
1. Identification of occupational titles and definition of the occupations bearing those titles
2. Classification of occupations in four major ways to compare job requirements and worker characteristics (Robinson, 1979):
   a. Occupational group arrangement (OGA)
   b. Industrial designation (Ind. Des.)
   c. Data, people, things (DPT)
   d. Worker trait groups (WTG).

Each occupational definition within the DOT contains six basic parts:
1. Occupational code
2. Occupational title
3. Industrial designation (Ind. Des.)
4. Alternate title
5. Body of the definition
6. Undefined related titles.

Occupational Code

This code consists of nine digits in sets of three: 000.000-000. For example, the occupational code for occupational therapist is 076.121-010. Each set of digits has a specific meaning. All 20,000 jobs in the DOT are assigned to one—and only one—occupational category or *occupational group arrangement* (OGA) (first digit), division (second digit), and group (third digit). With reference to the first set of three digits for occupational therapist, 076, the first digit identifies one of nine occupational categories (see Table 2-3a):

0/1   Professional, technical, and managerial occupations

The second digit, 7, indicates a more narrow division within the category (see Table 2-3b):

7   Occupations in medicine and health.

The third digit, 6, represents the occupational group within the division (see Table 2-3c):

6   Therapists

The middle three digits in the occupational code refer to the worker's requirements for dealing with data (fourth digit), people (fifth digit), and things (sixth digit) (see Table 2-3d). Each job in the economy requires a worker to interact to some degree with these *worker functions*. *Data* is defined as "information, knowledge, and conceptions related to data, people, or things resulting from observation, investigation, interpretation, visualization, and mental creation. Data are intangible and include numbers, words, symbols, ideas, concepts, and oral verbalization" (*Handbook for Analyzing Jobs,* 1972, p. 73). *People* is defined as "human beings; also animals dealt with on an individual basis as if they were human" (p. 76). *Things* is defined as inanimate objects, nonhuman substances or materials, machines, and tools. They are tangible and have shape, form, and other physical characteristics.

The number given for each function signifies the complexity of the function: the lower the number, the more complex the function. For example, analyzing and compiling are more

Table 2-3
Occupational Code as Defined in the *Dictionary of Occupational Titles*

The Occupational Code consists of 9 digits in sets of 3: 000.000-000.

a. The first digit identifies 1 of 9 Occupational Categories.

0/1	**Professional, technical, and managerial occupations**
2	Clerical and sales occupations
3	Service occupations
4	Agricultural, fishery, forestry, and related occupations
5	Processing occupations
6	Machine trades occupations
7	Benchwork occupations
8	Structural work occupations
9	Miscellaneous occupations

Occupational therapy   076.121-010

b. The second digit identifies 1 of 15 Professional, Technical, and Managerial Occupations.

00/01	Occupations in architecture, engineering, and surveying
02	Occupations in mathematics and physical sciences
04	Occupations in life sciences
05	Occupations in social sciences
07	**Occupations in medicine and health**
09	Occupations in education
10	Occupations in museum, library, and archival sciences
11	Occupations in law and jurisprudence
12	Occupations in religion and theology
13	Occupations in writing
14	Occupations in art
15	Occupations in entertainment and recreation
16	Occupations in administrative specializations
18	Managers and officials, n.e.c.
19	Miscellaneous professional, technical, and managerial occupations

Occupational therapy   076.121-010

c. The third digit identifies 1 of 10 Occupations in Medicine and Health.

070	Physicians and surgeons
071	Osteopaths
072	Dentists
073	Veterinarians
074	Pharmacists
075	Registered nurses
076	**Therapists**
077	Dietitians
078	Occupations in medical and dental technology
079	Occupations in medicine and health, n.e.c.

Occupational therapy   076.121-010

Table 2-3 (cont.)

d. The middle three digits identify Worker Function Ratings.

Each job in the economy requires a worker to function to some degree with Data, People, and Things.

Data (fourth digit)	People (fifth digit)	Things (sixth digit)
0 Synthesizing	0 Mentoring	0 Setting up
→ 1 **Coordinating**	1 Negotiating	→ 1 **Precision working**
2 Analyzing	→ 2 **Instructing**	2 Operating—controlling
3 Compiling	3 Supervising	3 Driving—operating
4 Computing	4 Diverting	4 Manipulating
5 Copying	5 Persuading	5 Tending
6 Comparing	6 Speaking—signaling	6 Feeding—offbearing
	7 Serving	7 Handling
	8 Taking instruction—helping	

Occupational therapy   076.121-010
↑

Example of the Data Function for Occupational Therapist

Data: Information, knowledge, and conceptions, related to data, people, or things, obtained by observation, investigation, interpretation, visualization, and mental creation. Data are intangible and include numbers, words, symbols, ideas, concepts, and oral verbalization.

0 Synthesizing: Integrating analyses of data to discover facts and/or develop knowledge, concepts, or interpretations.

→ 1 **Coordinating: Determining time, place, and sequence of operations or action to be taken on the basis of analysis of data; executing determination and/or reporting on events.**

2 Analyzing: Examining and evaluating data. Presenting alternative actions in relation to the evaluation is frequently involved.

3 Compiling: Gathering, collating, or classifying information about data, people, or things. Reporting and/or carrying out a prescribed action in relation to the information is frequently involved.

4 Computing: Performing arithmetic operations and reporting on and/or carrying out a prescribed action in relation to them. Does not include counting.

5 Copying: Transcribing, entering, or posting data.

6 Comparing: Judging the readily observable functional, structural, or compositional characteristics (whether similar to or divergent from obvious standards) of data, people, or things.

Note. Sections of the table explaining the interpretation of digits in the Occupational Code from *Dictionary of Occupational Titles* (4th ed.) (pp. xxxiv, xxxvi, xxxviii) by U.S. Department of Labor, 1977, Washington, DC: U.S. Government Printing Office. Section offering an example of the data function for occupational therapist from *Handbook for Analyzing Jobs* (pp. 73-76) by U.S. Department of Labor, Manpower Administration, 1972, Menomonie, WI: University of Wisconsin–Stout, Stout Vocational Rehabilitation Institute, Materials Development Center.

complex than comparing; supervising people involves more responsibility than persuading; and precision working is more complicated than handling.

In the example of occupational therapist, 076.121-010, the middle three digits are interpreted as follows:

> Data   1   Coordinating
> People   2   Instructing
> Things   1   Precision working

The last three digits of the occupational code indicate the alphabetical order of the listing of titles. Several jobs may have the same first six digits, but different jobs will not have the same nine digits. If there is only one occupation with a particular six digits, the last three digits of its code are always 010. If there is more than one with a particular six digits, the last three digits are assigned in multiples of four starting with 010—010, 014, 018, 022, and so on. For example:

> <u>O</u>ccupational therapist   076.121-010
> <u>P</u>hysical therapist   076.121-014

Occupational Title

The occupational title immediately follows the code. This base title, presented in boldfaced uppercase type, is the commonly used title for the job.

Industrial Designation

The industrial designation follows the base title in parentheses and notes one or more things about the occupation. It often differentiates between two or more occupations with identical titles, but different duties. For example, the occupations may differ in locations, types of duties, products manufactured, or processes used. The designation, "any industry," is used when an occupation occurs in a number of industries.

Alternate Title

The alternate title is a synonym for the base title, although not as commonly used. It is in boldface lowercase type.

Body of the Definition

The body of the definition is composed of a lead statement, a task statement, and statements of items or tasks that the worker may accomplish.

Undefined Related Titles

Undefined related titles represent specializations or variations of the base occupation.

Table 2-4
Occupational Therapist as Defined in the *Dictionary of Occupational Titles*

076.121-010. OCCUPATIONAL THERAPIST (medical ser.)
Plans, organizes, and conducts occupational therapy program in hospital, institution, or comunity setting to facilitate rehabilitation of mentally, physically, or emotionally handicapped: Plans program involving activities, such as manual arts and crafts, practice in function, prevocational, vocational, and homemaking skills and activities of daily living, and participation in sensorimotor, educational, recreational, and social activities designed to help patients regain physical or mental functioning or adjust to handicaps. Consults with other members of rehabilitation team to select activity program consistent with needs and capabilities of each patient and to coordinate occupational therapy with other therapeutic activities. Selects constructive activities suited to individual's physical capacity, intelligence level, and interest to upgrade patient to maximum independence, prepare patient for return to employment, assist in restoration of functions, and aid in adjustment to disability. Teaches patients skills and techniques required for participation in activities and evaluates patients' progress. Designs and constructs special equipment for patient and suggests adaptations of patient's work-living environment. Requisitions supplies and equipment. Lays out materials for patients' use and cleans and repairs tools at end of sessions. May conduct training programs or participate in training medical and nursing students and other workers in occupation's therapy techniques and objectives. May design, make, and fit adaptive devices, such as splints and braces, following medical prescription. May plan, direct, and coordinate occupational therapy program and be designated DIRECTOR, OCCUPATIONAL THERAPY (medical ser.).

Note. From *Dictionary of Occupational Titles* (4th ed.) (p. 59) by U.S. Department of Labor, 1977, Washington, DC: U.S. Government Printing Office.

Table 2-4 presents the complete entry for occupational therapist in the DOT.

"Selected Characteristics of Occupations Defined in the 'Dictionary of Occupational Titles'"

This two-part companion to the DOT provides more detailed data on occupational characteristics. "Part A clusters occupational titles using the coding system of the *Guide for Occupational Exploration* (GOE)" and physical demands. "This grouping of occupations helps the user to see relationships among requirements of jobs characterized by a predominant worker interest factor. Part B lists occupational titles in order of the nine-digit DOT code and specifies the physical strength required for each listed occupation" (USDOL, 1981, p. vi).

There are five appendixes to *Selected Characteristics*. They are described in the following sections.

Appendix A: Physical Demands (PD)

In Appendix A, seven factors—standing, walking, sitting, lifting, carrying, pushing, and pulling—are expressed in terms of five levels of strength:

S—Sedentary work
L—Light work
M—Medium work
H—Heavy work
V—Very heavy work.

These factors should be reviewed by the therapist in considering the injured worker's job choices. It must be stressed that these levels are generic, may vary from job to job, and do not specify, for example, lifting requirements at different body levels (T. Bryan, personal communication, November 1988). Other physical demands include climbing, balancing, stooping, kneeling, crouching, crawling, reaching, handling, fingering, feeling, talking, hearing, acuity (far), acuity (near), depth perception, visual accommodation, color vision, and field of vision.

Appendix B: Working Conditions (WC)

Appendix B describes the physical environmental conditions to which a worker is exposed while performing assigned tasks. Their effect on the injured worker must be considered.

1. Inside, Outside, or Both:
   (I) Inside: Protection from weather conditions but not necessarily from temperature changes.
   (O) Outside: No effective protection from weather.
   (B) Both: Inside and outside.
   A job is considered "inside" if the worker spends approximately 75 percent or more of the time inside, and "outside" if the worker spends approximately 75 percent or more of the time outside. A job is considered "both" if the activities occur inside and outside in approximately equal amounts.
2. Extremes of Cold Plus Temperature Changes:
   a. Extremes of Cold . . .
   b. Temperature Changes . . .
3. Extremes of Heat plus Temperature Changes:
   a. Extremes of Heat . . .
   b. Temperature Changes . . .
4. Wet and Humid . . .
5. Noise and Vibration . . .
6. Hazards . . .
7. Fumes, Odors, Toxic Conditions, Dust, and Poor Ventilation.

(USDOL, 1981, p. 467)

Appendix C: Mathematical Development and Language Development (Training Time)

This appendix states the level of training required to perform a job proficiently.

Appendix D: Specific Vocational Preparation (SVP) (Training Time)

Specific vocational preparation is the amount of time needed to learn the techniques, acquire the information, and develop the facility required for average performance in a specific job. Levels range from 1, short demonstration, to 9, over 10 years.

Appendix E: Occupational Aptitude Patterns (OAP)

Occupational aptitude patterns are described as specific abilities required of an individual to perform a given work activity. These nine aptitudes as measured on the USES General Aptitude Test Battery (GATB) are as follows:
G—Intelligence
V—Verbal aptitude
N—Numerical aptitude
S—Spatial aptitude
P—Form perception
Q—Clerical perception
K—Motor coordination
F—Finger dexterity
M—Manual dexterity.

"Classification of Jobs According to Worker Trait Factors"

The use of the *Classification of Jobs According to Worker Trait Factors* (COJ) is similar to that of *Selected Characteristics of Occupations Defined in the "Dictionary of Occupational Titles,"* but the COJ provides even more detailed information in its two volumes. Volume 1 contains 448 pages of computer entries representing the worker trait factors for all jobs in the 1977 DOT and the 1986 DOT Supplement. This totals 20,000 titles. The definitions of worker traits are provided in the appendix of this publication. These traits include the following:
1. Physical demands
2. Aptitudes
3. Working conditions
4. Specific vocational preparation
5. GOE interest areas
6. Interests (work activities)
7. Temperaments.

According to Taylor (1988), for the occupational therapist considering specific physical demands of a job, one of the most useful sections of the COJ is the "Physical Demands" classification section. One of the first criteria for determining a client's ability to do a job is his or her ability to lift the amount of weight which is ordinarily handled in a given job. For this reason, all jobs are classified, initially, by the primary "strength" requirements needed for successful performance of each job. The strength components include ability to lift, carry, push and pull. Consideration is given to the frequency with which the client's strength is employed. (p. 300)

"The Revised COJ also provides a 'cross-walk' between the DOT titles and codes and seven other coded databases and/or arrangements" (Field & Field, 1988, p. 6). This complete cross-walk is included in the Worker Trait Profiles section. For example, under the DOT number 076.121-010 OCCUPATIONAL THERAPIST is listed—

```
PHYS DEM L45            INTERESTS 3B4A
WORK CONDS I            TEMPS VPJ
GED RML 545             GOE 10.02.02
SVP 7                   CEN 099
SKL 1                   IND 573
APTITUDES               SOC 3032
  G 2                   MPS 939
  V 2                   WORK FLD 294
  N 2
  S 3
  P 3
  Q 4
  K 4
  F 3
  M 3
  E 4
  C 5
```

[Volume 2 of the COJ] contains two sections of the DOT titles that have been arranged numerically according to the *Guide for Occupational Exploration* (GOE) code for light and sedentary jobs, and numerically arranged data-people-things (DPT) codes, also of light and sedentary jobs. Each of these job arrangements lists also several of the worker trait factors in addition to a cross-referencing to the census code. The definitions of worker trait factors are included in Volume II. (Field & Field, 1988, p. 6)

According to the editors, the COJ does the following:

1. Provides a comprehensive listing of all jobs that are identified by the U.S. Department of Labor;

2. Provides a comprehensive "cross-walk" between the DOT and ten other coded databases and arrangements;
3. Provides useful and necessary information for job analyses, and
4. Sets forth a vital information base and format useful in finding related titles through the process of transferability of skills.

(Field & Field, 1988, pp. 6–7).

The entries in the COJ do not state the requirements directly, but in codes. To interpret the codes, the therapist must use one of the following sources: the appendix of the COJ, Appendixes A–E of *Selected Characteristics of Occupations Defined in the "Dictionary of Occupational Titles,"* or *A Guide to Job Analysis*.

An Illustration of the Use of the "Classification of Jobs"

Dan has been employed for nine years as a precision assembler. The DOT code number for precision assembler is 706.681-010 and includes the following worker traits:

Strength	Light
Physical demands	Stooping/bending, reaching/handling, vision
SVP	High school/two years
GED	
Reasoning	Average
Math	Below average
Language	Below average.

Unfortunately, because of an on-the-job accident, Dan has been restricted to sedentary exertion only, with no stooping and bending (other factors remain the same). The occupational therapist decides to evaluate Dan's physical capacities at all body ranges, for there is the possibility that Dan could work at a job that requires medium strength, but at midbody range.

To obtain data identifying related titles that have the reduced factors of sedentary exertion and no stooping or bending, the therapist refers to Volume 2 of the COJ. There are three ways of gaining access to relevant information in this volume:

1. By occupational interests (or the GOE)
2. By worker functions (or data-people-things, DPT)
3. By occupational groupings.

The occupational therapist uses Dan's worker function rating, or DPT level, of 681. The therapist turns to the DPT section and locates the page listing all jobs with a

DPT level of 681. The DPT numbers are arranged from high to low. The therapist finds 42 other titles listed in the DOT with the same 681 DPT level as precision assembler. Of these, 18 are sedentary jobs that require no stooping or bending. Further review eliminates 6 of them because they require higher SVP or GED levels than Dan's original job as precision assembler did. After this process of elimination, there remain 12 job titles within the 681 DPT cluster calling for residual functional capacity similar to Dan's. However, within the same industry area in which Dan is currently employed, benchwork (represented by the first digit in the DOT code number, 7), 5 titles are identified:

740.681-010 LINER
710.681-010 CALIBRATOR I
712.681-022 MEDICAL-INSTRUMENT-CABLE FABRICATOR
710.681-026 THERMOMETER MAKER
716.681-022 OPTICAL GLASS ETCHER.

Dan's occupational therapist uses this information to develop appropriate work simulations for his work hardening program.

This example has been provided as one solution for Dan. Other variables may need to be addressed that may have other vocational alternatives. For example, are Dan's skills actually higher than those he was using on his job before his injury? The occupational therapist can obtain an answer to this question by referring Dan for a comprehensive vocational evaluation. Occupational therapists should collaborate with other vocational rehabilitation professionals, but they should maintain their definitive role in this area of practice.

"Guide to Job Analysis"

This publication provides a structure for job analysis (see the Job Analysis section of this chapter for elaboration). It describes in depth two major types of job information used by the U.S. Employment Service: work performed and worker characteristics.

Work performed includes "those job analysis components that relate to the actual work activities of a job. The four work-performed components are as follows:

1. *"Worker functions*—the ways in which the job requires the worker to function in relation to data, people, and things.
2. *"Work fields*—categories of technologies that reflect how work gets done and what gets done as a result of the

work activities of a job and the purpose of the job. There are 94 work fields identified by the US Employment Service for classification of all jobs in the economy in terms of what gets done on the job. Work fields range from the specific to the general and are organized into homogeneous groups, based on related technologies or objectives, such as the movement of materials, the fabrication of products, the use of data, and the provision of services" (p. 121).

3. *Work devices*—the machines, equipment, tools, and work aids used by the individual to perform the specific activities of a job.
4. *Materials, products, subject matter, and services (MPSMS)*—"1) basic materials being processed, such as fabric, metal, and wood; 2) final products being made, cultivated, harvested, or captured, such as wild animals, sponges, field crops, trees, and automobiles; 3) data, when being dealt with or applied, such as in economics and physics; and 4) services being rendered, such as barbering and dentistry" (p. 11).

Worker characteristics include both information on work performed, previously described, and information on worker attributes that contribute to successful job performance with regard to the work activities themselves and the environment in which the work is performed. Worker characteristics include the following:

1. General educational development (GED)
2. Job training time (JTT) and specific vocational preparation (SVP)
3. Aptitudes
4. Interests
5. Temperaments, or the adaptability requirements made on the individual by specific types of jobs. There are 11 factors that the occupational therapist may consider:
   D—Directing activities
   R—Performing repetitive tasks
   I—Influencing people
   V—Performing a variety of tasks
   E—Expressing personal feelings
   A—Working alone
   S—Working under stress
   T—Attaining tolerances
   U—Working under specific instructions
   P—Dealing with people
   J—Making judgments and decisions
6. Physical Demands
7. Environmental Conditions.

The information provided in the *Guide to Job Analysis* is more detailed than that in the aforementioned references. For example, the COJ lists 21 physical demands, whereas the *Guide* identifies 28.

Application of the References

One of the easiest ways for the occupational therapist to use the information in the references that have been described is first to find the occupational code for the job in the DOT. The therapist would then turn to Part B of *Selected Characteristics of Occupations Defined in the "Dictionary of Occupational Titles"* to find the GOE code.

The occupational code for occupational therapist is 076.121-010, and its GOE code is 10.02.02. The strength factor required is listed as *L*, light. The GOE code 10.02, Nursing, Therapy and Specialized Teaching Services, is found in Part A of *Selected Characteristics of Occupations Defined in the "Dictionary of Occupational Titles."* The subcategory 10.02.02, Therapy and Rehabilitation, contains occupational therapy.

The DOT code is checked and the following additional information is now available on the job:

Physical demands	L 4,5,6
Environmental conditions	I
Mathematical (M) and language (L) development requirements	M4, L5
Specific vocational preparation (SVP)	7

Physical demands are listed as both the physical requirements of the job and specific physical traits that a worker must have to meet the job requirements. The *L* indicates that the average occupational therapist can expect to have to lift a maximum of 20 lbs., with up to 10 lbs. of frequent lift, and to have to carry the same weights. The primary expectations, as expressed in the numbers *4, 5,* and *6,* are these:

4 Reach, handle, finger, feel
5 Talk, hear
6 See (acuity, depth perception, field of vision, accommodation).

The occupational therapist is not expected to spend a major part of the job climbing and balancing *(2)* or stooping, kneeling, crouching, and crawling *(3).*

The *I* for environmental conditions indicates that 75 percent or more of the occupational therapist's time on the job is spent indoors. There is no expectation that the therapist work in extremes of cold or heat, work in wet or humid conditions, or be exposed to excessive noise, vibrations, hazards, fumes, odors, toxic conditions, dust, and poor ventilation.

The requirement for mathematical development, *4,* is the ability to handle algebra, geometry, and shop math and to make practical application of fractions, percentages, and ratios and proportions. The requirement for language development, *5,* is to be able to read scientific and technical journals, abstracts, financial reports, and legal documents; write journal articles, speeches, and manuals; and be conversant in the theory, principles, and methods of effective and persuasive speech. Specific vocational preparation, *7,* is in the two- to four-year category.

One cannot help but note that this description does not define all occupational therapy practice. Rather it represents the minimum skills needed to perform the job of occupational therapist.

In using these references with a disabled client, the therapist would follow the same procedure. It would then be possible to compare other more suitable occupations that were similar in skill, ability, and interests and that required strength levels that were appropriate to the individual's current physical and mental abilities.

Computerized Systems

The use of the DOT and its companion publications requires much "data shuffling," and it becomes obvious that some of these tasks could be performed by a computer. Fifteen software systems are described and compared in Botterbusch (1986), *A Comparison of Computerized Job Matching Systems.* The comparisons should be carefully considered in selecting a software system for a specific program or client population. If possible, contact should be made with a facility using the specific system to evaluate its applications and limitations before purchase.

Some of the more well-known systems are as follows:
1. Occupational Access System (OASYS), which is designed for a true transfer of skills analysis and can be used for client placement, career guidance, career exploration, and job analysis (Vertek Inc., Bellevue, Washington).
2. Labor Market Access, which is designed to determine the loss of employability from pre- to post-injury functioning level and the corresponding wage loss. This system can be used by vocational professionals, but is designed for the vocational expert in forensic rehabilitation (Elliot and Fitzpatrick, Athens, Georgia).
3. Vocational Information Processing System (VIPS), which is designed for disability assessment and includes job

matching, vocational guidance counseling, educational selection, and occupational information (Ability Information System, Spokane, Washington) (A. Walker, personal communication, November 1988).

4. ValSEARCH/JOB BANK, which is composed of an instructional manual and software designed for use with the Apple II, IIe, and II+ and the IBM-PC, -PC/XT, and -PS/II. This software is described in more depth as an example of a useful system.

ValSEARCH/JOB BANK: An Example

The ValSEARCH/JOB BANK program is very user friendly, with the manual providing step-by-step instructions and a program process flow chart. The software provides clear prompts. However, its usefulness and limitations are directly dependent upon the accuracy of the data input provided by the client in answering the evaluator's specific questions.

Before using the JOB BANK, the evaluator must develop a Worker Qualification Profile (WQP). The client-specific information that is used to develop the WQP can be collected in several ways:

1. By administering the Valpar Microcomputer Evaluation and Screening Assessment (MESA)
2. By using the Valpar Component Work Samples
3. By using any other vocational evaluations or tests that will provide reliable and consistent answers regarding a client's demographic information.

The nine major factors that compose the WQP are the same ones described in the COJ and defined earlier in this chapter:

1. *Guide for Occupational Exploration* (GOE) interests
2. Worker functions—data, people, things
3. Physical demands (PD)—sedentary, light, medium, heavy, and very heavy work
4. Environmental working conditions (WC)—indoor and outdoor exposure
5. General educational development (GED)—reasoning (R), mathematics (M), and language (L)
6. Specific vocational preparation (SVP)
7. Aptitudes
8. Interests
9. Temperament.

The information on the WQP is then entered into the computer and matched to the 20,000 jobs defined in the DOT. The ValSEARCH/JOB BANK program allows the user either to select a standard database or to design a custom application that fits a specific client population, that is, a specific age and/or disability group.

When the data on the client have been established, the program can—
1. determine the client's worker traits and the highest level of vocational functioning on each WQP factor;
2. conduct a number of job searches that can be used for vocational exploration and job placement;
3. print out the WQP for any one of the 20,000 jobs in the DOT database (Valpar International Corporation, 1985).

A report can be printed using a facility's title or on a facility's letterhead. This printout can compare the client's previous job with any other job under consideration. The program is designed to search out job matches in groups of 75, rank-ordered on the factors of intelligence, verbal and numerical aptitude, and general educational development. It is also possible to look at just the top 10 matches or at any one of the 75.

ValSEARCH/JOB BANK provides easy and quick access to data that are essential in vocational exploration. However, how these data are used always depends upon the skill and the knowledge of a therapist/evaluator in collaboration with a client. Therefore it is critical that the information about a client's previous job and skills be accurate. Whenever possible, a job analysis of the specific worker qualifications should be made on site (Valpar International Corporation, 1985). If circumstances preclude this—if, for example, a client is not physically able to return to his or her previous job and company, or if a client is in an adversary relationship with his or her previous employer, or if the distance to the workplace is too great—an interview and a job simulation can be used to identify the specific job tasks.

Job Analysis

Whether the therapist is collecting data independently or with a computer program, job analysis is a critical component in the development of a client's specific worker qualifications. The jobs defined in the DOT and its companion publications are integrally linked to job analysis in that the data used for developing the occupational definitions and the classification system were derived from 75,000 job analyses (Robinson, 1979). The best single basis for accurate job descriptions, job analysis is a systematic procedure for observing and describing the duties and the conditions of a particular job.

Purpose of Job Analysis

Although the content and the foci of job analyses may vary, the following list encompasses some of the objectives an occu-

pational therapist may have in performing a job analysis:
1. To identify the elements of a job
2. To determine the skill levels required in the various aspects of a job
3. To examine the suitability of an individual for a particular job or the need for therapeutic adaptation
4. To discover jobs available in the community to facilitate work placement
5. To ascertain the government classification of a job
6. To obtain information for industrial engineering (job, equipment, and tool design)
7. To conduct an ergonomic analysis of the work environment, which would focus on the biomechanical effects of external loads on posture and movement
8. To conduct a task analysis of selected job components used to develop and validate tests, design curricula, and restructure a job as a means of decreasing costs and obtaining efficient use of human resources
9. To meet Commission on Accreditation of Rehabilitation Facilities (CARF) standards for the development of work samples (an accurate description of the actual job).

Appendixes 2-A and 2-B present two sample formats for analysis of a job. The first one is the USDOL's Job Analysis Schedule; the other one was developed by Catherine Heck Edwards at the Rehabilitation Health Center in Ann Arbor, Michigan.

Typical Content of Job Analysis

The methods for all job analysis require that certain categories of information about jobs be collected, analyzed, and recorded in a systematic manner. Reynolds-Lynch (1985a) notes,

> There are various systems of job analysis, but all systems deal with the [following] information to some degree:
> 1. Physical demands
> 2. Mental factors
> 3. Stress factors
> 4. Breakdown of the job
> 5. Tools and machines used
> 6. Description of the work environment
> 7. Hazards. (p. 155)

Work Performed and Worker Characteristics

Work performed and worker characteristics are the two major types of job information used by the U.S. Employment Service in job analysis. Their components are summarized in an earlier section of this chapter that describes the publication, *A Guide to Job Analysis*.

Criteria for Assessing Physical Demands

Once again, the worker characteristic of physical demands is of primary interest to the therapist. Heck (1987) states,

> It is important to rate the frequency of physical demands in terms of the actual percentage of the total workday during which a particular demand (or combination of demands) is performed. If the task is performed frequently throughout the day, and is not continuous, it is useful to note the duration of the task and the interim amount of time between repetitions. (pp. 2–3).

Heck notes the following as additional criteria to use in assessing physical demands:

1. duration of static or dynamic posture, repetitive motion over time and the posture itself;
2. force required to adjust a knob, engage a press, gauge a part;
3. distance of reach, carry, push/pull;
4. shape, size and contour of objects and tools;
5. weight of parts or tools;
6. heights and direction of placement;
7. number of repetitions and/or production quotas (work speed);
8. variations in routine, operations present but not observed. (p. 3)

Methods of Job Analysis

There are various methods of performing a job analysis. The therapist can (a) contact the Materials Development Center at the University of Wisconsin–Stout to obtain a copy of *Job Analysis Exchange* (1988), which contains over 210 job analyses in an easy-to-read format; (b) interview the worker's supervisor; (c) interview the worker (obtain a subjective analysis); (d) observe a "normal/typical" person on the job; (e) perform the job himself or herself (conduct an introspective analysis); or (f) directly observe the worker performing the job. Whenever possible, photographic or video recording equipment should be used to document the job.

Preparation

In preparing to perform a job analysis, it is very useful for the therapist to consult the classic vocational references to obtain a basic knowledge of the job. Another excellent reference is "Methods of Classifying and Evaluating Manual Work,"

Chapter 7 in *Occupational Biomechanics* by Chaffin and Anderson (1984). The general information reviewed in this text will assist the therapist in planning the work demands to be measured and studied. In addition, in performing an ergonomic job analysis—that is, a study of work in terms of the productivity, the safety, and the health of the worker-machine system—Heck (1987) suggests that the therapist know first what components make up the job, what measurements must be taken, and what equipment is required.

Suggested Equipment for an On-Site Job Analysis

Heck (1987) suggests that the following equipment be taken by the occupational therapist to the job site to perform a job analysis:

1. A portable videocamera with an instant playback that operates well in low light.
2. A 50 ft. retractable steel tape measure.
3. A Rolatape or any wheeled measuring device.
4. A push-pull gauge with an accessory pack (Chatillon Dial Model DPH-250).
5. A 2 ft. welded chain with a locking link at one end and a minimum pull strength of 250 lbs.
6. A 3 ft. steel cable with formed loops at each end.
7. A scale for weighing (this may not be critical, for a therapist can usually have items weighed at the plant; however, the Norelco HS-10 is dependable).
8. Wide- and narrow-jaw vise-grip pliers, one pair each (to hold parts stable).
9. Heavy-duty work gloves and a hand towel.
10. A clipboard, a pencil, and graph paper.
11. A stopwatch.
12. A luggage cart to transport equipment.

(adapted from p. 3)

T. Bryan (personal communication, November 1988) suggests, in addition, a hard hat, safety glasses or goggles, and steel toes.

A final note on job analysis: The therapist is cautioned that when performing a job analysis, he or she is still dealing with a contrived situation because his or her presence and its influence on the individual's performance need to be taken into account.

Summary

The use of various references related to the study of jobs, work, and job analysis is described in this chapter. The information may be helpful to the occupational therapist operating alone or to the occupational therapist collaborating with a vocational evaluator. When functioning in work-related programs, the therapist needs a thorough understanding of this material to provide competent evaluation and treatment, not only of the injured worker but also of clients in mental health treatment programs, prison rehabilitation programs, and programs preparing the developmentally disabled to enter the job market. Familiarity with the material also aids in coordination of efforts with vocational rehabilitation specialists.

The development and management of work programs by occupational therapists has experienced tremendous growth in the 1980s. The high level of interest in this practice arena represents a return to the profession's basic values of work and occupation as a foundation of the profession.

Glossaries
Abbreviations

COJ—*The Classification of Jobs According to Worker Trait Factors*
DOT—*Dictionary of Occupational Titles*
DPT—data, people, things
GATB—General Aptitude Test Battery
GED—general educational development
GOE—*Guide for Occupational Exploration*
Ind. Des.—industrial designation
MPSMS—materials, products, subject matter, and services
OAP—occupational aptitude patterns
OGA—occupational group arrangement
OOH—*Occupational Outlook Handbook*
PD—physical demands
SVP—specific vocational preparation
USDOL—U.S. Department of Labor
USES—U.S. Employment Service
WC—working conditions
WQP—worker qualification profile
WTG—worker trait groups

Terms

Data, people, things (DPT)—see **Worker functions.**
Ginzberg's (1957) model of occupational choice—a developmental model of career choice, positing successive periods of fantasy, tentative choice, and realistic choice.
Interest area—one of 12 broad classifications of occupations used in the GOE; represented by the first two digits in a six-digit code (00.00.00) for occupations.

Job analysis—a systematic procedure for observing and describing the duties and the conditions of a particular job.

Materials, products, subject matter, and services (MPSMS)—what a worker in a given job processes, makes, applies (as with data), and/or renders; a component of work performed, relating to the actual work activities of a job; used in job analysis.

Mathematical development (M) and **language development (L)**—the level of training required to perform a job proficiently. See Appendix C of *Selected Characteristics of Occupations Defined in the "Dictionary of Occupational Titles."*

Occupational aptitude pattern (OAP)—specific abilities required of an individual to perform a given work activity; measured by the General Aptitude Test Battery (GATB) in nine areas: intelligence, verbal aptitude, numerical aptitude, spatial aptitude, form perception, clerical perception, motor coordination, finger dexterity, and manual dexterity. See Appendix E of *Selected Characteristics of Occupations Defined in the "Dictionary of Occupational Titles."*

Occupational code—a nine-digit code (000.000-000) used in the DOT to categorize occupations and uniquely identify them. The first digit represents the occupational group arrangement in which an occupation falls, and the next two digits each represent narrower classifications of the occupational groups. The middle three digits represent worker function ratings. The last three digits indicate an occupation's alphabetical order among all occupations with the same first six digits.

Occupational group arrangement (OGA)—one of nine broad classifications of occupations used in the DOT; represented by the first digit in a nine-digit code (000.000-000).

Physical demands (PD)—"both the physical requirements of the job and the physical capacities (specific physical traits) a worker must have to meet [them]" (USDOL, 1981, p. 465); expressed in terms of strength (ability to lift, carry, push, or pull while standing, walking, or sitting); climbing and/or balancing; stooping, kneeling, crouching, and/or crawling; reaching, handling, fingering, and/or feeling; talking and/or hearing; and seeing. See *Selected Characteristics of Occupations Defined in the "Dictionary of Occupational Titles,"* Appendix A; *Classification of Jobs According to Worker Trait Factors*, appendix; and *A Guide to Job Analysis*.

Specific vocational preparation (SVP)—the amount of time required to learn the techniques, acquire the information, and develop the facility needed for average performance in a specific job. See *Selected Characteristics of Occupations Defined in the "Dictionary of Occupational Titles,"* Appendix D; *Classification of Jobs According to Worker Trait Factors*, appendix; and *A Guide to Job Analysis*.

Subgroup—a classification of occupations used in the GOE, breaking down the broader classification of work group; represented by the third two digits in a six-digit code (00.00.00) for occupations.

Work devices—the machines, the equipment, the tools, and the work aids used by the individual to perform the specific activities of a job; a component of work performed, relating to the actual work activities of a job; used in job analysis.

Work field—one of 94 "categories of technologies that reflect how work gets done and what gets done" (USDOL, 1982, p. 121); a component of work performed, relating to the actual work activities of a job; used in job analysis.

Work group—a classification of occupations used in the GOE, breaking down the broader classification of interest area; represented by the second two digits in a six-digit code (00.00.00) for occupations.

Work performed—one of two types of information used by the U.S. Employment Service in job analysis, encompassing "those . . . components that relate to the actual work activities of a job" (USDOL, 1982, p. 121): worker functions, work fields, work devices, and materials, products, subject matter, and services (MPSMS).

Worker characteristics—one of two types of information used by the U.S. Employment Service in job analysis, encompassing worker attributes that contribute to successful job performance with regard to the work activities themselves and the environment in which the work is performed.

Worker functions—a system of classifying what a worker does in relation to data, people, and things; accompanied by a hierarchical system of numerical ratings reflecting complexity (the lower the number, the more complex the function); represented by the middle three digits in a nine-digit occupational code (000.000-000) used in the DOT.

Worker Qualification Profile—client-specific information fed into ValSEARCH/JOB BANK, a computerized system for matching clients with jobs.

Worker trait groups—a system of classifying occupations used in the DOT, making it possible to determine the degree to which aptitudes, interests, education, physical capacities, etc., are required for average successful job performance.

Working conditions (WC)—the specific physical environmental conditions to which a worker is exposed while performing assigned tasks; expressed in terms of exposure to weather, extremes of cold or heat, temperature changes, wetness and humidity, noise and vibration, hazards, and fumes, odors, toxic conditions, dust, and poor ventilation. See *Selected Characteristics of Occupations Defined in the "Dictionary of Occupational Titles,"* Appendix B; *Classification of Jobs According to Worker Trait Factors*, appendix; and *A Guide to Job Analysis*.

References

Botterbusch, K. F. (1986). *A comparison of computerized job matching systems.* Menomonie, WI: University of Wisconsin–Stout, Stout Vocational Rehabilitation Institute, Materials Development Center.

Chaffin, D. B., & Anderson, G. (1984). *Occupational biomechanics.* New York: John Wiley & Sons.

Field, T. F., & Field, J. E. (Eds.). (1988). *The classification of jobs according to worker trait factors.* Athens, GA: Elliot and Fitzpatrick. (Address: P.O. Box 19452, Athens, GA 30605).

Ginzberg, E. (1957). *Occupational choice: An approach to a general theory.* New York: Columbia University Press.

Heck, C. (1987). The job site analysis for work capacity programming. *Physical Disabilities Special Interest Section Newsletter, 10*(2), 2–3.

Job analysis exchange. (1988). Menomonie, WI: University of Wisconsin–Stout, Stout Vocational Rehabilitation Institute, Materials Development Center.

Reynolds-Lynch, K. (1985a). Job analysis. In M. Kirkland & S. C. Robertson (Eds.), *Planning and implementing vocational readiness in occupational therapy* (PIVOT) (pp. 155–157). Rockville, MD: American Occupational Therapy Association.

Reynolds-Lynch, K. (1985b). An orientation to the *Dictionary of occupational titles.* In M. Kirkland & S. C. Robertson (Eds.), *Planning and implementing vocational readiness in occupational therapy* (PIVOT) (pp. 315–340). Rockville, MD: American Occupational Therapy Association.

Robinson, C. (1979). *The "Dictionary of occupational titles" in vocational assessment: A self-study manual.* Menomonie, WI: University of Wisconsin–Stout, Stout Vocational Rehabilitation Institute, Materials Development Center.

Taylor, S. (1988). Occupational therapy in industrial rehabilitation. In H. Hopkins & H. Smith (Eds.), *Willard and Spackman's Occupational therapy* (pp. 299–307). Philadelphia: J. B. Lippincott.

U.S. Department of Labor. (1977). *Dictionary of occupational titles* (4th ed.). Washington, DC: U.S. Government Printing Office.

U.S. Department of Labor. (1979). *Guide for occupational exploration.* Washington, DC: U.S. Government Printing Office.

U.S. Department of Labor. (1981). *Selected characteristics of occupations defined in the "Dictionary of occupational titles."* Washington, DC: U.S. Government Printing Office.

U.S. Department of Labor. (1982). *Dictionary of occupational titles* (4th ed.), *Supplement.* Washington, DC: U.S. Government Printing Office.

U.S. Department of Labor. (1986). *Dictionary of occupational titles* (4th ed.), *Supplement.* Washington, DC: U.S. Government Printing Office.

U.S. Department of Labor, Employment and Training Administration. (1982). *A guide to job analysis.* Washington, DC: U.S. Government Printing Office.

U.S. Department of Labor, Labor Statistics Bureau. (1988). *Occupational outlook handbook 1986–87.* Washington, DC: U.S. Government Printing Office.

U.S. Department of Labor, Manpower Administration. (1972). *Handbook for analyzing jobs.* Menomonie, WI: University of Wisconsin–Stout, Stout Vocational Rehabilitation Institute, Materials Development Center.

Valpar International Corporation. (1985). *ValSEARCH/JOB BANK.* Tucson, AZ: Author.

Related Reading

Botterbusch, K. F. (1987). *Vocational assessment and evaluation systems: A comparison.* Menomonie, WI: University of Wisconsin–Stout, Stout Vocational Rehabilitation Institute, Materials Development Center.

Job analysis exchange catalog. (1988). Menomonie, WI: University of Wisconsin–Stout, Stout Vocational Rehabilitation Institute, Materials Development Center.

Kester, D. L. (1985). The job search. In M. Kirkland & S. C. Robertson (Eds.), *Planning and implementing vocational readiness in occupational therapy* (PIVOT) (pp. 291–313). Rockville, MD: American Occupational Therapy Association.

Chapter 2, Appendix A

U.S. Department of Labor
Manpower Administration

OMB 44-R0722

Estab. & Sched. No. _____

Job Analysis Schedule

1. Estab. Job Title _____

2. Ind. Assign. _____

3. SIC Code(s) and Title(s) _____

4. Job Summary:

5. Work Performed Ratings:

Worker Functions	D Data	P People	T Things

Work Field _____

M.P.S.M.S. _____

6. Worker Traits Ratings:

GED	1	2	3	4	5	6			
SVP	1	2	3	4	5	6	7	8	9
Aptitudes	G__	V__	N__	S__	P__	Q__	K__	F__	M__ E__ C__
Temperaments	D	F	I	J	M	P	R	S	T V
Interests	1a	1b	2a	2b	3a	3b	4a	4b	5a 5b
Phys. Demands	S	L	M	H	V	2	3	4	5 6
Environ. Cond.	I	O	B	2	3	4	5	6	7

Code _____ WTA Group _____ DOT Title _____ Ind. Desig. _____

MA 7-36

From *Handbook for Analyzing Jobs* (pp. 33–36) by U.S. Department of Labor, Manpower Administration, 1972, Menomonie, WI: University of Wisconsin–Stout, Stout Vocational Rehabilitation Institute, Materials Development Center.

7. General Education

    a. Elementary _____ High School _____ Courses _____

    b. College _____ Courses _____

8. Vocational Preparation

    a. College _____ Courses _____

    _____

    b. Vocational Education _____ Courses _____

    _____

    c. Apprenticeship _____

    _____

    d. Inplant Training _____

    e. On-the-Job Training _____

    f. Performance on Other Jobs _____

9. Experience _____

10. Orientation _____

11. Licenses, etc. _____

12. Relation to Other Jobs and Workers _____

    Promotion: From _____ To _____

    Transfers: From _____ To _____

    Supervision Received _____

    Supervision Given _____

    _____

13. Machines, Tools, Equipment, and Work Aids

14. Materials and Products

15. Description of Tasks:

16. Definition of Terms

17. General Comments

18. Analyst _____ Date _____ Editor _____ Date _____

    Reviewed By _____ Title, Org. _____

    National Office Reviewer _____

Chapter 2, Appendix B

Rehabilitation Health Center
2010 Hogback Road, Suite 6
Ann Arbor, MI 48105
313-971-9790

Occupational Therapy
Job Analysis

Date: _____

Patient: _____

SS#: _____

Date(s) of Service(s): _____

Referral Source: _____

Attending Physician: _____

Employer: _____

Insurance Company: _____

Case Manager: _____

Job Site Analysis

Job Title: _____

Type of Industry: _____

Site: _____

Contact Person: _____

Present: _____

Date of Injury/
Subsequent Injuries: _____
_____

Time off Work: _____

Date of Hire: _____

© 1989 by Catherine Heck Edwards, OTR, formerly employed at Rehabilitation Health Center, now employed at Ingham Medical Center, 401 West Greenlawn Avenue, Lansing, MI 48910-2819. Reprinted by permission.

RHC Patient: _____ Date: _____ Sh 2 of 10

Work Hours: From   _____ a.m. to _____ p.m.

Days of week _____ to _____

Breaks from   _____ a.m. to _____ p.m.

_____ a.m. to _____ p.m.

_____ not scheduled

Lunch   _____ a.m. to _____ p.m.

Overtime   _____

Departments Viewed: _____

Machine or Station No.: _____

Production Quota: _____

Time of Analysis: _____

Videotaped: _____ Yes _____ No

Physical Demands Analysis
1. Stand

    Task: _____

    Estimated total hours per shift: _____

    Maximum continuous time: _____

    Surface: _____

    Foot controls: _____ Yes   _____ No   _____ Right   _____ Left

    Toe clearance: _____ Yes   _____ No

2. Walk

    Task: _____

    Frequency: _____

    Distance: _____

    Duration: _____

Chapter 2, Appendix B: Occupational Therapy Job Analysis

RHC Patient: _____ Date: _____ Sh 3 of 10

Surface: _____

Pace: _____ Slow   _____ Normal   _____ Fast   _____ Run

Distance from parking lot to job: _____

Distance to break area: _____

Distance to bathroom: _____

3. Sit

   Task: _____

   Chair Seat Height: _____

   Backrest: _____ Yes   _____ No   Type: _____

   Adequate Leg Room Below Work Station: _____ Yes   _____ No

   Swivel Chair: _____ Yes   _____ No

   Estimated Total Hours Per Shift: _____

   Maximum Continuous Time: _____

   Is Chair Appropriate to Task (s):   _____ Yes   _____ No

   Footrest: _____ Yes   _____ No   (Height _____)

   Armrest: _____ Yes   _____ No

4. Lift

   Object(s): _____

   Dimensions: _____ Length   _____ Width (Depth)
                    _____ Height   _____ Girth

   Maximum Weight:
   - Start/End Point: _____ to _____
   - Frequency: _____
   - Body Position: _____

   Most Common Weight:
   - Start/End Point: _____ to _____
   - Frequency: _____
   - Body Position: _____

RHC Patient: _____ Date: _____ Sh 4 of 10

Obstructions: _____
_____
_____
_____

Load Balanced: _____ Yes   _____ No

Hand Used: _____ Right   _____ Left   _____ Both

5. Varied Weight Demands Chart

   (A = Lifted with Another's Assistance)

	Total Hours Performed Daily				
	Never	< 1	1–2	3–4	5–6	7–8
Lift under 10#						
Lift 11–25#						
Lift 26–50#						
Lift 51–75#						
Lift 76–100#						
Over 100#						

	Total Hours Performed Daily				
	Never	< 1	1–2	3–4	5–6	7–8
Carry under 10#						
Carry 11–25#						
Carry 26–50#						
Carry 51–75#						
Carry 76–100#						
Over 100#						

6. Carry

   Objects: _____

   Maximum Weight:
   - Distance: _____
   - Frequency: _____
   - Hands Used: _____ Right   _____ Left   _____ Both

   Most Common Weight:
   - Distance: _____ 0–10 feet   _____ 50–100 feet
                 _____ 10–25 feet   _____ Over 100 feet
                 _____ 25–50 feet   _____ Over 100 yards
   - Frequency: _____
   - Hands Used: _____ Right   _____ Left   _____ Both

   Obstructions: _____

Chapter 2, Appendix B: Occupational Therapy Job Analysis

RHC Patient: _____   Date: _____   Sh 5 of 10

7. Push   Position: _____

  Object _____ Force _____ Weight _____ Surface _____

  Height from Floor _____   Distance _____ Frequency _____

8. Pull   Position: _____

  Object _____ Force _____ Weight _____ Surface _____

  Height from Floor _____   Distance _____ Frequency _____

9. Climb

  Task: _____

  Device: _____ Stairs _____ Ladder _____ Other

  Height: _____

  Duration: _____

  Frequency: _____

  Under Load: _____ Yes _____ No   (Description: _____

  _____)

  Footing: _____

  Associated Tasks/Demands: _____

  _____

10. Balance

  Task: _____

  Device: _____

  Height: _____

  Frequency: _____

  Surface: _____

  Safety Equipment/Precautions: _____

  Associated Tasks/Demands: _____

RHC Patient: _____ Date: _____ Sh 6 of 10

11. Stoop/Bend

   Task: _____

   Frequency: _____

   Associated Tasks/Demands: _____

   Duration: _____

12. Crouch/Squat

   Task: _____

   Frequency: _____

   Associated Tasks/Demands: _____

   Duration: _____

13. Kneel

   Task: _____

   Frequency: _____

   Duration: _____

   Leg Used: _____ Right   _____ Left   _____ Both

   Surface: _____

14. Reach

   Task: _____

   Hand(s) Used: _____ Right   _____ Left   _____ Both

	Direction	Frequency	Duration	Weight
0–20"				
20–36"				
37–54"				
54–72"				
Above 72"				

| RHC Patient: | Date: | Sh 7 of 10 |

NOTE: The following is to be completed only in the case of a hand or arm injury.

The following scale is used to interpret work demands in the following section:

    Infrequently: Happens less than once per day
    Occasionally: 1–33% of the time
    Frequently: 34–66% of the time
    Continuously: 67–100% of the time

Use of the word "required" indicates that activity must be performed due to employer demands or for acceptable performance level to be maintained.

15. Hand Tasks

Job Demands	Right	Left	Both	Neither	Frequency
Major Hand					
Grasp: Overhead	_____	_____	_____	_____	_____
Sidehand	_____	_____	_____	_____	_____
Underhand	_____	_____	_____	_____	_____
Finger Grasp	_____	_____	_____	_____	_____
Up & Down Flexion of Wrist	_____	_____	_____	_____	_____
Side to Side Bending of Wrist	_____	_____	_____	_____	_____
Hand Controls	_____	_____	_____	_____	_____
Hand Twisting	_____	_____	_____	_____	_____
Sensory Discrimination	_____	_____	_____	_____	_____

16. Description of Items Handled/Fingered (include weight/size of object)

_____
_____
_____
_____
_____
_____
_____
_____

RHC Patient: _____ Date: _____ Sh 8 of 10

17. Prehension Patterns Used

    Cylindrical Grip _____   Lateral Pinch _____
    Ball Grip _____   Palmar Pinch _____
    Hook Grip _____   Tip Pinch _____

18. Comments

    _____
    _____
    _____

19. Gloves Used   _____ Yes   _____ No

20. Static Tasks

    _____
    _____
    _____

21. Work Conditions

    Exposure to   Yes   No

    Hot Temperatures   _____   _____
    Cold Temperatures   _____   _____
    Sudden Changes in Temperature   _____   _____
    Noise   _____   _____
    Fumes   _____   _____
    Cramped Quarters   _____   _____
    Cold Surfaces/Tools   _____   _____
    Hot Surfaces/Tools   _____   _____
    Sharp Edges   _____   _____
    Vibration   _____   _____

    _____ % inside _____ % outside

22. Cervical Injury

    Does Job Require?   Yes   No

    Extreme Neck Extension   _____   _____
    Extensive Neck Flexion   _____   _____
    Side to Side Turning   _____   _____

    Length of Time Position Maintained _____

Chapter 2, Appendix B: Occupational Therapy Job Analysis

RHC Patient: Date:

23. Other Job Demands

	Yes	No		
Crawl	_____	_____	Distance _____	Duration _____
Jump	_____	_____		
Lie on Back/ Stomach	_____	_____	Duration _____	
Twist	_____	_____	Weight _____	

24. List Tools, Equipment, and Materials Used

   _____

   _____

   _____

25. Tools

   Handle Length: _____

   Handle Diameter: _____

   Handle Span: _____

   Handle Angle: _____

   Frequency Used: _____

   Pinch Points: _____

26. Work Surface Height

   _____

   _____

27. Possible Modifications

   _____

   _____

   _____

   _____

   _____

RHC Patient: _____ Date: _____ Sh 10 of 10

Comments: _____

_____

_____

_____

_____

_____

_____

_____

_____

_____

28. Job Analyst: _____
                              Signature

29. Plant Attendant: _____
                              Signature

Catherine Heck Edwards, OTR
1/88

3

Work Hardening

Melanie T. Ellexson, OTR/L

The term *work hardening* was first seen in current literature in the late 1970s and early 1980s. As the body of knowledge related to work hardening has grown, both practice and definition have gone through a metamorphosis. Principles that now apply to this treatment approach are applicable to a wide variety of individuals whose primary goal is employment. However, *work hardening* is most widely accepted as applying to the rehabilitation phase of returning the industrially injured worker to the workplace (Isernhagen, 1988).

This chapter presents many considerations and principles in the development of a work hardening program. Particular emphasis is placed upon individuals injured at work and covered by workers' compensation. However, most programmatic information is applicable to anyone whose goal is competitive employment.

A few terms need clarification. *Worker* is used to denote the individual receiving direct treatment. The terms *referral source, company,* and *payer source* represent the client because they identify a business relationship.

Many professionals involved in work hardening programs find themselves serving two masters. They are providing a means of improving function for the injured worker and at the same time offering answers and case resolution services to the insurance company or the employer. In most instances this means that each case has both a worker and a client component.

The concept of work hardening is rooted in treatment done in the early 1920s by occupational therapists in Veterans Administration hospitals in the United States. Services were provided to bring work-oriented programs to the men disabled in the Spanish-American War and World War I who were of an age to need future employment (Matheson, 1987).

In 1920 the Smith-Fess Act, often referred to as the Civilian Vocational Rehabilitation Act, gave government support and sanction to rehabilitation efforts. This law focused on retraining disabled people and placing them in suitable jobs. Occupational therapy was covered under this act only if it was part of a medical treatment program (Kirkland & Robertson, 1985).

Amendments to the original act, made in 1943 and 1954, added coverage for people with psychiatric conditions and developmental disabilities and provided greater financial support for training, research, and program development. The Rehabilitation Act of 1973 expanded services to the more severely disabled and called for affirmative action in the workplace. There exists a very comprehensive overview of work-related history (Kirkland & Robertson, 1985) in *Planning and Implementing Vocational Readiness in Occupational Therapy,* published by the American Occupational Therapy Association.

Work and occupation are at the foundations of the occupational therapy profession. Both legislation and occupational therapy principles have placed the occupational therapist in the position of having a unique combination of skills and knowledge to practice in the area of work hardening.

In 1913 Herbert Hall, an occupational therapy leader, recommended that Massachusetts General Hospital in Boston start a workshop "'to fill the dangerous interval immediately after hospital discharge and before regular work can be attempted'" (Kirkland & Robertson, 1985, p. 18). This describes the work hardening phase of rehabilitation at its most complete. Recently *work hardening* was defined by the Commission on Accreditation of Rehabilitation Facilities (CARF, 1989) as being

> interdisciplinary in nature [and using] conditioning tasks that are graded to progressively improve the biomechanical, neuromuscular, cardiovascular/metabolic, and psychosocial functions of the individual in conjunction with real or simulated work activities. Work hardening provides a transition between acute care and return to work while addressing the issues of productivity, safety, physical tolerances, and worker behaviors. Work hardening is a highly structured, goal-oriented, individualized treatment program designed to maximize the individual's ability to return to work. (p. 69)

The CARF definition is used as the basis for program development in this chapter.

Workers' Compensation Laws

As previously mentioned, industrially injured workers are the largest group currently benefiting from work hardening programs. Workers' compensation laws are a product of the 20th century and were developed as the United States moved beyond the Industrial Revolution. The first federal Workmen's Compensation Act was written in 1908, and by 1915, 30 states had adopted compensation acts of their own (U.S. Chamber of Commerce, 1987). The workers' compensation system was developed to protect injured workers by dispensing benefits necessary for basic subsistence during the recovery period, and to ensure that the families of workers seriously injured or killed would not be without food or shelter. It was not intended to be a permanent welfare system or a means of improving a worker's occupational skill level through advanced education or training.

Although each state law is different in its administration, interpretation, and benefit level, there are some common principles:

1. The burden of proof of injury lies with the injured worker.
2. The weekly benefit amount is available during the period of nonwork.
3. The injured worker must cooperate in his or her medical/rehabilitation care.
4. No benefit will be paid if the injury or the illness is intentionally self-inflicted or if the worker is intoxicated.
5. All claims must be reported promptly. There is a time limit on the filing of claims.
6. A review process exists for disputed claims.

Recent changes in many states have mandated benefits covering both physical and vocational rehabilitation. A number of states now recognize *cumulative trauma,* or repetitive-motion-type injury, as a compensable disability. The recognition of cumulative trauma has enabled individuals who have developed significant problems over a period of years to obtain paid medical care and compensation. Previously a specific incident had to be documented for workers' compensation to be applied.

These changes and others have served to increase the cost of workers' compensation. American society has been called litigious in the last few decades. More information about workers' rights and the influence of the legal profession, often supported by unions, have encouraged employees to seek greater compensation.

Ever-increasing compensation costs have led to the development of programs and technology to try to stem these rising expenses to industry. The concept of work hardening has developed as a step toward solving this problem. As both the profession's involvement and work-related technology continue to evolve, occupational therapists may find themselves with many new and diverse models of practice in industrial rehabilitation and occupational medicine. For now, work hardening, which has principles deeply rooted in occupational therapy theory and history, appears to be a very effective method of returning the injured worker to the workplace.

The material that follows is a presentation of significant components for the development and the operation of work hardening services. Special emphasis is placed upon those elements and activities particularly identified with occupational therapy.

Program Development
Market Analysis

In developing any new product line, the merchandiser must complete a careful study of the marketplace to determine the demand for and the probability of selling the product. Product-line development has now become an accepted approach to marketing medical/rehabilitation services.

Before one establishes a work hardening program, it is best to get a picture of future demand by looking at various demographics:

1. Competition: What programs are established? Where are they located? What is their design? What do they charge? Are they accepted by the community? Who refers people to them?
2. Community unemployment rate: High unemployment may mean fewer workers needing services. There is no exposure to work-related injuries when people are not working because of economic problems.
3. Industrial growth rate: No new industry and older companies moving out of an area together mean fewer workers needing services. An aging population without younger workers may also lower exposure.
4. Industry mix: Communities in which major employment is in retail sales or in sedentary, service-type industries may generate very few workers' compensation injuries.
5. Average household income: High income per household may indicate more residents with professional or executive employment than residents with hands-on jobs that generate greater risk of injury.

6. Perceived needs of the community: Some state laws do not encourage the development of work hardening programs because they do not support rehabilitation. Very low benefits for injury may be found. This serves to limit treatment to the basic medical/rehabilitation expenditures.

Elements for Site Location

Once one has a good picture of the general area one will be serving, a specific site must be identified. The selection of a site to provide work hardening services is a critical decision. One has two choices basically: either to be within an established hospital or rehabilitation facility or to develop as a freestanding entity. There are advantages to each, but being autonomous and having separate space in which work hardening services can be provided is the trend (Isernhagen, 1988). Further, the concept of a separate area is supported by the CARF (1989) work hardening guidelines. If one chooses to be identified with an established facility, space within the facility that has a private entrance is most desirable. This offers convenience, avoids the mingling of work hardening workers with general hospital patients, and encourages work/wellness roles rather than patient/sick roles. In a multidisciplinary team approach, programs may become fragmented when the various components of work hardening take place in different departments. Work hardening workers are better able to see the combination of work simulation and exercise as a total program when all activity is performed in the same area. Strengthening through conditioning exercises and practice through work simulations should be alternated throughout the daily treatment sessions; this gives added support to a single work hardening location.

Freestanding sites, when chosen, should be on the ground level, have good access from major thoroughfares, be easy to locate, and have ample parking available. Locations in an industrial park, a strip shopping mall, or a rehabilitated factory area can offer excellent rental opportunities.

Staffing Patterns and Ratios

Once the market is known and the site has been located, staffing becomes the next critical decision to be made. Work hardening programs provide options for many different staffing patterns. In most models the occupational therapist plays a major role. Regardless of the scope of staffing, the core team should include an occupational therapist, a physical therapist, a vocational services professional, and a psychologist. Depending upon the size and the goals of the program, additional or adjunct staff could include a rehabilitation engineer, an exercise physiologist, an industrial arts teacher, an ergonomist, a rehabilitation nurse, an occupational health nurse, a lay foreman with an industrial background, an industrial hygienist, and a nutrition counselor. All of these individuals need not be present at one time. Many, including core team members, may be consultants or part-time employees. This is particularly true for the vocational evaluator and the psychologist, who may not be involved in every case (CARF, 1989). Both occupational therapy assistants and physical therapy assistants can play significant roles in the daily operation by providing supervision of work hardening activities and by developing work-simulation tasks.

A ratio of one professional for every six to eight workers receiving work hardening services is recommended (Ellexson, 1987). Because work hardening programming is a daily treatment approach and may involve two to eight hours of activity for each individual, the daily time and work intensity required of staff dictate worker/professional ratios lower than those found in other treatment settings.

Space Requirements

Typically, work hardening programs require 1,200 square feet or more (Matheson, 1987). At the STEPS Industrial Injury Clinics, satellite programs of Schwab Rehabilitation Center in Chicago, the experience has been that 2,500 square feet will accommodate 12–14 work hardening workers at various stages in their treatment program. The need to offer a wide variety of job-simulation work stations, open areas for gross motor activities (such as pushing carts and carrying objects), and quiet areas for testing and evaluation means that work hardening programs demand not only flexible space but high space/worker ratios. Figure 3-1 is an example of a possible layout for a work hardening clinic. Figures 3-2 and 3-3, which picture two established clinics, serve as examples currently in use.

Several elements can influence the effectiveness of programming for both staff and workers. These should be kept in mind as one either adapts existing facility space or seeks a freestanding center.

1. Workers have needs related to many kinds of work environments. Not all people relate to factory-like settings.
2. "Work" and "return to work" do not equate with dirty, dingy settings.
3. The design of a space and the colors used in it can positively or negatively influence staff-worker and worker-worker interaction.

Figure 3-1
Work Hardening Center Layout

Rough, final dimensions: 48.5 feet by 50 feet. Scale: 1/6 inch = 1.25 feet

Note. © 1988 by M. T. Ellexson, OTR/L. Reprinted by permission.

Figure 3-2
Theracom, Livonia, Michigan

Note. © 1989 by Theracom, Inc. Reprinted by permission.

4. Adequate and properly positioned lighting is essential to prevent injuries in the work hardening setting and to improve individual participation.
5. Giving workers access to the outside and using outdoor work simulations should be considered.

Equipment

Increasing acceptance of the concept of return-to-work rehabilitation programs and the rapid growth in the number of programs available have led to the development of much new equipment and technology to match changing job demands. Thus in planning a new program one must consider new as well as traditional equipment needs. Work hardening today may employ very elaborate machines that provide isokinetic or isodynamic evaluation of motion, such as the Cybex products. Alternatively it may rely on manual or computerized work simulation "samples" that have been standardized and professionally manufactured—for example, the Ergos equipment; evaluation equipment for manual lifting such as

Figure 3-3
Schwab STEPS Industrial Injury Clinic, South Holland, Illinois

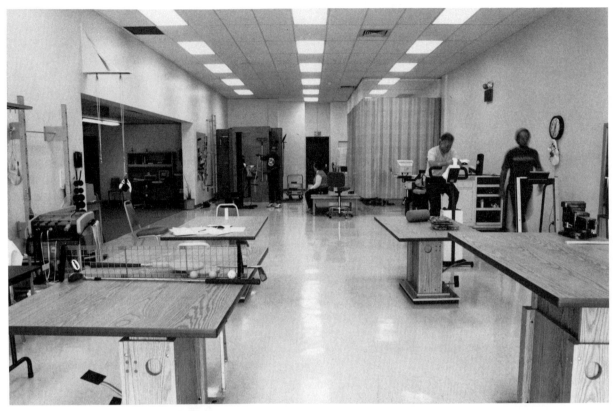

Note. Photograph by Susan Matczak. © by Schwab STEPS Industrial Injury Clinic. Reprinted by permission.

that of WEST; the dynamometer produced by Baltimore Therapeutic Equipment (BTE) (see Figure 3-4), which evaluates static movement, grip strength, and work force; and Valpar evaluation tools (see Figure 3-5).

One must also consider homemade work simulations involving bricks, crates, hand tools, garden tools, ladders, and other items typically used in manual jobs. Further, many programs are using computer activities such as word processing and data processing, which are frequently found in the service industries. A partial list of equipment and resources appears in Appendix 3-A.

In many instances workers being treated may have jobs that require specialized tools or equipment. If so, they may need to bring such equipment to the center for practice. Industries may give or loan specialized equipment, such as cutting tools, railroad switches, assembly parts, or specialized safety equipment. This is particularly true if the company plans to have employees treated frequently in a facility.

Figure 3-4
A Worker Using the Baltimore Therapeutic Equipment (BTE) Work Simulator at the Schwab STEPS Industrial Injury Clinic, Chicago, Illinois

Note. © by Schwab STEPS Industrial Injury Clinic. Reprinted by permission.

Finally, an important point to remember in setting up a work hardening program is to have evaluation tools and systems that measure basic functions and skills and that provide reproducible test results showing a worker's capacities. Also, materials that allow the building or the development of work stations simulating the actual activities necessary in work offer the most realistic measures of workers' skills and endurance.

Milieu

People recovering from serious illness or injury often have many doubts about their return to work. The clinic's environment, or milieu, can be critical to a successful return. It has been found that an effective work hardening setting encourages activity and emphasizes good worker traits such as regular attendance, punctuality, personal industry, and safety (Matheson 1987; Taylor, 1988). Such a work environment

Figure 3-5
A Worker Using the Valpar Dynamic Physical Capacity Evaluation 19 at the Schwab STEPS Industrial Injury Clinic, Chicago, Illinois

Note. © by Schwab STEPS Industrial Injury Clinic. Reprinted by permission.

should be maintained by establishing work rules, break times, and meal times. Interaction similar to that found among coworkers and between workers and supervisors is also to be encouraged. Figure 3-6 is one example of rules provided to workers at the start of a program. Staff should serve and be viewed more as work or activity supervisors than as caregivers. Individuals in the program should be held responsible for their own productivity just as they would be in a competitive-employment situation.

Establishing and maintaining the milieu may mean not accepting workers for rehabilitation whose cognitive or physical disability makes them poor candidates for return to competitive employment. Examples might be a person with significant brain injury, a person with high-level spinal cord injury, or a young person who has suffered a stroke and has both physical and cognitive residuals. Although such people

Figure 3-6
Sample Statement of Work Rules and Procedures

Work Rules and Procedures

Your evaluation or work hardening program at Schwab is set up to be as similar to normal work as possible. To help make your experience as realistic as possible and to provide for the health and safety of everybody, we have a few simple work rules:

Hours: Work hardening begins at 8:30 a.m. each day. Work capacity evaluation begins at a scheduled time. You will have a mid-morning break and afternoon break of 15 minutes. Lunch is from 12:00 noon to 1:00 p.m. Sign in and out on sheets upon arrival to and departure from program. Sign in break time and lunch time on sheet.

Absence: If you are unable to attend the program, you must call in. Call _____ from 8:00 a.m. on. If during the evaluation, you have an appointment scheduled, please let us know.

Clothing: Comfortable work clothes should be worn at all times. Comfortable shoes with good traction on soles should be worn at all times. Do not wear sandals, long necklaces or bracelets.

Smoking: Smoke only in break room. Chewing tobacco is acceptable.

Telephone Use: You may receive calls here only on your breaks. Outgoing calls can be made on an emergency basis only.

Safety: Safety equipment must be utilized as necessary at all times. Protective eye wear must be worn at all times when operating power equipment. Do not use any electrical equipment without being cleared by staff. Never exceed the limits set for you in the program by the supervising therapist.

Reviewed rules _____ Date _____

Note. © 1986 by Schwab STEPS Industrial Injury Clinic. Reprinted by permission.

may benefit from various forms of functional capacity evaluation and from a group environment, they may not make gains in work hardening because their potential to work at greater than sedentary levels may be neglible. Also, mixing them with more typical candidates for work hardening (workers with back injury, traumatic hand injury, etc.) may prevent the latter from moving steadily toward the worker role.

Structure

Work hardening has come to mean both a treatment approach offered by health care professionals to prepare an injured worker for return to employment, and an all-encompassing program provided by health care teams aimed at the

Figure 3-7
Stage Model of Industrial Rehabilitation
Leonard N. Matheson, PhD

Stage	Area Assessed	Measured by or in Terms of . . .
One	Pathology	Studies of tissue and bone
Two	Impairment	Anatomy, physiology, psyche
Three	Functional limitation	Symptoms and limitations
Four	Occupational disability	Social consequences of functional limitations
Five	Vocational feasibility	Acceptability of the patient as an employee in the most general sense
Six	Employability	Ability to become employed
Seven	Vocational handicap	Ability to perform a particular job
Eight	Earning capacity	Earned income measured over expected worklife

Note. From *Work Capacity Evaluation* (p. I-11) by L. N. Matheson, Anaheim, CA: Employment and Rehabilitation Institute of California. © 1986 by L. N. Matheson. Used with permission.

---

same goal of return to the workplace. This more global work hardening concept has been termed *industrial rehabilitation* by several experts in the field (Lett, McCabe, Tramposh, & Tate-Henderson, 1988; Matheson, 1988).

The programmatic view of work hardening encompasses a broad group of service providers and involves the worker in activities from the Functional Limitation through the Earning Capacity stages of recovery, as defined by Matheson (see Figure 3-7). Work hardening as a treatment approach, on the other hand, complements the Vocational Feasibility, Employability, and Vocational Handicap stages. The trend in the United States is toward offering programmatic approaches to work hardening. This model is congruent with one of the CARF criteria for a work hardening program, that it be interdisciplinary.

There are at least two models currently in practice for the provision of work hardening services. The first is the menu or cafeteria approach. It permits the referral source (the client), the therapist, and the physician to choose among services available, depending on the worker's need. Many believe this allows for more individualized treatment. Further, referral sources often think it is a more cost-effective method and one that offers the client more control over the services provided.

A typical menu of services might include the following:
- Physical capacity screening
- Functional capacity evaluation
- Work hardening
- Occupational therapy
- Physical therapy
- Vocational evaluation
- Psychological counseling
- Physician evaluation
- Work-site evaluation
- Worker/family education and training
- Preplacement screening
- Ergonomic site evaluation.

With the menu approach, services are generally billed as separate items within a time period. One problem with this approach is the need for physicians' orders/referrals to reflect each of the various services requested—for example, physical therapy versus work hardening—because laws in various states require specific orders for services provided by some disciplines.

Hypothetical charges are used here to illustrate billing procedures in many programs. Each item on the menu would be costed separately—for example, work hardening (four hours), $100; physical therapy (one hour), $75. Most patients would receive a combination of services recommended by the treatment team and approved by the client. An individual receiving work hardening five times per week for four hours per day, plus physical therapy three times per week for one hour per visit, could accumulate weekly charges of $725 (based on the previous hypothetical charges). The addition of service from psychology twice per week at $55 per hour could bring charges to $835 for the week.

A problem that occurs with the separate charges in a menu-driven program is the revenue that many providers lose by not charging for missed appointments. Accordingly, some providers now charge a small fee for missed treatments, and others charge full rates unless certain pre-agreed conditions are met. Such charge schedules are viewed by clients differently from company to company, and even from person to person within a given company. Charges must therefore be carefully discussed with each client.

The second approach to service provision is to offer packaged programs. This may be done in one of two ways: Either everyone receives the same services, regardless of level of function, and is charged a set cost; or everyone is charged a set cost regardless of services received in a given time period. Both models exist in practice. Programs that are designed to serve people with disabilities, such as workers with hand injuries, may do better by making the same services available to everyone for a set fee. Likewise, centers serving a certain industry or group of companies may find greater acceptance by charging a flat fee that includes any or all services available.

In general, the daily or weekly charges in packaged programs tend to be about the same as those for an individual with the same needs receiving care under the menu-driven plan. An advantage to packaged programs is that charging for missed sessions does not become such an issue; the client expects to owe a set amount regardless of a worker's attendance. However, charges may become a point of serious conflict if a client is not notified promptly of a worker's absenteeism.

Some therapists have expressed concern that by offering packaged programs, centers do not encourage individualized treatment planning, and staff may overlook the special needs of an individual. Clients often feel that there is not as much control over what their worker will receive and further that a package arrangement is not as cost-effective as a menu approach. One example of this might be seen in a packaged program that provides treatment for a variety of injuries, but puts all workers through formal body mechanics training or "back school." If a worker has already received this training elsewhere, the client may resent having to pay a second time for the service. Another example might be the packaged program that provides each worker with some degree of vocational evaluation or counseling. If a worker is to return to his or her former position, the service is unnecessary and may create concern on the part of the worker that he or she will be unable to return to the previous job. Clients may not only resent this service, but stop referring if it becomes an issue.

Centers that offer only a system of set fees regardless of services provided certainly could prove less cost-effective to the client for the worker requiring fewer services. For example, if a particular client refers mainly higher-functioning individuals with fewer needs, the client may well feel that menu-type service providers are more cost-effective.

Some packaged programs are defined by both service and length, say, three to five weeks. Such programs are criticized as not being individualized. In most programs operated for a set number of weeks, the worker is discharged with work recommendations at the level of physical demand attained within the time period allotted. Clients may become confused by programs of set length, thinking that workers always emerge at their highest level of function and are ready to return to their former jobs. This is not necessarily the case.

Program Design

Scheduling

Work hardening programs are usually arranged so that after initial evaluation, an individual starts in a program for two to four hours per day, gradually increasing both time and activity demands to an eight-hour work day. CARF (1989) has recommended that agencies design programs to ensure participation five days per week. This is actually the most common practice. The five-day-a-week program matches the average workweek and encourages the worker to view and accept work hardening as he or she would a competitive-employment situation.

Work hardening centers generally design programs that involve daily schedules of structured job cycles, interspersed with work projects, exercise, and rest periods, that match as nearly as possible the worker's job situation (Matheson, 1987). Job cycles are specific task sequences found in a worker's daily routine and performed repeatedly during the work day. Examples of tasks found in a job cycle are *small parts assembly* for 30 minutes, *packing activities* for 10 minutes, *lifting* 10 pounds from floor to waist level five times, and *carrying* five cartons to a loading cart. Such a cycle might be repeated six times per day. Work projects are activities that may or may not relate directly to an individual worker's job, but that build tolerance for certain body positions, promote good body mechanics, and require physical activity and endurance typical of working, office tasks, domestic activities, computer operations, or craft-type activities.

Special group classes in such subjects as body mechanics, stress management, safety, and energy conservation may be added as part of a weekly schedule. Alternatively these activities may be incorporated into an individual's program on a continuing basis when particularly relevant to job demands.

Evaluation

Before beginning work hardening activities, an individual is evaluated to establish his or her current level of physical function and to determine behavioral and attitudinal positives and negatives. The evaluation process may involve several hours or several days and numerous types of assessments. Evaluation categories defined and recommended by CARF (1989) follow. They may incorporate a facility's evaluation battery as appropriate.

1. Baseline capacity evaluation: a baseline "assessment of functional ability to perform work activities which include the physical demand factors on which the *Dictionary of Occupational Titles* [DOT] is based" (CARF, 1989,

p. 70). The DOT is published by the U.S. Department of Labor. Chapter 2 discusses the physical demand factors in detail.

2. Job capacity evaluation: "an assessment of the match between the individual's capabilities and the critical demands of a *specific job*" (CARF, 1989, p. 70). For example, the therapist might compare Mr. Smith's functional status with the requirements for driving a truck for the XYZ Company.
3. Occupational capacity evaluation: "an assessment of the match between the individual's capabilities and the critical demands of an *occupational group*" (CARF, 1989, p. 70). In this case the therapist would compare Mr. Smith's abilities and level of physical functioning with the level of physical demand required of any truck driver.
4. Work capacity evaluation: "an assessment of the match between the individual's capabilities and the demands of *competitive employment*" (CARF, 1989, p. 70). In this process the therapist must pay particular attention to the physical function, the knowledge, the skills, the attitudes, and the habits of the individual worker.

The entire evaluation process in a work hardening program should take place within the context of the demands of actual work. Its purpose, of course, is to provide a basis for establishing a treatment plan or to justify disposition of the worker. Depending on a worker's disability and its severity, as well as the job goals, special assessments may need to be incorporated into the evaluation phase of treatment.

There are evaluation packages available commercially, and many traditional occupational therapy evaluations and assessments are regularly used (see Appendixes 3-B and 3-C). The experienced therapist can, over time, develop useful evaluation tools that yield reproducible results related to work demands by incorporating both standardized therapy equipment and work simulations from industry. There is no need to reinvent the wheel. Careful study and review of existing assessments must be undertaken as one designs a new program. Along with functional capacity evaluations, there should be in-depth interviews with workers to establish their perceptions of their current abilities, activity levels, anticipated job duties, satisfactions, support systems, and personal goals, as well as their current understanding of their physical status and prognosis (Taylor, 1988).

Armed with the data revealed from both the multiple functional assessment and any specialized evaluations and interviews with the worker, the therapist is able to develop treatment goals and strategies for the work hardening program. Other data contributing to the final plan are the reports from the medical record, reports of other professionals, information from employer representatives, and job-site evaluations. Only with the complete picture of both assets and potentials, and deficits, can a meaningful and viable return-to-work program be designed.

Content

In developing an individual's specific work hardening program, one should incorporate work simulation tasks, conditioning tasks, activity, and education. Regardless of who supervises the day-to-day activity, planning requires team input. Appendix 3-D shows typical programs for different diagnostic categories. Programs should be reviewed daily and upgraded for both time and physical demand level as indicated by progress.

In selecting work simulation activities for a worker, one must try to pick specific functional components that are as similar to the actual job as possible. Using actual tools, safety equipment, and materials is always the first choice. Simulating both tools and motions necessary to complete a task is possible. The therapist needs to evaluate muscle groups, motions, repetitions, and forces required by the work. The bulk or the dimensions of items to be lifted or carried, pushed or pulled, should be considered.

Education can be a major benefit of work simulation. Body mechanics can be taught as the worker simulates job activity. All tasks that may have previously caused injury or pain should be evaluated, and safe practices should be incorporated into the simulations.

Workers must be monitored in all activities for safe work practice as well as for good body movement. Monitoring an action to correct or encourage attitude; cooperation with start times, break times, and work rules; and activity compliance are all critical to success.

Activities are sequenced in different ways. Some centers may have all workers do their general-conditioning exercises at one time or even as a group activity. In other programs workers are allowed to develop their own sequences as long as all activities are completed in the time allowed. The most common approach is for the therapist to intersperse static and/or heavy work simulations with periods of conditioning exercise, which allows for stretching of muscle groups and perhaps more active motion. Usually the exercise activity is gradually decreased as work simulations increase to approximate the job situation more closely. Workers may need to be taught simple stretching and flexibility exercises and encouraged to perform the exercises intermittently at their workstations to avoid muscle fatigue and possible reinjury.

Documentation

Good documentation of status, progress, potential, and problems is one of the important elements in successful operation of a treatment program. In work hardening programs it is critical. Test results, goals, and objective physical capacity measures must be reported clearly and concisely, so that those who must make decisions about a worker's status can find answers to their questions and individuals engaged in treatment can return to a safe work environment. A plan for both treatment and return to work should be presented in a goal-directed format that makes clear the time frame of the program. Results of evaluations should be reported as measurements and described in understandable language. They should always be stated in terms related to physical function, and one should be able to replicate the tests and the results. For example, many times a 10- to 15-degree loss of range of motion in a major joint is not significant in terms of the person's full function. Unless this is made clear in a report, the loss may be considered disabling, and the individual may be compensated at a higher rate than is realistically justified.

When reporting, specific periods of time must be identified for accomplishing goals. For example:

> Mr. Brown must be able to lift 50 pounds from floor to waist level in order to return to his job as a shipping clerk at Acme Fabricating Company. He normally must repeat this activity 12 to 15 times per hour. On 9/25/88 he is able to lift 30 pounds from floor to waist level 12 times per hour using a two-handed lift. His goal is to lift 50 pounds from floor to waist level 12 times per hour by 10/10/88.

How a goal is accomplished or what equipment is used to achieve it may not appear important to report. However, if Mr. Brown is using a two-handed lift in treatment and will be required to use a one-handed lift on the job, he is not accomplishing what is necessary for return to work, and the client does not know important facts.

Qualifying statements regarding such matters as the significance of specific findings, the worker's attendance and punctuality, his or her willingness to participate in and cooperate with evaluation and treatment, and the appropriateness of dress and behavior are all important elements of behavior and function, and should be reported. Subjective comments by the worker and observations of him or her away from the activity area should also be reported if relevant. The therapist is expected to record such observations accurately and in a nonbiased manner. It is very easy to convey negatively the poor attendance of a difficult worker, but to overlook treatments missed by the cooperative individual.

Because of current workers' compensation laws and an increased awareness of litigation possibilities, the courts are often involved in industrial injury cases. This places even greater importance on carefully written, time-referenced documentation. A therapist may be asked to serve as an expert witness in a compensation hearing or a legal proceeding as late as two to three years after treatment is completed. A person cannot remember the details that records convey. Reports of the results of evaluations that include measures of specific body movement, or notations of behavioral or physiological findings such as range of joint motion, muscle strength, grip strength, and endurance in certain activities, will be accepted in court, whereas estimates or opinions of those same findings may not.

Results of evaluations in which certain special equipment has been employed have been tested in the courts. One example of this type of equipment is the Cybex II plus (Farmer, 1979). Many therapists think that other tests and measurements will find similar acceptance, but to date these instruments have not been verified.

Work program reports of performance that fairly and accurately describe a worker's functional ability clarify the worker's potential for return to work, provide cues to the chance of reinjury on the job, and supply information necessary for a fair case settlement. Good data assist the employer in determining if reemployment or job accommodation is possible. Such reporting may also identify ergonomic changes in the job site that might reduce or prevent the likelihood of further injuries. (Chapter 4 discusses ergonomics and its applications in occupational therapy.) Further, efficient and effective record keeping provides insurance companies, workers' compensation boards, or company claims officers with the information they need to represent the company and the worker fairly and to bring about both return to work and case settlement in a timely and cost-effective manner.

Occupational therapists are no strangers to regular reporting of treatment. However, in work hardening programs new terminology and a greater degree of specificity must be used if reports are to be understandable and useful in resolving work-related injury cases.

Reimbursement

The increasing number of facilities offering work-related programs attests to their popularity and acceptance as a viable treatment approach for the injured worker. This means work hardening services are becoming readily reimbursable. However, like payer sources in many other areas today, clients of work hardening expect the procedures that they have set forth for billing to be followed. With good documentation to support charges, full and prompt payment is likely. Thus it behooves the therapist involved in work programs to be sensitive to the requirements. A few guidelines are discussed.

Bills for services should *never* be sent unaccompanied by evaluation or progress reports. Further, both the date and the service given should be listed with each daily charge. For many facilities this may be difficult under existing fiscal policy and procedure. Bills may need to be prepared manually, or some special arrangement for preparing them may need to be made to ensure that they and the reports are mailed together. Insurance companies and industry require records to support payment. Failure to comply will cause endless delays or no payment.

Today, charges submitted for workers' compensation cases are usually paid in full. The possible exception to this is with the preferred provider organizations (PPOs) that are developing to handle workers' compensation medical costs at discounted rates. Turn-around time for most workers' compensation billing is 30 to 45 days. The cash flow that results is very attractive to the provider of service, compared with the delays in reimbursement for health care common from other payers. A facility offering work hardening services may choose to pursue contractual arrangements with individual companies and offer discounted rates for volume referrals or exclusivity agreements.

Marketing and Public Relations

Documentation about the individuals receiving service—their job categories, diagnoses, time between injury and work hardening treatment, time away from work, timing of return to work or other disposition after discharge, and activity 30, 60, or 90 days after discharge—is important to support quality control and marketing, not just to have complete and usable records. Such strategies as noting the length of time a worker spends in the program at various levels and durations of activity and physical challenge and his or her rate of increase in levels of physical demand over the course of the program, will help the staff determine program effectiveness, problem areas, and assets.

Further, it is important that staff in work hardening programs keep these kinds of statistics (and share the information on both a local and a national level) in order to show the effectiveness of the concept of work hardening. Such data can help ensure the future of these programs.

Typical sources of referral to work hardening programs include claims representatives of insurance companies, rehabilitation nurses, vocational specialists, physicians, personnel safety or risk managers in industry, state department of vocational rehabilitation representatives, other professionals, and attorneys. All of these sources need to know about a given facility's programs and the services it offers. This calls for active marketing and public relations.

One marketing technique is to establish a referral advisory council or a focus group composed of some of the foregoing kinds of individuals. Such a group may be able to assist in the initial and the continuing development of a program by identifying unmet needs and service requirements unique to given demographic areas. Involvement in a group of this type means an investment of time and effort and ties the referral sources closely to the program. A caution to the facility using this approach is that facility personnel must remain in control, not allowing the outside representatives' "ideals" to affect their objectivity and good practice.

It is very important to use various ways to keep referral sources aware and updated about one's program and its needs, successes, and changes. Several strategies that might be employed with good results are as follows:
- Producing periodic newsletters
- Preparing press releases featuring one's own activities and success stories
- Submitting articles to trade publications or business journals
- Passing on legislation updates
- Providing information packets about the program that recipients can use in discussions with personnel in their own and other agencies.

Other marketing strategies relate to both goals and current needs. For example, many centers offer short (whole- or half-day) invitational workshops directed at the concerns of their referral sources. Such sessions help identify the program as being in touch with the needs of the referral sources and assist in tightening bonds between referrers and center staff. Another practice is to hold an open house annually or semiannually, both to attract new referral sources and to express appreciation to current clients. Having staff available to speak to groups of various kinds on behalf of the program and work hardening in general has proven to be an excellent method of contact. Examples of groups frequently interested in hearing speakers on this topic are the following:

Self-insured associations
Claims representatives groups
Rehabilitation nurses associations

Occupational health nurses associations
Local chambers of commerce
Local business associations.
Specialty groups, such as fire or police chiefs associations.

Still another useful public relations activity is to develop exhibits or displays depicting the scope of work hardening programs and demonstrating equipment. These can be set up at shopping malls as part of Wellness Weeks, at civic centers when they are featuring health care programs or issues, and at both local and national safety council meetings or gatherings of trade associations.

Administrators of work hardening programs are hiring medical sales specialists to sell their particular clinical services directly to industry. Such specialists, to be effective, must be fully knowledgeable about the concept of work hardening: what it is, how it works, what is involved, what services are offered in the specialty centers, and what makes work hardening cost-effective. Wide exposure within a community is as much a key to obtaining steady referrals as are good documentation and effective results. Successfully rehabilitated and satisfied "graduates" of a program are often its best ambassadors in the community. In any case a conscientious program of marketing and public relations is an essential ingredient to growth and success in this relatively new rehabilitation activity.

Summary

The goal of this chapter has been to provide the occupational therapist new to work hardening with a general exposure to programs and to some basic information one must have regarding the components necessary for developing such programs. The following list of suggested principles is meant as a quick reference or checklist to guide program development and service provision and can serve as a summary of major points covered. These suggested principles are in no special order of priority.

1. Work hardening programs should be physically separated from other kinds of treatment programs and give the appearance that work is to be accomplished in the area (CARF, 1989).
2. Activities used for work hardening must combine real or simulated job tasks along with physical conditioning (CARF, 1989; Matheson, 1987).
3. The work hardening team should be multidisciplinary and include or have regular access to an occupational therapist, a physical therapist, a vocational specialist, and a psychologist (CARF, 1989).

4. Work hardening programs serve two masters, the injured worker and the referral source (Ellexson, 1987).
5. Work hardening programs should be located in areas with high concentrations of industry and be readily accessible to those served (Ellexson, 1987).
6. Staff/worker ratios should be near one to six (Ellexson, 1987).
7. Work hardening must involve workers in a daily program of activities that are graded in both duration and activity level (CARF, 1989).
8. Staff should function and be viewed by workers more as first-line supervisors than as caregivers (Ellexson, 1987).
9. Services offered in the program should be defined and comprehensively described in such a way that the referral community will have full knowledge of what a referred worker will receive.
10. Design of programs should be such that the individual needs of the worker with his or her disability are addressed and of prime concern.
11. Regular, complete, and timely documentation is one of the most critical elements in the treatment of the worker because almost all workers served are involved in some claim process (Ellexson, 1987).
12. Evaluation of the worker should be planned and done in the context of competitive employment (CARF, 1989).
13. Test results should be stated as measurements and be reported in objective terms that are related to function. Also, they should be reproducible (Ellexson, 1987).
14. Goals established for each worker should be clear, concise, and time referenced in order to be useful to referral sources (Ellexson, 1987).
15. Evaluation reports and progress reports should be concise and offer only the information needed by the referral source. Twenty-page reports are not cost-effective (Ellexson, 1987).
16. Reports should always accompany the bill for service (Ellexson, 1987).
17. Quality control programs demonstrating program improvement and the future of work hardening concepts depend upon the accumulation of outcome data (Ellexson, 1987).
18. Flexibility of staff in meeting the often divergent goals of the worker and the referral source is vital to success.
19. Competent use of the newest and the best of technology for both evaluation and treatment will contribute to the growing acceptance of work hardening programs by those in the medical, legal, insurance, and industrial communities.

20. Physicians' orders, as mandated by state laws, may be required in order for services to be reimbursable.
21. Insurance authorization must be obtained before program implementation so that reimbursement is ensured (Ellexson, 1987).
22. Research into the effectiveness of program design and activities strengthens program acceptance and assists with reimbursement issues (Ellexson, 1987).
23. Market surveys can guide program administrators to locations and give valuable information necessary to design programs that will be an asset to the community served.
24. Appearance and milieu of the work environment must be considered in relation to the population served (Ellexson, 1987).

Case Study: Doug Ramm

A case study is presented to illustrate the occupational therapist's role in work hardening and to offer a possible treatment scenario.

Doug Ramm, 36 years old, had worked as a pipefitter-welder for ABC Chemical Company for 12-1/2 years. He was referred for a baseline functional capacity evaluation on 8/1/88 with a diagnosis of musculo-ligamentous back strain with neurological involvement. An EMG found nerve-root irritation at L^5-S^1. Doug had first been injured on 1/8/88 while "yanking" on a pipe wrench. His initial symptoms were back and left-leg pain. Doug lost very little time from work in the beginning. He received several physical therapy treatments consisting of hot packs, massage, and ultrasound. Doug was viewed by the company as a "good" worker. He continued to work, but repeatedly reinjured his back. The company referred him to the work hardening center to determine what he could safely do at work and if treatment would help him get better and be able to perform full duty.

Before the baseline functional capacity evaluation, the occupational therapist interviewed Doug. During this interview he described his job duties as laying pipe of 1/2 inch to 6 inches in diameter and up to 20 feet in length; replacing valves of 1/2 to 6 inches in diameter; working on all levels, from floor to overhead; working in tight places to break flanges loose; and handling 14- to 24-inch pipe wrenches. Motions used in his job included yanking, stooping, bending and twisting, sitting, balancing, standing, walking, kneeling, crouching, and reaching. He had to lift 50 to 75 pounds and carry it for 25 feet or more. Tools of his trade were welding and cutting torches, hammers, wrenches, hacksaws, a come-along, and other small tools. To move the welding equipment took two men, one to push while the other pulled a weight of up to 500 pounds. Positions of function were frequently on the extremes of the range for the arms or lying in a twisted position supine. This information was verified by the company safety manager.

Doug lived with his wife and five children. He was independent in all areas of activities of daily living. He did some light chores around the home, including child care and shopping. He was able to drive for short distances without discomfort. Doug was having a "great deal" of difficulty with yard work and car maintenance, which he had always enjoyed. He was working in a "light duty" capacity when evaluated. Light duty at ABC Chemical simply meant that he could ask for help and might be able to get out of overtime. He did not appear angry about his work situation; however, he was concerned about his job because he had a large family to support.

During the interview the occupational therapist explained how the evaluation would proceed and what was expected of Doug. He appeared to be very cooperative and appreciative of the help that the company was providing. He expressed the hope that the work hardening program could help him "feel better" and continue to work.

The occupational therapist administered the baseline functional capacity evaluation, with the following results:

Lifting: The lifting evaluation was performed using the WEST II equipment. Doug was able to lift 30 pounds from 18 to 78 inches. He attempted 40 pounds and was able to lift the bar from 36 to 60 inches. He rested for one minute before moving it to 72 inches and then was unable to take the bar any higher or lower. Using the wire crate, he was able to lift 37 pounds from floor to overhead level and 47 pounds from knuckle to shoulder level. He was able to move this 47 pounds three times in 10 minutes within the knuckle-to-shoulder range. Good body mechanics were noted during the lifting task.

Carrying: Doug was able to carry a maximum of 47 pounds in a wire crate for a distance of 25 feet. Then he began to limp.

Pushing/pulling: Static pushing at waist level using the Chatillon gauge was 80 pounds; pulling was 60 pounds. Dynamic pushing and pulling, tested using a low four-wheeled dolly, was 150 pounds for 50 feet, with no complaints of pain.

Repetitive squatting: Doug performed repetitive squatting with a purposeful activity for 35 seconds with seven repetitions.

Kneeling: Doug was able to maintain a kneeling position for 3 minutes while performing a purposeful activity.

Crouching: Doug did attempt this task, but was unable to maintain the position because of a "pinching in his back."

Climbing: Doug had no difficulty climbing five stairs five times in 1 minute and 35 seconds. He was able to climb three steps on a ladder for three repetitions. He tended to lead with his left foot.

Standing/sitting: Both areas were normal, with no complaints of pain or discomfort after 1 hour.

Endurance: Doug was evaluated using the WEST II equipment. He was able to complete the small parts assembly from 18 inches off the floor to 78 inches overhead. He was able to work for 14 minutes without complaints. He required the support of one hand to return to a standing position.

	Right Hand	Left Hand
	(in inch-pounds)	
Hand Function		
Grip strength	138	120
Lateral pinch	15	15
2-point pinch	14	12
3-jaw chuck	13	12
Graded Grip Strength		
(average of 3 trials)		
Span		
1-1/4"	68	76
1-3/4"	115	110
2-1/4"	118	113
2-3/4"	118	107
3-1/4"	100	83

Doug's right-hand grip strength fell into the 90th percentile for his age group. His left-hand grip strength fell above the 75th percentile, the 90th percentile for the nondominant hand being 128 pounds. Given his occupation, his grip strengths were expected to fall in the 90th percentile or above. His pinch strength fell in the 10th percentile on all three methods.

Doug was found to be functional at the medium-light level of physical demand (lifting 20 pounds frequently, 35 pounds occasionally) (Matheson, 1987). However, he needed to function at the heavy level of physical demand (lifting 50 pounds frequently, 100 pounds occasionally)

(U.S. Department of Labor, 1986) to perform his job duties fully. Decreased hand strength added to his problems, particularly when much of his work required the use of heavy equipment and welding tools and called for climbing and reaching. Doug had to learn and use proper body mechanics to work safely without further injury.

The occupational therapist recommended an eight-week work hardening program stressing upper-extremity strengthening, general strengthening of the abdominals and the lower extremities, improvement of endurance, position changes, use of proper lifting techniques, and good body mechanics. The therapist also requested a physical therapy evaluation to determine if specific treatment could reduce the pain and the spasm present when Doug engaged in activity, and to assist in developing conditioning exercises appropriate for Doug's needs.

The program director, also an occupational therapist, contacted the company, fully explaining the plan and the recommendations. What was being proposed would require that Doug be away from work and receive workers' compensation benefits for at least eight weeks. A careful explanation of Doug's current level of safe function, compared with what the job demanded, resulted in permission for Doug to enter the program. In this particular case the employer notified the insurance carrier of the plan and the company's desire to have Doug involved in work hardening. The office manager verified insurance approval.

On 8/3/88 Doug was evaluated by the physical therapist, who recommended Cybex exercises and assisted the occupational therapist in setting up the conditioning components of the program. Work activity records for Doug's first, fifth, and eighth weeks of treatment appear in Appendix 3-E. His work hardening program consisted of both simulated activity and conditioning. Mat exercises were designed for him to use as both a warm-up before and a cool-down after his program. A woodworking project was introduced at week 4. It was set up on a high-low hydraulic table in order to change the height of the work and to introduce position changes. The project, a toy chest for his children, offered Doug a sense of accomplishment and an opportunity to make something for his family during a time when he felt he was not giving as much time to his children as he usually did.

Doug was discharged from the program on 9/30/88. He had been seen by his physician on 9/23/88 and had been tentatively released for return to work pending successful completion of work hardening.

Doug had demonstrated the following increases in physical demand at the time of discharge:

1. His weight capacities were secure in the medium-heavy work level. He was able to lift and carry 50 pounds a distance of 110 yards 20 times per day. In a crate-lift activity he was able to lift 50 pounds from floor to chest to overhead for seven repetitions twice each day. He was able to execute repetitive push/pull motions on the Baltimore Therapeutic Equipment with low resistance at a slow pace for 10 minutes.
2. He had been tolerating eight hours of work hardening daily for the previous three weeks.
3. He was able to tolerate kneeling for 27 minutes with an activity three times per day.
4. His standing balance appeared good for all tasks assigned to him during his work hardening program. He was able to tolerate walking and standing for 60 minutes without resting, and walking at a fast rate of 3.5 miles per hour for 15 minutes two times per day.
5. He was able to tolerate working in a crouch and in an overhead position for 30 minutes without increased discomfort.
6. He had met the goal of performing squats for 10 repetitions, 10 times per day.
7. He was able to demonstrate good body mechanics, including assuming lordosis lift position and maintaining spinal alignment during work performance tasks 90 percent of the day.
8. Tolerance for activity and general endurance had improved, as had his ability to maintain different positions (i.e., kneeling, reaching overhead, and squatting).

Doug went back to work on 10/3/88. He returned to the clinic once every two weeks for rechecking by the occupational therapist. At 30 days after discharge he was working a 40-hour week, with an average of 10 hours of overtime per week. Doug complained of some bad days, but had not missed any work and stated that he felt he was 110 percent compared with when he had entered the program.

This scenario represents the ideal candidate, who is well motivated, has a position that he or she enjoys, has a job to which he or she can return, and has not been sitting at home for extended periods before entering a work hardening program. Many workers may require more direct physical therapy treatment, psychological intervention, and even vocational evaluation and counseling. Doug's situation, however, is a good example of the important role the occupational therapist plays in a work hardening program, using his or her unique combination of skills and knowledge to rehabilitate the injured worker.

Glossary

Biomechanics—the study of the effects of energy and forces on the human anatomy as a structural basis for human performance (Biomechanics Corp. of America, 1986).

Critical job demands—"those job tasks which, when considered in light of the evaluee's disability, will cause significant vocational handicaps. These job demands are termed 'critical' because they provide the frame of reference within which vocational exploration occurs. The physical demand factors of work that are considered to be critical for a given evaluee will be determined by the nature of his or her injury, symptomatic history, work restrictions outlined by the physician, as well as the goals of the referral. Critical physical demands of work include (but are not limited to) whole body range of motion under load, speed and dexterity for fine manipulation at bench level, speed and dexterity for tool handling with light resistance at bench level, speed, dexterity, and endurance for light tool use with variations in posture, strength and endurance for tool handling with moderate to heavy resistance at bench level, and strength and endurance for tool handling with moderate to heavy resistance with variations in posture" (Matheson, 1987, Appendixes, pp. 3–4).

Ergonomics—the art or the science of making a workplace or a job as compatible as possible in physical demands with the people who must perform it (Biomechanics Corp. of America, 1986).

Evaluation—

Baseline capacity evaluation—"an assessment of functional ability to perform work activities which include the physical demand factors on which the *Dictionary of Occupational Titles* is based" (CARF, 1989, p. 70).

Job capacity evaluation—"an assessment of the match between the individual's capabilities and the critical demands of a *specific job*" (CARF, 1989, p. 70).

Occupational capacity evaluation—"an assessment of the match between the individual's capabilities and the critical demands of an *occupational group*" (CARF, 1989, p. 70).

Work capacity evaluation—"an assessment of the match between the individual's capabilities and the demands of *competitive employment*" (CARF, 1989, p. 70).

Job cycle—a specific task sequence found in a worker's daily routine and performed repeatedly during the work day. Compare **Work project.**

Job task—a single work activity, which together with other single work activities constitutes the effort in which a worker is involved in his or her job (Matheson, 1987).

Levels of physical demand—

Sedentary work—"lifting 10 lbs. maximum and occasionally lifting and/or carrying such articles as dockets, ledgers, papers and small tools. Although a sedentary job is defined as one which involves sitting, a certain amount of walking and standing is often necessary in carrying out job duties" (USDOL, 1986, p. 465).

Light work—"lifting 20 lbs. maximum with frequent lifting and/or carrying of objects weighing up to 10 lbs." Jobs in this category may require significant walking or standing. They may nonetheless involve sitting most of the time with a degree of pushing and pulling of arm and/or leg controls (USDOL, 1986, p. 465).

Medium work—"lifting 50 lbs. maximum with frequent lifting and/or carrying of objects weighing up to 25 lbs." (USDOL, 1986, p. 465).

Heavy work—"lifting 100 lbs. maximum with frequent lifting and/or carrying of objects weighing up to 50 lbs." (USDOL, 1986, p. 465).

Very heavy work—"lifting objects in excess of 100 lbs. with frequent lifting and/or carrying of objects weighing 50 lbs. or more" (USDOL, 1986, p. 465).

Maximum voluntary effort—"a measured level of performance which is stable in a manner consistent with the evaluee's biomechanical, psychophysical, and metabolic/cardiovascular capacity" (Matheson, 1987, Appendixes, p. 5).

Physical demands—"the occupationally significant physical demands factor(s) generally required of an individual in the performance of a specific job-worker situation" (USDOL, 1986, p. vii). Examples are lifting, bending, reaching, walking, and climbing.

Simulated job station—"a work setting which has the following characteristics: (1) [involves] replication of all aspects of a job (not limited to job tasks) or a work process as realistically 'duplicated' as possible; (2) does not necessarily require payment to the evaluee; (3) . . . is controlled by the evaluator; and (4) is located within the evaluation facility" (Matheson, 1987, Appendixes, p. 6). An example would be a pipe-tree or a plumbing-fixture setup.

Task analysis—"breakdown of a particular job into its component parts" (Matheson, 1987, Appendixes, p. 6). "Information gained from task analysis can be utilized to develop training curricula and/or to price a product or service" (p. 6). It can also be used by a therapist/evaluator in developing central job demands for a person being evaluated.

Work hardening—programs that are "interdisciplinary in nature [and] use conditioning tasks that are graded to progressively improve the biomechanical, neuromuscular, cardiovascular/metabolic, and psychosocial functions of the individual in conjunction with real or simulated work activities. Work hardening provides a transition between acute care and return to work while addressing the issues of productivity, safety, physical tolerances, and worker behaviors. Work hardening is a highly structured, goal-oriented, individualized treatment program designed to maximize the individual's ability to return to work" (CARF, 1989, p. 69).

Work project—an activity that may or may not relate directly to an individual worker's job, but that builds tolerance for certain body positions, promotes good body mechanics, and requires physical activity and endurance typical of working, office tasks, domestic activities, computer operations, or craft-type activities. Compare **Job cycle.**

Work simulation tasks—activities that closely simulate or imitate real work tasks in competitive employment. An example is word processing exercises using a computer (Ellexson, 1987).

Work site evaluation—an evaluation of the job tasks, the biomechanics, the positioning, and the training required to perform a job and the stress and the noise present on it (Ellexson, 1987).

References

Biomechanics Corporation of America (for the Occupational Safety and Health Administration). (1986). *Principles of ergonomics* (Vol. 1). Roslyn, NY: Author.

Civilian Vocational Rehabilitation (Smith-Fess) Act of June 2, 1920, 41 Stat. 735 (1920).

Commission on Accreditation of Rehabilitation Facilities. (1989). Work hardening programs. In *Standards manual for organizations serving people with disabilities* (pp. 69–72). Tucson, AZ: Author.

Ellexson, M. T. (1987). *Work hardening programming*. Speech delivered at the annual conference of the American Occupational Therapy Association, Indianapolis, IN.

Farmer, M. (1979, January-February). Measurement of physical impairment in personal injury. *Missouri Bar Journal,* p. IF0-11.

Isernhagen, S. J. (1988). *Work hardening programs and ergonomics.* Rockville, MD: American Physical Therapy Association.

Lett, C. F., McCabe, N. E., Tramposh, A. K., & Tate-Henderson, S. (1988). Work hardening. In S. J. Isernhagen (Ed.), *Work injury: Management and prevention* (pp. 193–230). Rockville, MD: Aspen.

Kirkland, M., & Robertson, S. C. (1985). The evolution of work-related theory in occupational therapy. In M. Kirkland & S. C. Robertson (Eds.), *Planning and implementing vocational readiness in occupational therapy* (PIVOT) (pp. 17–26). Rockville, MD: American Occupational Therapy Association.

Matheson, L. N. (1987). *Work capacity evaluation.* Anaheim, CA: Employment and Rehabilitation Institute of California.

Matheson, L. N. (1988). *Meeting the market's needs.* Speech delivered at the Industrial Rehabilitation Regional Conference, Chicago.

Rehabilitation Act of 1973, Pub. L. No. 93-112, 29 U.S.C. § 701 (1982).

Taylor, S. E. (1988). Occupational therapy in industrial rehabilitation. In H. L. Hopkins & H. D. Smith (Eds.), *Willard and Spackman's Occupational therapy* (pp. 299–307). Philadelphia: J. B. Lippincott.

U.S. Chamber of Commerce. (1987). *1987 analysis of workers' compensation laws.* Washington, DC: Author.

U.S. Department of Labor. (1986). *Selected characteristics of occupations defined in the "Dictionary of occupational titles."* Washington, DC: U.S. Government Printing Office.

Workmen's Compensation Act of May 30, 1908, 35 Stat. 556 (1908).

Related Reading

U.S. Government Publications

Biomechanics Corporation of America (for the Occupational Safety and Health Administration). (1986). *Principles of ergonomics* (Vol. 1). Roslyn, NY: Author.

U.S. Department of Labor. (1977). *Dictionary of occupational titles* (4th ed.). Washington, DC: U.S. Government Printing Office.

U.S. Department of Labor. (1986). *Selected characteristics of occupations defined in the "Dictionary of occupational titles."* Washington, DC: U.S. Government Printing Office.

U.S. Department of Labor, Employment and Training Administration. (1982). *A guide to job analysis.* Washington, DC: U.S. Government Printing Office.

General Reading

Anderson, A. (1985). Work potential evaluation in mental health. *American Journal of Occupational Therapy, 39,* 659–663.

Armstrong, T., & Kochhar, D. (1981). Work performance and handicapped persons. In G. Salverdy (Ed.), *Industrial engineering handbook.* New York: John Wiley & Sons.

Benner, C. L., Schilling, A. D., & Klein, L. Coordinated teamwork in California industrial rehabilitation. *Journal of Hand Surgery, 12,* 936–939.

Bettencourt, C. M., Carlstrom, P., Brown, S. H., Lindau, K., & Long, C. M. (1986). Using work simulation to treat adults with back injuries. *American Journal of Occupational Therapy, 40,* 12–18.

Carlton, R. (1987). The effects of body mechanics instruction on work performance. *American Journal of Occupational Therapy, 41,* 16–20.

Caruso, L. A., Chan, D. E., & Chan, A. (1987). The management of work-related back pain. *American Journal of Occupational Therapy, 41,* 112–117.

Cranfield, H. V. (1947). Assessment of the working capacity of the physically disabled person. *Occupational Therapy and Rehabilitation, 26,* 128–135.

Cromwell, F. (1984). *Occupational therapy in health care: Occupational therapy and the patient with pain.* New York: Hawthorne Press.

Cromwell, F. (1985–86). *Occupational therapy in health care: Work-related programs in occupational therapy.* New York: Hawthorne Press.

Greenburg, L., & Chaffin, D. (1976). *Workers and their tools.* Midland, MI: Pendell Publishers Press.

Holmes, D. (1985). The role of the occupational therapist—work evaluator. *American Journal of Occupational Therapy, 39,* 308–313.

Jacobs, K. (1985). *Occupational therapy: Work-related programs and assessments.* Boston: Little, Brown.

Kirkland, M., & Robertson, S. C. (Eds.) (1985). *Planning and implementing vocational readiness in occupational therapy* (PIVOT). Rockville, MD: American Occupational Therapy Association.

Matheson, L. N., Ogden, L. D., Violette, K., & Schultz, K. (1985). Work hardening: Occupational therapy in industrial rehabilitation. *American Journal of Occupational Therapy, 39,* 314–321.

Reuss, E., Rawe, D. E., & Sundquist, A. E. (1958). Development of a physical capacities evaluation. *American Journal of Occupational Therapy, 12,* 1–8, 14.

Tramposh, A. K. (1988). Work-related therapy for the injured reduces return-to-work barriers. *Occupational Health and Safety, 57*(4), 55–56, 82.

Chapter 3, Appendix A
Resources: Work Hardening

American Therapeutics, Inc. P.O. Box 5084 Macon, GA 31208	The Sled II dynamometer, workshops, training
Baltimore Therapeutic Equipment (BTE) 7455 New Ridge Road Hanover, MD 21076	BTE work simulator
Best Priced Products P.O. Box 1174 White Plains, NY 10602	General supplies
Biodex Corporation P.O. Drawer S Shirley, NY 11967	Ergonomic assessment, work hardening equipment
Creative Specialists P.O. Box 213 Cloquet, MN 55720	Push/pull sled, pipe tree, weight boxes
Cybex 2100 Smithtown Avenue Ronkonkoma, NY 11779	Cybex systems
EBSCO Curriculum Materials P.O. Box 262 Chelsea, AL 35043	Prevocational training material
Employment and Rehabilitation Institute of California (ERIC) 1160 North Gilbert Anaheim, CA 92801	WEST equipment, consultation, residency training, workshops
Functional Capacity Assessment Polinsky Medical Rehabilitation Center 530 East Second Street Duluth, MN 55805	Work hardening evaluation system training
Isotechnologies P.O. Box 1239 Elizabeth Brady Road Hillsborough, NC 27278	B-200 back dynamometer
Loredan Biomedical, Inc. 1632 DaVinci Court P.O. Box 1154 Davis, CA 95617	LIDO workset, LIDO lift

Master Gauge 1150 West Grand Avenue Chicago, IL 60622	Chatillon push/pull dynamometer
Milliken Physical Therapy Center 5 Oak Hill Plaza P.O. Box 1450 Scarborough, ME 04074	Workshops, consultation
N.G.G. Associates P.O. Box 27517 Milwaukee, WI 52377	Valpar evaluation samples
North Coast Medical 450 Salmar Avenue Campbell, CA 95008	General supplies, e.g., JAMAR dynamometer
Physio-Tek, Inc. P.O. Box 190 Martinez, CA 94553	Human engineering center, computerized force platform
Singer Educational Systems New Concepts Corporation 1161 North El Dorado Place Tucson, AZ 85715	Singer educational systems
STEPS Industrial Injury Clinics Schwab Rehabilitation Center 1401 South California Chicago, IL 60608	Residency training, consultation
Work Evaluation Systems Technology 1950 Freeman Long Beach, CA 90804	WEST equipment
Work Recovery Systems 1141 North El Dorado Place Tucson, AZ 85715	Ergos work simulator
The Work System Lake Forest Health Services 31740 Franklin Fairway Farmington Hills, MI 48018	The Work System

Chapter 3, Appendix B

Schwab STEPS Industry Injury Clinic
Occupational Therapy Physical Capacities Evaluation

Name: _____ Date: _____

Referral: _____ Physician: _____

Diagnosis: _____

I. Injury: Date: _____ Description: _____
   _____
   _____

II. Medical Course
   A. Hospitalizations
      1) When _____
      2) Where _____
      3) Reason _____
      4) Tx/Tests _____

      1) When _____
      2) Where _____
      3) Reason _____
      4) Tx/Tests _____

   B. Diagnostic Tests
      1) Test _____
      2) When _____
      3) Where _____
      4) Outcome/Results _____

      1) Test _____
      2) When _____
      3) Where _____
      4) Outcome/Results _____

      1) Test _____
      2) When _____
      3) Where _____
      4) Outcome/Results _____

   C. Surgeries
      1) What Kind/Type _____
      2) When _____
      3) Where _____

© Schwab STEPS Industrial Injury Clinic. Reprinted by permission.

    D. Therapies Received
       1) Type _____
       2) Place _____
       3) Times per Week _____
       4) Length of Time _____
       5) Tx/Modalities _____

       1) Type _____
       2) Place _____
       3) Times per Week _____
       4) Length of Time _____
       5) Tx/Modalities _____

III. Other Medical Problems/Precautions
_____
_____

IV. Present Condition
    A. Current Symptoms/Problems
_____
_____

    B. Current Medications
_____
_____

    C. Assistive Devices
_____
_____

V. Lifestyle/Education
    A. Living Where _____
    B. Living With _____
    C. Type of Home/Apt. _____
    D. Self-care Activities

                 Independent   Independent but with Difficulty   Requires Assistance

       1) UE/LE Dressing _____
_____

       2) Grooming/Hygiene _____
_____

       3) Shower/Bathing _____
_____

    E. Homemaking Activities
       1) Light Chores (vacuuming, mopping, cooking, washing dishes, laundry, trash removal, dusting)
       2) Heavy Chores (mowing lawn, shoveling snow, car/home maintenance, grocery shopping)

F. Estimated Tolerances For
   1) Sitting _____
   2) Standing _____
   3) Walking _____
   4) Lifting _____
   5) Driving _____
   6) Sleeping _____

G. Hobbies/Interests
   _____
   _____

H. Typical Day Involves
   _____
   _____

I. Education Level (School, Where, Highest Level Completed)
   _____
   _____

J. Technical/Vocational Training
   _____
   _____

VI. Plan for Return to Work. Reason Why You Were Sent Here. What You Hope to Gain from This Program
   _____
   _____
   _____
   _____

VII. Two Previous Jobs
   A. Employer
      1) City _____
      2) Job Title _____
      3) Length of Time Worked _____

   B. Employer
      1) City _____
      2) Job Title _____
      3) Length of Time Worked _____

VIII. Job Description (Present Job)
   A. Job Title _____
   B. Employer _____
   C. Length of Time Worked _____
   D. Off Work Since _____
   E. Work Schedule/Breaks/Overtime/Pace
      _____
      _____

F. Equipment/Tools/Machinery/Safety Devices

G. Description of Duties

H. Physical Demands
    1) Lifting: Weights of

                                Distance
                                Frequency

    2) Carrying: Weights of

                                Distance
                                Frequency

    3) Pushing/Pulling: Weights of

                                Distance
                                Frequency

    4) Standing/Walking: Situation

                                Frequency

    5) Sitting: Situation

                                Frequency

    6) Climbing: Situation

                                Frequency

    7) Balancing: Situation

                                Frequency

    8) Stooping: Situation

                                Frequency

9) Kneeling: Situation _____
_____
Frequency _____

10) Crouching: Situation _____
_____
Frequency _____

11) Crawling: Situation _____
_____
Frequency _____

12) Reaching: Situation _____
_____
Frequency _____

Sitting Tolerance (End of Interview) _____

Comments/Observations
_____
_____
_____
_____
_____
_____
_____

IX. Evaluation

Brief Tool Use

	L	ON	R		L	OFF	R	
		<				<		
-10-		<	-78"-			<		-10-
		<				<		
-9-		<	-72"-			<		-9-
		<				<		
-8-		<	-66"-			<		-8-
		<				<		
-7-		<	-60"-			<		-7-
		<				<		
-6-		<	-54"-			<		-6-
		<				<		
-5-		<	-48"-			<		-5-
		<				<		
=================	=	-42"-	=================
		<				<		
-4-		<	-36"-			<		-4-
		<				<		
-3-		<	-30"-			<		-3-
		<				<		
-2-		<	-24"-			<		-2-
		<				<		
-1-		<	-18"-			<		-1-
		<				<		

Time (ON) _____   Time (OFF) _____

Observations:
Body mechanics when working at lower levels appears good/fair/poor, requiring no/occasional/frequent/constant verbal and/or physical cues to maintain upright back posture in spinal alignment and negotiating occasional position changes in/out of kneeling/half-kneeling/crouching with no/minimum/moderate/high difficulty (pulling on vertical bar to assist with stand).

Limitations and/or complaints include: _____
_____

Range of Motion

Client reported height was _____ feet, _____ inches. Client was able to reach from _____ to _____ height with both hands executing squat to stand.

WEST II Lift

	< T1	< T2	< T3	< T4	< T5	< T6	< T7	< T8	< T9	< T10	<
Lbs.	< ___	< ___	< ___	< ___	< ___	< ___	< ___	< ___	< ___	< ___	<
	<	<	<	<	<	<	<	<	<	<	<
-10-	<	<	<	<	<	<	<	<	<	<	< -78"-
	<	<	<	<	<	<	<	<	<	<	<
-9-	<	<	<	<	<	<	<	<	<	<	< -72"-
	<	<	<	<	<	<	<	<	<	<	<
-8-	<	<	<	<	<	<	<	<	<	<	< -66"-
	<	<	<	<	<	<	<	<	<	<	<
-7-	<	<	<	<	<	<	<	<	<	<	< -60"-
	<	<	<	<	<	<	<	<	<	<	<
-6-	<	<	<	<	<	<	<	<	<	<	< -54"-
	<	<	<	<	<	<	<	<	<	<	<
-5-	<	<	<	<	<	<	<	<	<	<	< -48"-
	<	<	<	<	<	<	<	<	<	<	<
======	====	====	====	====	====	====	====	====	====	====	-42"-
	<	<	<	<	<	<	<	<	<	<	<
-4-	<	<	<	<	<	<	<	<	<	<	< -36"-
	<	<	<	<	<	<	<	<	<	<	<
-3-	<	<	<	<	<	<	<	<	<	<	< -30"-
	<	<	<	<	<	<	<	<	<	<	<
-2-	<	<	<	<	<	<	<	<	<	<	< -24"-
	<	<	<	<	<	<	<	<	<	<	<
-1-	<	<	<	<	<	<	<	<	<	<	< -18"-
	<	<	<	<	<	<	<	<	<	<	<
___	< ___	< ___	< ___	< ___	< ___	< ___	< ___	< ___	< ___	< ___	< ___

Observations:
Client requires <u>no/occasional/frequent/constant</u> verbal and/or physical cues to assume lordosis lift position, demonstrates <u>good/fair/poor</u> body mechanics with <u>normal curves/flat low back/ forward flexed trunk.</u>

Limitations and/or complaints include: _____

Crate Lift (5 repetitions MAX. lifts)

Level	<	Trial 1	<	Trial 2	<	Trial 3	<	Comments
	<		<		<		<	
Floor to Knuckle	<		<		<		<	
_____	< ___		< ___		< ___		< ___	
	<		<		<		<	
12" to Knuckle	<		<		<		<	
_____	< ___		< ___		< ___		< ___	
	<		<		<		<	
Knuckle to Chest	<		<		<		<	
_____	< ___		< ___		< ___		< ___	
	<		<		<		<	
Chest to Overhead	<		<		<		<	

Observations:
Client requires <u>no/occasional/frequent/constant</u> verbal and/or physical cues to assume lordosis lift position, demonstrates <u>good/fair/poor</u> body mechanics with <u>normal curves/flat low back/ forward flexed trunk.</u>

Weight Carry
Carrying a maximum of _____ lbs. one time for 100 feet using weighted crate held at waist level.

Limitations and/or complaints include: _____

Pushing
    Dynamic (100 feet) _____ lbs., using <u>2-/4-</u>wheel cart.
    Static _____ lbs., using Chatillon gauge.

Pulling
    Dynamic (100 feet) _____ lbs., using <u>2-/4-</u>wheel cart.
    Static _____ lbs., using Chatillon gauge.

Limitations and/or complaints include: _____

Repetitive Squatting (3-minute trial)
Squatting with <u>upright back posture and normal curves/flat low back/forward flexed trunk</u> at <u>slow/moderate/fast</u> pace for _____ repetitions in _____ minutes, _____ seconds.

Limitations and/or complaints include: _____

Sustained Crouching (3-minute trial)
Crouching sustained for _____ minutes, _____ seconds, while performing light work task.

Limitations and/or complaints include: _____

Tall Kneel (3-min trial)
Maintaining tall kneel position for _____ minutes, _____ seconds while performing small tool task.

Limitations and/or complaints include: _____

Climb
Ascending/descending 10 steps on stairs for _____ (5) repetitions with rail/assistive device for support, demonstrating good/questionable/unsafe balance and with reciprocal/foot by foot/slow climbing pattern.

Climbing 3 steps on ladder for _____ (5) repetitions with good/questionable/unsafe balance and with reciprocal/one-step-at-a-time/slow climbing pattern.

Limitations and/or complaints include: _____

Crawl
Crawling 10 feet forward and 10 feet backward negotiating position change in/out of quadruped position with no/minimum/moderate/high difficulty.

Limitations and/or complaints include: _____

Balance
Walking heel to toe forward, backward, and sideways for 3 lengths each. Errors (stepping off beam) _____

Limitations and/or complaints include: _____

Comments/Observations:
Pain behaviors—minimal/moderate/excessive including _____
_____
_____
_____

Working at slow/moderate/fast pace, demonstrating cautious/deliberate work behaviors and/or good/questionable/poor awareness of physical limitations.

Standing tolerance of up to _____ minutes during the evaluation.

Requiring no/occasional/frequent/constant breaks up to _____ minutes at a time in sitting/supine position throughout the evaluation.

Client appeared to be working to maximum abilities/questionable to this therapist whether client was exerting maximum effort/client appeared to be self-limiting.

Occupational Therapy
Upper Extremity Evaluation

Part	Action	A/ROM R	A/ROM L	Strength R	Strength L		A/ROM			
						Right Digits	II	III	IV	V
Shoulder	Flexion					MP				
	Extension					PIP				
	Abduction					DIP				
	Int. Rotation									
	Ext. Rotation					Left Digits	II	III	IV	V
Elbow	Flexion					MP				
	Extension					PIP				
Forearm	Supination					DIP				
	Pronation									
Wrist	Flexion					Thumb R/L				
	Extension					CMC				
	Radial Deviation					MP				
	Ulnar Deviation					IP				

	R	L
Gross Grasp		
Lateral Pinch		
2-Point Pinch		
3-Jaw Chuck		

Trials	1	2	3	Average	Trials	1	2	3	Average
Grip Strength: R					Grip Strength: L				

Sensation	Intact	Impaired	Comments
Temperature Discrimination			
Pain/Pressure (sharp/dull)			
Light Touch			
Two-Point Discrimination			
Position Sense/Proprioception			
Stereognosis			

Comments:

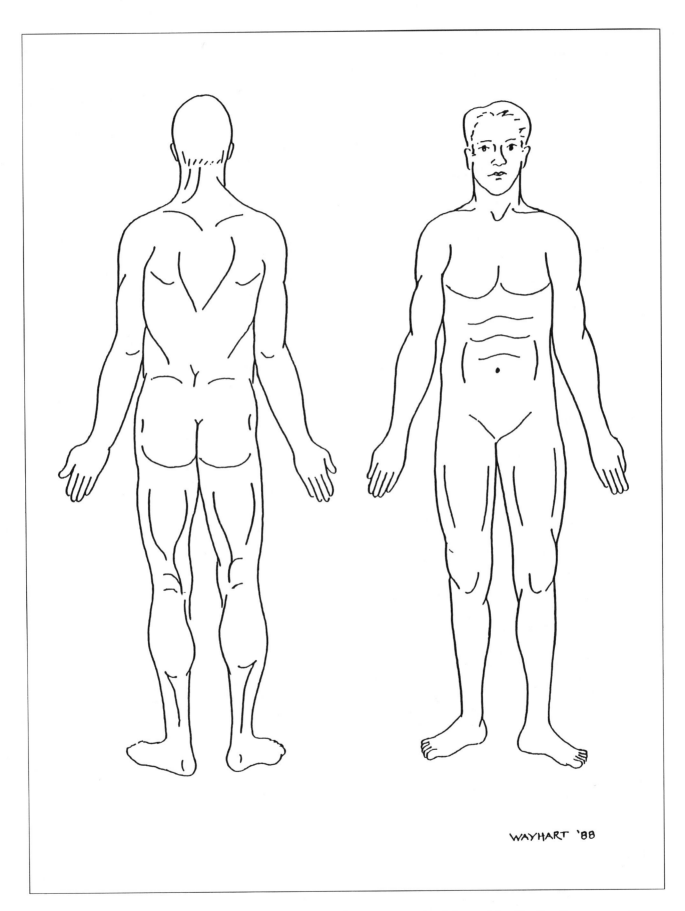

Chapter 3, Appendix C

HealthLine
THE CENTER FOR
EVALUATION AND REHABILITATION

Date of Service
Work Performance Evaluation for
(Name)

DOI: **DOB:**   **SS#:**

Referring Physician:

Date of Referral:

Diagnosis:

Precautions:

Job Information:
   Company:
   Title:
   Classified at the _____ Work Level.

Summary of Findings

Maximum Lift: _____ lbs. floor to _____ " overhead.
                _____ lbs. _____ " to _____ ".

Primary Limiting Factor for Return to Job:

Problems to Be Addressed in Work Hardening Therapy:

_____ Inconsistencies in performance.

_____ Limited reaching.

_____ Limited maximum lifting performance.

_____ Limited repetitive lifting performance.

_____ Limited pushing and pulling performance.

_____ Limited fingering performance.

_____ Decreased lower extremity function.

© 1988 by Sallie E. Taylor, MEd, OTR, HealthLine Corporate Health Service. Reprinted by permission.

_____ Limited lateral and forward bending.

_____ Limited neck movement.

_____ Limited work range.

_____ Report of increased pain with activity.

_____ Limited performance of safe body mechanics.

_____ Decreased endurance for work.

_____ Limited carrying performance.

_____ Limited sitting tolerance.

_____ Limited standing tolerance.

_____ Diminished balancing performance.

_____

Comments (therapist's assessment of performance):

Prognosis for Return to Work:

Anticipate _____ **weeks of work hardening.**

Plan

Begin work hardening/physical therapy   (date)
Focus initially on stretching, body mechanics, job simulation.

Data base supporting this summary is available upon request.

_____
Therapist

Date
Name
Data Base

The following subjective and objective sections of this report are provided for review of the client's comments and performance on specific tests performed during evaluation this date.

Contents
Subjective Information
Objective Tasks

Subjective Information
Provided by Client

Present Complaints:

Present Medication:

Hospitalizations Associated with Worker's Compensation Claim:

Other Medical Conditions Reported by Client:

Client's Statement of Expected Limitations for Work:

Objective Findings

Hand Strength Measures:
Tested with JAMAR dynamometer in 5-position grip strength testing:

Comments:

Pinch Strength was tested using B&L Pinch Gauge.

                                Performance   Norm for age

Lateral pinch (3 measures)

3-point pinch

Muscle Strength (reported in standard manual muscle testing nomenclature with normal = 5/5): Strength was generally _____ for both upper and lower extremities except for the following muscle groups:

        Right   Muscle Group   Left

Range of Motion (goniometric measures recorded in degrees of movement, each joint): Within normal limits for all planes of movement (shoulders, elbows, wrists, hands, hips, knees, and ankles) except for the following:

        Right   Motion   Left
                                    (Normal value in degrees)
                                  Trunk forward bend (80–90) = _____
                                  Trunk backward bend (30) = _____
       _____   Trunk sidebend (30)   _____
       _____   Trunk rotation (45)   _____

Balance
Static and dynamic sitting and standing balance was within normal limits against challenge.

Client showed _____ backward, forward displacement to the right/left when challenged in sitting/standing.

Heel to Toe Walking:

Sustained Postures:

Posture	Time	Assessment	Comments
Bending	(not timed)	Good, Fair, Poor, Unable	
Crouching	(30 sec)	Good, Fair, Poor, Unable	
Kneeling	(30 sec)	Right: Good, Fair, Poor, Unable	
		Left: Good, Fair, Poor, Unable	
		Together: Good, Fair, Poor, Unable	

Functional Mobility:

Walking: 1. Comment on limp or deviation.
          2. Comment on arm movement.

Carrying:

Maximum weight tested for carrying up and down stairs was _____ lbs.
Maximum weight tested for carrying on slanting/vertical ladder was _____ lbs.

Climbing:

Client climbed one flight of stairs:
1. Use of handrails:
Client climbed slanting _____ ft. ladder, carrying _____ lbs. load _____ , safely.

Handling (tested with Minnesota Rate of Manipulation Test):

Test	Total Time	% Normal
Displacing test		
Turning and placing test		
Bilateral turning and placing test		

Multilevel Assembly (tested with Valpar VCWS 9):
Results: Difficulty in upper range (above shoulder level) due to limited reaching, _____ upper extremity. Difficulty in lower range (knuckles to floor) due to back pain with forward bending, crouching, kneeling.

Maximum Lifting Performance (in standard protocol, using WEST II lifting apparatus):
Results: Floor to overhead   _____ " to _____ " = _____ lbs.
         Floor to shoulder   _____ " to _____ " = _____ lbs.
         Knee to shoulder   _____ " to _____ " = _____ lbs.
         Bench to bench   _____ " to _____ " = _____ lbs.

Body Mechanics (tested with maximum lifting and with multilevel assembly test):
 Back position:
 Leg position:
 Foot placement:
 Position of weight:
 Control of weight:

Simulated Work Cycle

A work cycle simulating components of the client's job was included in the testing. Simulated work tasks included:
 1. Task A
 2. Task B
 3. Task C
 (Up to 6 or 7 tasks simulating job)

Client completed this _____ -minute cycle _____ times during the evaluation.

Direction following was

Work rate was

Endurance was

End of Test

_____
Therapist

Chapter 3, Appendix D, Work Activity Record Program Samples

Schwab STEPS Industrial Injury Clinic
Work Activity Record

Name: *Anita Doctor*

Position: Data entry operator
Dx: S/P bilateral carpal tunnel releases

Start of Program: 6/17/88
Week of Program: 4
Length of Program: 6–8 wks.
Hours in Clinic: 6

Complete 1 through 5.

Activity/Position	Time	Reps	Sets	Wt.						Date T in / T out
Bike	15 min	1x								Total Reps/Sets
Theraputty on wall Shoulder flexion activity	10 min	1x								Total Reps/Sets
Bin sort	10 min	1x								Total Reps/Sets
1. Data entry machine	45 min									Total Reps/Sets
2. Weight carry	10 min			10 lb						Total Reps/Sets
3. Typing at computer	45 min									Total Reps/Sets
4. Filing	10 min									Total Reps/Sets
5. Stair climb		10 flights								Total Reps/Sets

© by Schwab STEPS Industrial Injury Clinic. Reprinted by permission.

Schwab STEPS Industrial Injury Clinic
Work Activity Record

Name _Easy Does It_
Position: Laborer
Dx: S/P laminectomy, L4–5

Start of Program _5/4/88_
Week of Program _7_
Length of Program _8 wks._
Hours in Clinic _8_

Complete 1 through 10; repeat.

Activity/Position	Time	Reps	Sets	Wt.						Date / T in / T out
Walk	30 min	2x								Total Reps/Sets
Bike	25 min	2x								
Wall slides		10x	x4							Total Reps/Sets
Quad strengthening										
Cybex—knee flex. & ext.	60/90/120	1x								Total Reps/Sets
1. Push cart		1 lap		275 lb						Total Reps/Sets
2. Ladder climb		3 steps	x5							
3. Crate lift—				45 lb						Total Reps/Sets
floor to knuckle		5x								
knuckle to chest		5x								
chest to overhead		5x								
4. Kneel—small tool Valpar	5 min									Total Reps/Sets
5. Weight carry	15 min			45 lb						
6. Bin sort	15 min									
7. Max. lift—floor to knuckle		2x		80 lb						Total Reps/Sets
8. Balance beam—forward, backward, sideways		5x ea.								Total Reps/Sets
9. Brief tool use—WEST II										Total Reps/Sets
10. Shoveling	15 min									

122   *Work in Progress: Occupational Therapy in Work Programs*

Schwab STEPS Industrial Injury Clinic
Work Activity Record

Name _Stonewall Reddy_

Position: Bricklayer
Dx: S/P right rotator cuff repair

Start of Program __5/9/88__
Week of Program __6__
Length of Program __6–8 wks.__
Hours in Clinic __8__

Complete 1 through 9; repeat.

Activity/Position	Time	Reps	Sets	Wt.						Date T in / T out
Walk	30 min	2x								Total Reps/Sets
Bike	20 min	2x								
BTE #181—right shoulder flex.	5 min	2x		Level 30						Total Reps/Sets
BTE #701—right shoulder circ.	5 min	2x		Level 10						
BTE #191—pull-down Latissimus Dorsi	5 min	2x		Level 15						Total Reps/Sets
Cybex push/pull		30/60/90								
Cybex int./ext. rot.		30/60/90								Total Reps/Sets
1. Brief tool use—WEST II										
2. Kneel—small tool Valpar 1	5 min									Total Reps/Sets
3. Bin sort	15 min									
4. Bricklaying		75 brks.								
5. Crouch—Valpar 9, panels 3–4 only	5 min									Total Reps/Sets
6. Crate lift— floor to knuckle		5x		60 lb						Total Reps/Sets
knuckle to chest		5x		55 lb						
chest to overhead		5x		40 lb						
7. Ladder climb	3 steps	5x								Total Reps/Sets
8. Squats		10 x								
9. Max. lifts		2x								
										Total Reps/Sets

Chapter 3, Appendix D: Work Activity Record Program Samples

Chapter 3, Appendix E, Work Activity Records: Doug Ramm

Schwab STEPS Industrial Injury Clinic
Work Activity Record

Name: _Doug Ramm_

Start of Program: _8/8/88_
Week of Program: _1_
Length of Program: _8 wks._
Hours in Clinic: _4_

Activity/Position	Time	Reps	Sets	Wt.	8/8 7:00/11:00	8/9 7:00/11:00	8/10 7:00/11:00	8/11 7:00/11:00	8/12 7:00/11:00	Date T in / T out
Mat exercises		2x			xx	xx	xx	xx	xx	Total Reps/Sets
Table squats 5		2x			xx	xx	xx	xx	xx	
Overhead chain	7 min	2x			xx	xx	xx	xx	xx	
Bike—seat ht. 11	10 min	5x	x2		x	x	xx	xx	xx	Total Reps/Sets
Wooden crate— waist to overhead		5x	x2	10 lb	x	x	x	xx	xx	
BTE steering wheel, horizontal				600 lb	x	x	x	x	x	Total Reps/Sets
BTE push/pull				700 lb	x	x	x	x	x	
Valpar nuts & bolts box, kneeling	5 min	3x			x	x	xx	xx	xxx	Total Reps/Sets
Plumbing corner	15 min	2x			x	x	xx	xx	xx	
Treadmill—speed 3.5 mph	10 min	3x			xx	xx	xx	xxx	xxx	Total Reps/Sets
Valpar panels 3-2-4			8 pcs		x	x	x	x	x	
Cybex—shoulders, legs					x	x	x	x	x	Total Reps/Sets

Isokinetic exercises are employed to strengthen leg musculature used in lifting and other functional activities. They are also employed with the shoulder musculature used in most activities for motion or stabilization of that joint.
Knee extension/flexion and shoulder IR/ER with modified position are used.

Total Reps/Sets

Total Reps/Sets

© by Schwab STEPS Industrial Injury Clinic. Reprinted by permission.

Schwab STEPS Industrial Injury Clinic
Work Activity Record

Name: _Doug Ramm_

Start of Program __8/8/88__
Week of Program __5__
Length of Program __8 wks.__
Hours in Clinic __6__

Activity/Position	Time	Reps	Sets	Wt.	9/5 7:00/2:00	9/6 7:00/2:00	9/7 7:00/2:00	9/8 7:00/2:00	9/9 7:00/2:00	Date T in/T out
Mat exercises		2x			xx	xx	xx	xx	xx	**Total**
Table squats 5		2x			xx	xx	xx	xx	xx	**Reps/Sets**
Wooden crate— waist to overhead		7x	x3	35 lb	xx	xx	xx	xx	xx	**Total**
Bike—seat ht. 11	15 min	3x	x2		xx	xx	xx	xx	xx	**Reps/Sets**
WEST II nuts & bolts #1–10	3 min	2x			xx	xx	xx	xx	xx	**Total**
Plumbing corner	15 min	3x			xx	xx	xx	xx	xx	**Reps/Sets**
Computer	10 min		x2		xx	xx	xx	xx	xx	
Treadmill—speed 2.5–3.5 mph	10 min		x3		xxx	xxx	xxx	xxx	xxx	**Total**
Valpar nuts & bolts box, low kneeling	5 min	2x			xx	xx	xx	xx	xx	**Reps/Sets**
BTE large steering wheel	15 min	2x			xx	xx	xx	xx	xx	**Total**
BTE push/pull	15 min	2x			xx	xx	xx	xx	xx	**Reps/Sets**
Cybex					x	x	x	x	x	
Wall ladder		5x	x2		xx	xx	xx	xx	xx	
Project	30 min				x	x	x	x	x	**Total Reps/Sets**
										Total Reps/Sets
										Total Reps/Sets
										Total Reps/Sets

Schwab STEPS Industrial Injury Clinic
Work Activity Record

Name: _Doug Ramm_

Start of Program: _8/8/88_
Week of Program: _8_
Length of Program: _8 wks._
Hours in Clinic: _8_

Activity/Position	Time	Reps	Sets	Wt.	9/26 7:00–4:00	9/27 7:00–4:00	9/28 7:00–4:00	9/29 7:00–4:00	9/30 7:00–4:00	Date / T in / T out
Mat exercises		3x			xxx	xxx	xxx	xxx	xxx	Total Reps/Sets
Table squats 5		2x			xx	xx	xx	xx	xx	
Wire crate		5 laps	x1	50 lb	x	x	x	x	x	Total Reps/Sets
Wooden crate		5 laps	x2	10 brks.	xx	xx	xx	xx	xx	
Cybex, knees					x	x	x	x	x	
Wooden crate—waist to overhead, waist to knuckle		7x	x2	75 lb	xx	xx	xx	xx	xx	Total Reps/Sets
Bike—seat ht. 11	20 min	3x			xxx	xxx	xxx	xxx	xxx	
Treadmill—speed 3.0–3.5 mph	15 min	3x			xxx	xxx	xxx	xxx	xxx	Total Reps/Sets
Valpar nuts & bolts box, low kneeling	7 min	2x			xx	xx	xx	xx	xx	
WEST II nuts & bolts #1–10	5 min	2x			xx	xx	xx	xx	xx	Total Reps/Sets
Computer	10 min	3x			xxx	xxx	xxx	xxx	xxx	
Plumbing corner	20 min	3x			xxx	xxx	xxx	xxx	xxx	
BTE large steering wheel, flat	600 sec				x	x	x	x	x	Total Reps/Sets
BTE push/pull	600 sec				x	x	x	x	x	
BTE V.E. crank	500 sec				x	x	x	x	x	
Wall ladder		5x	x3		xxx	xxx	xxx	xxx	xxx	Total Reps/Sets
Standing project	60 min		x2		xx	xx	xx	xx	xx	
Sorting	15 min		x3		xxx	xxx	xxx	xxx	xxx	
Push dolly		5 laps		100 lb	x	x	x	x	x	
										Total Reps/Sets
										Total Reps/Sets

4
Ergonomics and the Occupational Therapist

Ellen Rader Smith, MA, OTR

Occupational therapists are expanding their role in industrial settings. This expansion involves interaction with new personnel, outside the traditional practice arena. Training in the basic and applied sciences, knowledge of medical conditions, emphasis on the total person within the context of the home or work environment, and understanding of activity and work analysis methods make the occupational therapist well qualified to enter the industrial arena. In industry as in any new setting, occupational therapists must define their roles clearly and be confident of the skills that they can offer to their industrial clients.

Ergonomics is a subject receiving increased attention in the industrial and occupational medicine communities. The incorporation of ergonomics into medically oriented programs is seen in the expansion of programs for assessment of functional capacity and disability, work-injury rehabilitation, return to work, proactive injury prevention, and wellness. These programs are currently being implemented by occupational and physical therapists, occupational physicians and nurses, industrial hygienists, safety and engineering personnel, and specifically trained ergonomists or human factors specialists. In efforts to attract clients to these newly developed programs, many health service providers are using the word *ergonomics* to help market their programs. The author believes that to maintain credibility, all health care professionals providing ergonomics as part of their programs should receive formal training in the subject at the university level or through continuing education.

The occupational therapist's focus is on the person as a whole. The therapist's psychophysical frame of reference adds a special perspective when one is applying ergonomic concepts to various industrial situations. It involves maintaining a broad focus at all times on workers' physical, psychological, and adaptive behaviors in response to their workplace environment. This differs from the more unidimensional focus of the safety or rehabilitation engineer, the loss control or workers' compensation manager, or other industry personnel. However, the aforementioned health and safety professionals must work together in industry to provide a multidisciplinary approach to health and safety in the workplace. This is key to the success of any program in industry.

This chapter summarizes some aspects of ergonomics that may be incorporated into occupational therapy industrial programs. The goal is to show therapists how they can enrich their roles in industry by incorporating ergonomic concepts. The material should be viewed as introductory and not all-inclusive. Further readings are recommended for the interested therapist.

Introduction to Ergonomics

Ergonomics is derived from the Greek words *ergos* meaning work and *nomos* meaning laws (Eastman Kodak, 1983). Thus ergonomics is the study of work and more specifically the study of the interaction or fit between workers and their total workplace environment. Applying ergonomics means using a multifaceted approach to examine this interaction. The overall goal is to improve worker performance and safety by maximizing the fit between workers and the work they do. The fit involves many factors, as illustrated in Figure 4-1.

Ergonomics is an interdisciplinary, applied science whose foundations, much like occupational therapy's, integrate the tenets of engineering, medicine, anatomy and physiology, kinesiology, biomechanics, psychology, the behavioral sciences, and anthropology. Ergonomics is not a new discipline, but it may not be a familiar one to the public or to many therapists. In the automotive and furniture industries, the term *ergonomics* is used regularly in advertising to explain the fit between the product and the consumer.

Both occupational therapy and ergonomics are concerned with the individual's adaptation to and interaction with the physical environment. Working within a medical framework and using various rehabilitative techniques, occupational therapists have traditionally established goals directed at enhancing the injured or disabled person's physical abilities to return to the work force. Upon return to work, these individuals have had to adapt their level of skill performance to the demands of their jobs. In contrast, the ergonomist's goal is to accommodate the design of the workplace and the job to the worker's capabilities. In a sense the two fields have diametri-

Figure 4-1
Interactions Between the Workplace, the Job, and the Worker
The goal of ergonomics is to optimize these interactions. Individual components can be adapted to improve workers' health, safety, and productivity.

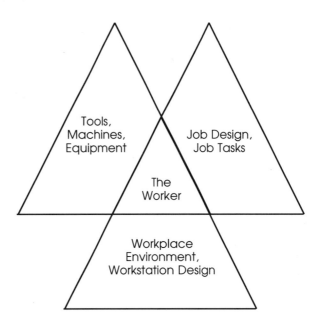

cally opposing views, but both strive toward the same outcome: maximizing the fit between workers and their jobs. This relationship is illustrated in Table 4-1.

The process of returning injured workers to the work force or providing disabled people with initial entry into the workplace can be assisted by ergonomics. An individual's current medical and physical status (which for an injured worker may reflect "maximum medical progress") may require modifications in the workplace to ensure a successful return. Therapists, ergonomists, and rehabilitation or safety engineers may be among the professionals who recommend and implement these changes. The point of entry for each professional will vary; this usually relates to respective referral sources and reasons for initial consultation.

Historical Background

Tichauer (1978) notes that as early as the 1700s, the physician Ramazzini described the negative health effects of work: "'The cause I assign [to] certain violent and irregular motions and unnatural postures ... by which ... the natural structure of the living machine is so impaired that serious diseases gradually develop'" (p. 1). However, not until shortly after

Table 4-1
The Relationship Between Occupational Therapy and Ergonomics

	Occupational Therapy	Ergonomics
Focus	Disabled/injured person	Worker
Goal	Rehabilitate the client to meet job demands upon return to work	Modify the job to meet the worker's needs

World War II did the field of ergonomics become truly recognized and those in it active in promoting worker health and safety.

In 1949 the British ergonomist K. F. H. Murrell coined the word *ergonomics*. Whether *ergonomics* or *human factors engineering* is used, the concern is the human performance element in the context of work. Moreover, similar to the therapist's interest in the total person, the ergonomist's interest is the total work environment. This includes biomechanical as well as human performance factors.

In the introduction to *Industrial Ergonomics* (Alexander & Pulat, 1985), Pulat states, "The basic assumption of ergonomics is that equipment, object, and environment characteristics influence human and thus total man-machine system performance" (p. 5). It follows that if products, equipment, workstations, and work methods are designed by considering human capabilities and limitations, the performance of the resulting system will be optimum.

Conversely, Pulat adds, "If ergonomics is ignored during design, one should be prepared to accept the costs" (p. 5). These costs include diminished production; greater lost time and down time; higher medical, workers' compensation, and material costs; an increased incidence of sprain and strain injuries; higher rates of absenteeism; lower-quality work; a higher probability of accidents and errors; an increased labor turnover; and less spare capacity to deal with emergencies.

Therefore a primary goal of ergonomics is to improve worker performance and safety by optimizing the efficiency of the "human machine." This involves reducing the effects of fatigue and musculoskeletal stress and strain on the body that work can produce. Of particular interest to occupational therapists is the field of *occupational biomechanics* emerging within ergonomics. According to Chaffin and Anderson (1984), occupational biomechanics is the matching of human physical capacities and human performance requirements in industry. It can be defined as "the study of the physical interaction of workers with their tools, machines, and materials so as to enhance the worker's performance while minimizing the risk of future musculoskeletal disorders" (pp. 1–2).

Some basic concepts of industrial ergonomics are now discussed.

Anthropometrics

Each job places its own physical and psychological demands on the worker. *Anthropometry* deals with the measurement of body dimensions and the differences in human physical characteristics. At any workstation, concern should be given to how workers of different sizes and shapes are able to perform their work, given existing conditions of job design.

Anthropometric data are available that delineate the 95th, 50th, and 5th percentile measurements of various body dimensions for men and women (Chaffin & Anderson, 1984; Dreyfuss, 1967; Eastman Kodak, 1983; Grandjean, 1980; Kroemer, 1978; McCormick & Sanders, 1982; Sahley, 1981; Woodson, 1981). These anthropometric charts and illustrations are useful in planning, designing, and adapting workstations, equipment, and products to make them fit the intended users' needs and capacities to reach, grasp, lift, and manipulate.

The issue then becomes, design for whom—the tall person, the short person, or the average person? Unfortunately, if a workstation is designed for the average person, workers at either end of the height spectrum will be unable to perform the task efficiently. Likewise, if the job is designed for one of the extremes—for example, tall people—then only this group will be able to perform optimally. The limiting design dimension varies in each situation: The height of the tall person may be more important when determining doorway heights or shelf locations, whereas the short person's maximum arm reach or feet-to-floor distance must be considered in the design of seated work tasks. It follows that principles of workplace and job task design are based upon different limiting dimensions and the way in which they affect, as well as permit, the greatest number of people to perform work. Clearly an element of adjustability is necessary in all workstations to meet the varied anthropometric needs of the work force. In addition, a job's physical demand levels should be designed to fit the capabilities of the majority of the intended worker population.

Biomechanics and Work Load Factors

The occupational therapist's training in anatomy, physiology, biomechanics, kinesiology, and medical pathology is helpful in analyzing the efficiency of different work methods and the ways in which the work methods of people with various disabilities can be affected. Ergonomists consider the impact of these factors on job design and operator efficiency. The therapist's medical training can be an asset to the ergonomist when dealing with disabled, injured worker, and aging populations. This pertains to the use of ergonomics in the design and the modification of work and home environments and in the growing field of rehabilitation technology.

Many biomechanical factors affect each person's work performance abilities: the structure, the function, and the optimal power ranges of muscles; the differing effects of static and dynamic muscle loading on the joints; energy sources; and resultant metabolic demands (Brunnstrom, 1972; Kelley, 1971; Wells & Luttgens, 1976). According to Grandjean (1980), these factors further combine with the age, the sex, the physical strength, the skill, and the worker's motivation of the moment to yield a truer performance profile.

In physics, work is defined as

$$Work = Weight \times Distance$$

It is important to realize that not all work involves significant changes in either variable. For this reason therapists and engineers generally differentiate between dynamic and static muscle loading forces. In dynamic work, as force is exerted, the contraction of muscles is generally visible. Concurrently blood is actively pumped to the muscles, and waste products are removed. This contrasts with static work, in which muscles must rely upon their own energy reserves. In this case, although energy is being used, it is not visible, there is no active blood flow through the muscles, and a build-up of metabolic waste products results.

The differences between dynamic and static work have implications for both the net energy exertion and the cumulative musculoskeletal stress on all workers. For these reasons sedentary work can be as demanding as it is, despite the lack of dynamic muscle activity. Workers are subject to the effects of static muscle loading on the back when lifting and lowering loads at the initial and terminal lift points, on the shoulders when reaching and placing loads, and on the hands during fine manipulation tasks.

Job Analysis

Analysis of activity, task, and job is generic to occupational therapy. All job analysis methods are based upon careful observation. Methods in traditional rehabilitation are well documented (Botterbusch, 1987; Field & Field, 1988; U.S. Department of Labor, 1972, 1982) and are described in Chapter 2, "Use of Department of Labor References and Job Analysis."

Today an increasing number of vocational rehabilitation professionals are realizing that traditional analysis methods and job descriptions such as those found in the *Dictionary of Occupational Titles* (U.S. Department of Labor, 1977) are inadequate for placing new or injured workers. New methods of analyzing the physical demands of jobs are helping rehabilitation professionals better understand the actual job requirements before worker placement (Florida Occupational Information Coordinating Committee, 1984; Lytel & Botterbusch, 1981). It is important, however, not to overlook the fact that much information about individual job requirements can be obtained from on-line supervisors, workers themselves, and a review of a company's own job analyses.

Job analysis is also fundamental to the work of ergonomists and industrial engineers. Ergonomic methods of job analysis can enhance or complement traditional methods by helping to define clearly the human factor in work performance. Traditional industrial engineering methods have been briefly reviewed by Chaffin and Anderson (1984). In the early 20th century these work, time study, and motion analyses were performed by Frederick Taylor (often referred to as the father of modern time analysis) and Frank and Lillian Gilbreth. The analyses involved describing the required work tasks, the fundamental task movements or elements, and the time necessary to complete the job. In 1924 the Gilbreths coined the term *therbligs* to define the movements they used in their analysis of elemental motions basic to task performance—for example, select, search, reach, grasp, move, hold, position, assemble, disassemble, use, inspect, plan, or idle. This categorization led to Maynard, Stegmerten, and Schwab's (1948) development of a job analysis system using systematic, predetermined motion-time methods, commonly known as Methods-Time Measurement (MTM).

The MODAPTs (Modular Arrangement of Predetermined Time Standards) system is a current method of job analysis developed in Australia by Heyde (1978, 1983). It delineates a systematic way to characterize motion and task components within a job description. The various motion components of a job are described as a series of gets, moves, and puts that involve different degrees of strength, visual cues, conscious control, and mental processing. MODAPTs helps determine the reasonable time that a worker may be expected to take in performing a specific task. Today the wage rates in many vocational workshops and manufacturing companies are established by using various time study methods to assess the expected time necessary to complete specific job tasks.

The foregoing discussion has focused on the more traditional job analysis methods that identify individual task components, motions, and time factors. Today the work of ergonomists and biomechanics specialists is assisted by the analysis of slow-motion videotape replay for the identification of the fundamental elements of job tasks. Then further biomechanical analysis can be performed by using various computer programs (e.g., Chaffin & Anderson, 1984) that assess resultant joint forces and muscle loading factors in both static and dynamic muscle modes of performance. Often ergonomists perform an additional level of job analysis for the identification of known "musculoskeletal risk factors" that relate to the possible subsequent development of cumulative trauma disorders and manual material handling injuries (discussed in a later section). At the next level of analysis, associations between specific job task components, known risk factors, and resultant medical conditions can be assessed and addressed.

Occupational therapists working with industrial populations can assist ergonomists in reviewing the foregoing types of data with respect to the performance of specific disabled populations or injured worker groups seen in their clinics. Together occupational therapists and ergonomists can design modifications in the job, the tool, or the workplace to minimize the chance of further injury and to prevent new injuries. Such information can also be applied as part of preemployment screening criteria to the placement of suspect, injured, or disabled workers.

Job Station Design

The ways in which workstations have been planned have not traditionally given full consideration to worker health, worker safety, and ergonomics. Principles of ergonomic workstation design are concerned not only with the actual elements of the job task but with the entire job process and the worker's interactions with all components of the job and the workplace environment. Given that the workplace is composed of workers with different needs, from both physical and psychological vantage points, adjustability is a critical feature of all workplaces. Most workstations currently lack the adjustability features that are necessary to accommodate varied workers' needs and permit workers to adapt their workplaces for optimal comfort, performance, and efficiency.

Basic to the design and the structure of any work task is consideration for physical work demands; required working postures; reach distances; work counter heights; locations of fixed machines and controls; required tools, materials, or other equipment; static and dynamic work-performance elements; component task processes; visual work demands; and psychological work demands. Some of these aspects are discussed in the following paragraphs.

Jobs should be designed to minimize excessive force, stress, and effort by and on the worker. Job design must consider anthropometric factors and the biomechanical efficiency of the body in different working postures. The body can be considered a set of links, or a kinematic chain, in which motion of one part affects the resultant postures and muscle forces at adjacent locations.

Chaffin and Anderson (1984), Eastman Kodak (1983), and Grandjean (1980), among others, have delineated ideal working-arm positions for benchwork and office jobs. These postures should be used as guides when adapting both seated and standing workstations. They include an elbow position of approximately 90 degrees of flexion and a straight or neutral wrist. Small deviations from this position are recommended when work involves either greater than normal strength or fine dexterity.

The limitations in workers' effective arm reaches must also be considered. The ideal horizontal arm reach applies to a semicircle distance around the worker. Work areas for frequent tasks should be kept within approximately a 10-inch reach of the worker, and areas for occasional tasks, within a 20-inch distance (see Figure 4-2). Vertical-reach distances should minimize forward elevation of the shoulder to less than 90 degrees and sideward reaches to less than 60 degrees. This reduces any muscle fatigue that might result from increases in arm elevation, especially if these arm positions must be sustained for a time. It is also known that compressive forces on the shoulder joint increase significantly when arm abduction angles exceed 15 to 20 degrees. According to Tichauer (1966), such increased abduction angles can be caused by either the location of the work task or negative differences of 2 inches or less in seat-height dimension. Reaches behind or to the sides that require twisting should be avoided at all times. If necessary, a swivel-based chair can eliminate the effects of torquing on the spine.

The visual demands of a job must be examined too. These can contribute not only to visual fatigue and stress but to musculoskeletal postural stress and strain, particularly if corrective lenses are indicated.

Generally the level of work tasks should be about 2 inches below the elbow for normal light assembly tasks, just above elbow height for more precise work, and 4–8 inches below elbow height for more manual work (see Figure 4-3). When reviewing work counter heights, it is important to remember that the actual work heights are not determined by the work

Figure 4-2
Preferred Distances of Work Areas

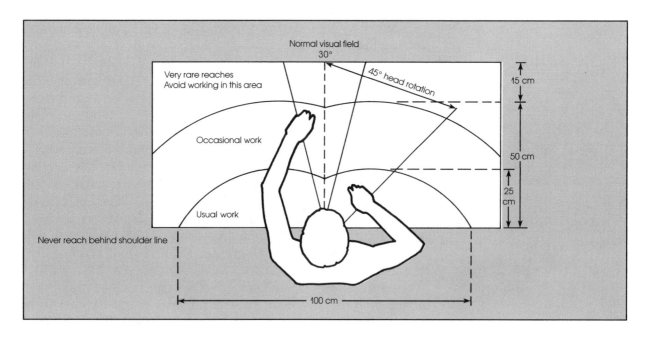

Note. From *Industrial Ergonomics* (p. 5) by Industrial Accident Prevention Association, 1982, Toronto, Ontario: Author. © 1982 by Industrial Accident Prevention Association. Reprinted by permission.

counter itself. Rather they are determined by the locations of machines and their controls, keyboards, and any other work items or fixtures on the counter. Desk heights should vary about 2 inches for typing and writing tasks, with additional allowances necessary for height differences among workers (Grandjean, 1980). The seated dimensions for typists differ from those for secretaries, data-entry workers, and computer programmers because although all of these jobs involve keying, it is only one aspect of the overall job, and the actual workstation must be designed according to the total demands of the job (Rader, 1986). Various researchers have determined different ideal working heights and dimensions; representative ranges are illustrated in Figure 4-4.

In offices with computers the equipment must often be adapted to facilitate optimal hand positioning by the user during keying tasks. Detachable and redesigned keyboards, slide-out trays, and wrist rests allow computer operators to make adjustments in their hand placement on the keyboard. Adjustments in chair height are often the necessary link in helping workers accommodate to generally fixed work-counter heights.

Figure 4-3
Recommended Heights of Bench for Standing Work
The reference line (± 0) is the height of the elbows above the floor, which averages 105 cm for men and 98 cm for women.

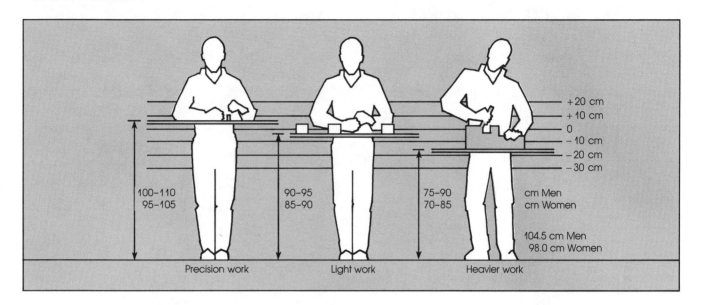

Note. From *Fitting the Task to the Man: An Ergonomic Approach* (3rd ed.) (p. 42) by E. Grandjean, 1980, Philadelphia: Taylor & Francis. © 1980 by Taylor & Francis Ltd. Reprinted by permission.

The worker's line of sight should be direct, assist eye-hand coordination, and minimize straining of the neck, the head, and the eye muscles (Chaffin & Anderson, 1984; Eastman Kodak, 1983; Grandjean, 1980).

Psychological work demands must also be considered. These include the cumulative effects of mental stress and fatigue as a result of repetition, boredom, job demands, scheduling, deadlines, and organizational issues. The worker's overall general mental health is important as well, from a holistic point of view. A discussion of occupational stress issues is beyond the scope of this chapter, but they merit consideration as factors affecting each worker's performance.

The next sections address methods of modifying workplaces using principles of ergonomic design.

Adapting Seated Work

The importance of a comfortably fitting and supportive chair cannot be overlooked for all workers who perform sedentary work, whether it be in office or manufacturing settings. Therapists are already familiar with the wheelchair user's seating needs for comfort, proper support, and productivity.

Figure 4-4
Recommended Video Display Terminal (VDT) Workstation

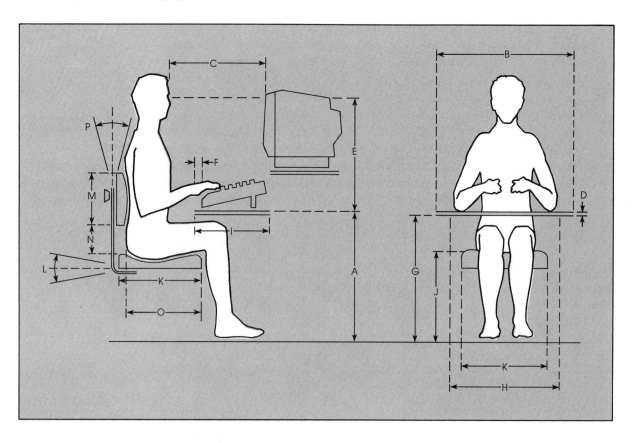

A — Height of work surface: adjustable 23 to 28 inches (584 to 711 mm)
B — Width of work surface: 30 inches (760 mm)
C — Viewing distance: minimum 12 inches (305 mm); hard copy distance 12 to 16 inches (305 to 406 mm); typical eye to keyboard distance 18 to 20 inches (457 to 508 mm)
D — Thickness of work surface: 1 inch (25 mm)
E — Height of screen: top of screen at approximately eye level (maximum 0° to horizontal, or 0° to -60°)
F — Palm rest: 1-1/2 inches (40 mm)

G — Knee room height: minimum of 26.2 inches (665 mm) non-adjustable surface; 20.2 inches (513 mm) adjustable surface
H — Knee room width: 20 inches (510 mm) minimum
I — Knee room depth: minimum of 15.0 inches (381 mm) knee level; 23.5 inches (597 mm) toe level

J — Seat height: adjustable 16 to 20.5 inches (400 to 521 mm)
K — Seat size: 15 to 17 inches (381 to 432 mm) depth; 17.7 inches (450 mm) width; "waterfall" front edge
L — Seat slope: adjustable 0° to 10° backward slope
M— Back rest size: 7 inches high (180 mm); 13 inches wide (330 mm)
N — Back rest height: adjustable 3 to 6 inches (80 to 150 mm) above seat
O— Back rest depth: adjustable 14 to 17 inches (350 to 430 mm)
P — Back rest tilt: adjustable ± 15°

Other — Angles between back rest and seat 90° to 105°; between seat and lower leg 60° to 100°; between upper arm and forearm 70° to 135°

Note. From *Workplace Design: Recommended VDT Workstation* (LP 186 R1) by Liberty Mutual Insurance Company, Loss Prevention Department, n.d., Boston, MA: Author. Reprinted by permission.

Chairs that provide the necessary back support are essential to the performance and the well-being of all seated workers. Chairs in corporate offices have always been given high priority, but rarely have those on shop or office floors. Most chairs found in industry are old, lack adjustable features or the proper supports, and include makeshift padding adaptations. Proper chair design and selection can reduce fatigue and enhance musculoskeletal comfort and circulation. In the author's experience with sewing machine operators, significant changes in worker comfort and posture have resulted from the introduction of new chairs (A.C.T.W.U.-N.Y.S. Education Training Grant, 1988).

Chair heights must be adjustable to meet the wide range of human needs. Because work counter heights are generally fixed, the chair is usually the easiest workplace item to adjust. Often workers are either unable to adjust their chairs or unaware that they can do so. In many cases, educating workers about how they can adjust their chairs can help improve their seating comfort. However, the solution is not always that simple because most chairs on manufacturing and office floors lack the necessary features to permit proper adjustments to individual worker needs. (Likewise, wheelchair users may require specific work-counter height and space modifications and removable armrests to permit access to their work area. Discussion of these modifications is beyond the scope of this chapter.)

The purchase of new chairs must be considered when workers experience musculoskeletal discomfort that is in part due to chairs lacking adjustable features. The overall cost of this purchase is relatively minor when compared with other changes in workplace design. Improvements in worker productivity are known to occur concurrently with increased user comfort and reduced musculoskeletal fatigue. Enhancing musculoskeletal comfort is also a good prevention method. Because shift work is common to many manufacturing companies, a chair with adjustable features can help accommodate the same workstation to more than one user. There is a need to educate all employers whose work forces perform sedentary work about the benefits of using properly designed chairs.

The features of a good chair are as follows (Chaffin & Anderson, 1984; Eastman Kodak, 1983; Grandjean, 1976, 1980):

1. An adjustable height mechanism
2. An adjustable backrest
3. Padded and contoured seat cushions
4. A seat fabric that breathes
5. A swivel post and a five-point base of support.

The ideal seated work position can be described thus:
1. A series of approximately 90-degree links at the hip, knee, foot, and elbow joints
2. The upper arms relaxed at the sides
3. The forearms parallel to the floor
4. The wrists straight and the hands resting comfortably
5. The feet resting flat on the floor, on controls, or on a footrest.

Chair design should also include or permit the following:
6. Adequate clearance between the thighs and the work counter
7. Proper support to the lumbar curve
8. The opportunity for unrestricted arm motion
9. A seat-pan angle that prevents any forward sliding from the upright posture
10. Easy adjustments by the chair's occupant.

Each worker's sitting posture should be reviewed and compared with the preceding recommendations. Further fine-tuning can be done with footrests, lumbar supports, seat cushions, and forearm supports. For example, the short worker's feet may not touch the floor or the base chair rim. In this case, footrests are indicated to help maintain the knees and the hips in approximately 90 degrees of flexion and to promote venous return from the legs. Otherwise, swollen ankles and fatigue of the hip muscles may become problems.

Adapting Standing Workplaces

Fatigue is a common problem among workers who stand for prolonged periods. The concrete floors of most factories offer no shock absorption to the spinal column of standing workers. This results in cumulative stress and static loading on back and leg muscles (Snook, 1988). Poor posture habits can then develop. In addition to alterations in the job design to avoid continuous standing, relatively small modifications in the workplace can be made to minimize the negative effect on the body of continuous standing. Standing workers should have the opportunity to alleviate some of the back strain and fatigue that results from continuous standing. This includes using footrests or counter rails and intermittently performing work in a seated position—for example, working from sit-stand stools. The cumulative effects of continuous standing on the back and the legs can be further alleviated by resilient floor matting—for example, antifatigue mats in specific workplace locations—and by a requirement that workers wear good supportive rubber-soled shoes or Sorbothane-type insoles (made by Sorbothane, Inc.). These latter suggestions also apply to the standing worker who performs manual work throughout the day, not necessarily in one fixed location.

Musculoskeletal Injury Prevention

Occupational musculoskeletal stress and strain injuries, including cumulative trauma disorders and back injuries, occur in high frequencies in industry. Ergonomics is an integral component of any injury prevention program.

Cumulative Trauma Disorders

Cumulative trauma disorders are soft-tissue injuries that are the result of repeated hand or arm use, day after day, year after year. According to the National Institute for Occupational Safety and Health (NIOSH, 1988), more than half of the nation's workers have jobs with the potential for cumulative trauma disorders. The major industries that NIOSH cites are construction, services, manufacturing, and clerical work. A review of occupational illnesses by the Bureau of Labor Statistics, reported in the National Safety Council's 1988 edition of *Accident Facts,* indicates that cumulative trauma disorders occur most frequently in the manufacturing industry.

The overall prevalence of cumulative trauma disorders is not known. An exact recording of incidence rates is difficult because symptoms generally develop slowly, over time. It is not always possible to establish a single causative event. Precisely how many motions are too much has not yet been determined.

According to Armstrong, Radwin, and Hansen (1986), up to 25 percent of the workers in some industries require medical attention for these problems. Cumulative trauma disorders, including carpal tunnel syndrome, tendinitis, tenosynovitis, and ganglionic cysts, are a major cause of lost time and workers' compensation dollars in many hand-intensive industries. A recent NIOSH (1988) publication attributes the increase in the incidence of these disorders to changes in the work force: more service and "high-tech" jobs, an aging worker population, and a reduction in turnover. Numerous epidemiological and industry-specific studies are available on this topic (Buckle, 1987; Dimberg, 1987; Feldman, Goldman, & Keyserling, 1983; Hadler, 1977; Kelsey, 1980, 1982; Keyserling, Donoghue, Punnett, & Miller, 1982; Kilbom, Perrson, & Jonsson, 1986; Kuorinka & Koskinen, 1979; Kvarnstrom, 1983; Luopajarvi, Kuorinka, Virolainen, & Homberg, 1979; Silverstein, Fine, & Armstrong, 1987; Stroud, 1985; Vihma, 1982; Waris et al., 1979; Wells, Zipp, Schuette, & McEleney, 1983).

Many ergonomic factors are known to contribute to the development of cumulative trauma or repetitive motion disorders in the workplace. Causal factors include the following

(Armstrong, 1983; Armstrong & Chaffin, 1979; Armstrong, Foulke, Goldstein, & Joseph, 1981; Armstrong, Radwin, & Hansen, 1986; Armstrong & Silverstein, 1987; Cannon, Bernaacki, & Walter, 1981; Hoyt, 1984; Silverstein, Fine, & Armstrong, 1987; Wehrle, 1976):

1. Repetitive arm, wrist, or finger motions
2. Awkward postures
3. Extended reaches
4. Repetitive twisting and turning
5. Prolonged pinching
6. Static limb positioning
7. Mechanical pressure
8. Increased stress and force concentrations
9. Tools or objects causing pressure on the volar hand/wrist surface
10. Exposure to low temperatures
11. Use of vibratory hand tools or components
12. Wearing of gloves that interfere with hand use
13. Lack of job rotation
14. Any combination of the above factors.

Gelberman, Hergenroeder, Hargens, Lunborg, and Akeson (1981) have found that working with the wrist in either extreme flexion or extreme extension significantly increases the pressure within the carpal canal. Silverstein, Fine, and Armstrong (1986) have examined the variables of short and long cycle times and high and low forces among various industrial populations. They report that the workers at greatest risk to develop cumulative trauma disorders are those in jobs that involve high force and high repetition.

Engineering changes have been found to assist in the reduction of cumulative trauma injuries (Armstrong, 1983; Armstrong & Chaffin, 1979; Armstrong, Foulke, Goldstein, & Joseph, 1981; Armstrong, Radwin, & Hansen, 1986; Armstrong & Silverstein, 1987). These interventions include redesigning jobs to eliminate aggravating hand or wrist positions and forces, reorienting locations of tasks or products on which employees are working, designing tasks to include straight-wrist working postures whenever possible, modifying or changing tools, reducing task frequencies, and adjusting seat or table heights.

Manual Material Handling Injuries

Back pain and injuries are known to affect large segments of the industrial population. NIOSH (1981) cites National Safety Council reports that about 25 percent of all work injuries result from overexertion to the back during manual material handling. The result is over $10 billion in compensation costs annually (NIOSH, 1981; Snook, 1978, 1988). According to Snook (1978, 1988) and others, more than half of all compensable back pain incidents are related to the manual handling of objects.

Many job factors related to the development of back injuries extend beyond the individual's actual physical abilities to lift. They include the following (Chaffin & Anderson, 1984; Eastman Kodak, 1984; Rowe, 1983; Snook, 1978, 1988):

1. The actual horizontal- and vertical-lift distances—for example, loads that are too low to or too high from the floor, or involve extended forward reaches
2. High task frequency
3. Short cycle times
4. Repetitive or sustained bending or lifting or awkward body postures
5. Asymmetric loading on the spine and the body
6. Twisting of the torso while lifting
7. Handling of very heavy, bulky, or unstable loads
8. Inadequate grip control
9. Poor floor or shoe traction
10. Space constraints
11. Total body vibration during heavy tool usage
12. Working in cold environments
13. Externally paced job demands
14. The unavailability of co-workers to assist with load handling
15. The lack of proper assistive equipment.

The occupational therapist treating industrial clients with back injury serves an important role as educator. This includes training the clients in proper lifting and posture techniques, biomechanics, energy conservation, and injury prevention methods consistent with maintaining a healthy back. The occupational therapist must analyze how each of the 15 factors related to back injuries contributes to the performance of material handling tasks. Then the best methods of lifting, holding, carrying, or bending can be determined, with respect to the individual worker and the design characteristics of the job.

According to Snook (1978, 1988) and Manuele (1984), "back schools" have flourished in recent years, yet longitudinal follow-up studies have not found them to be the answer in reducing industrial back injuries. Back injuries are known to have high recurrence rates. Returning injured workers to the same job site can negate medical and rehabilitation progress unless changes in the workplace itself have been made. For this reason, instruction in lifting techniques, by itself, is not the answer. An ergonomics intervention program, which may involve engineering redesign, is required concurrently to help rectify the causal factors at the job site and to help prevent back injuries in the future, for both returning workers and "to-date-noninjured workers."

Ergonomic interventions to reduce back injury involve both biomechanical studies and the redesign of material handling tasks. Biomechanical studies, including vector, force, and motion analyses, assess the resultant forces on the various body joints. Currently computer programs incorporating two- and three-dimensional cinematography, developed at the University of Michigan (e.g., Chaffin & Anderson, 1984), are being used for this purpose. Ergonomists throughout the country are developing and employing similar programs.

NIOSH (1981) has developed a comprehensive formula to assess various factors affecting safe lifting loads and the resultant forces on the back during symmetric lifts. Known as the NIOSH lifting guide, the formula is useful for estimating what are safe and unsafe lifting loads on the body and how different loads, under different frequencies and lift distances, concur with established safe lifting limits. It is important to realize that this formula deals with symmetric lifting patterns and not the torsional forces that accompany most lifts. The rehabilitation professional or the ergonomics or safety specialist using the NIOSH guide to assess safe lifting loads can introduce data about variables into the formula manually or electronically.

Snook (1978) has delineated different acceptable weight lifts and lowers, carrying loads, and push/pull exertions of force for different percentiles of the industrial population. Chaffin and Park (1973) conclude that the incidence of back pain increases as the lifted load exceeds 35 pounds. Correlations of the known lifting demands of jobs with both injured and noninjured individuals' abilities to perform physically demanding tasks are essential to the safe placement of all workers in industry. Many of the rehabilitation professionals who specialize in assessing workers' physical capacities are beginning to expand their job analysis methods to include these physical demands assessments and consideration of ergonomic factors.

Tools

Tools, according to Tichauer (1977), should be designed to extend and reinforce the range, the strength, and the effectiveness of the limb(s) engaged in performing a given task. The purpose of most tools is to transmit forces generated within the human body onto the specific workpiece. Basic principles of tool design are these:
  1. The grips and the handles of the tool should fit comfortably in the hands.

2. Pressure on vulnerable tissue structures should be avoided.
3. The resultant working-hand posture should minimize pressure on nerves and tendons.
4. The grasp required to hold and use a tool should incorporate the largest muscle groups whenever possible.
5. Pinch and trigger forces should be minimized.

Anthropometrics related to hand size are important in selecting the proper tool (Kaplan, 1981). Workers who wear gloves must exert additional force during tool use because they do not receive the same sensory feedback as workers with ungloved hands do. For this reason glove-to-skin contact areas should be kept to a minimum whenever possible, providing the wearer with the opportunity for maximum sensory feedback. Wearing gloves can also contribute to reduced power grip strength (Isernhagen, 1988; Rodgers, 1988).

Both Tichauer (1978) and Grandjean (1980) have found that workers note beneficial effects when a needed bend is placed in a tool rather than in the user's wrists. Recently some tool manufacturers have developed a new line of ergonomic tools that place the bend in the tool. This helps to avoid the musculoskeletal stress and strain on the user's hands that result from awkward positioning during tool use. Modified tools include hammers, utility and kitchen knives, and pliers. A list of tool manufacturing companies appears in Appendix 4-A.

It is important to realize that the newly designed ergonomic tools cannot fit the needs of all users because tools are task specific. The orientation of a tool relative to each work surface must be considered. For example, as seen in Figure 4-5, the pistol-grip drill and the straight-nozzle drill are intended for work on different surfaces. If either tool is used inappropriately, the result is the unhealthy flexed-wrist position.

Both industrial and home tool users should become knowledgeable about which tools are available and most appropriate for each task. Many new tools on the market can make work easier—for example, ratchet-type screwdrivers that reduce the required torquing force. Tool users need to be alerted to certain pain warning signals that can result from awkward hand positioning or pressure during tool use.

Not only are tools task specific, but the type of machine control—for example, knob, push button, dial, switch, crank, or pedal—also varies with each job. The choice of control is determined by the complexity of the task, safety factors, the required amount of muscular control and precision, and the degree of mental concentration and skill necessary to guide worker actions.

Figure 4-5
Proper Tool Selection
Proper tool selection is task specific. Biomechanics are affected by resultant hand positioning with respect to different work surfaces.

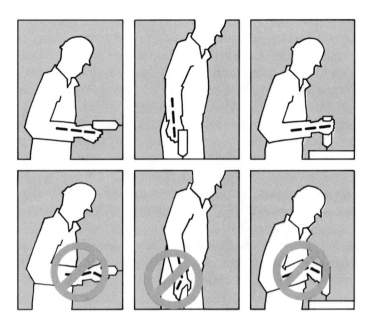

Pistol and cylindrical tools showing wrist in desired nearly straight postures

Pistol and cylindrical tools showing wrist in undesirable bent postures

Note. Adapted from *Occupational Biomechanics* (p. 361) by D. Chaffin and B. J. Anderson, 1984, New York: John Wiley & Sons, which was in turn adapted from *An Ergonomics Guide to Carpal Tunnel Syndrome* (p. 4) by T. Armstrong, 1983, Akron, OH: American Industrial Hygiene Association. © 1983 by American Industrial Hygiene Association, © 1984 by John Wiley & Sons. Reprinted by permission of the publishers.

Ergonomic Principles

The occupational therapist working in an industrial setting can apply basic ergonomic principles to new and existing workstations, benefiting both the employer and the employee. The goal of ergonomic interventions is to minimize or alleviate the effects of cumulative musculoskeletal stress and strain on the worker.

The basic principles that have been reviewed in previous sections are presented again in a format that can be directly used by workers (see the box). Most ergonomic principles relate to reducing the load weight, the force required, the distance moved, or the frequency of an activity.

Information-Processing and Environmental Issues

The domain of ergonomics is not restricted to the purely biomechanical aspects of work. Both occupational therapists and ergonomists are concerned with the capacities of humans

Ergonomic Principles for the Informed Worker

1. Avoid any sustained bent or unnatural postures—for example, extreme wrist positions (up, down, or sideward) or bending of the back.
2. Avoid lifts directly from the floor level; use platforms or conveyors that are located between knee and shoulder heights to eliminate extreme lifting postures.
3. Position yourself as close as possible to the object to be lifted, transferred, or manipulated.
4. Avoid excessive bending whenever possible; tilt large containers, not your back, for unloading; use sloped containers to retrieve and place small assembly pieces.
5. Avoid twisting while lifting or placing objects; turn with your whole body, rather than with the torso alone.
6. Use pushing rather than pulling actions whenever possible.
7. Minimize forward and sideward reaches to below shoulder-level height.
8. Arrange the work area so that you can work with your elbows at an angle of about 90 degrees.
9. Limit the areas of frequent work to a semicircle within 10 inches of your body, the areas of occasional work to within 20 inches.
10. Keep the wrists as straight as possible while working.
11. Use tools that are task specific and that distribute forces throughout the hand.
12. Use controls that are contoured or padded and that allow use of maximum hand surface.
13. Avoid unnecessary repeated and rapid arm or hand movements.
14. Avoid isolated finger trigger-control motions.
15. Pad counter edges or use forearm supports to lessen the weight on the hand while performing hand-intensive work.
16. Arrange work areas to be within a direct field of vision; be sure proper lighting is present at the work area.
17. Perform work sitting down if you can. Alternate standing tasks with sitting ones whenever possible.
18. Use chairs with adjustable features and good back support.
19. Rotate job tasks whenever possible.
20. Use all available visual, auditory, and tactile sensory cues to enhance information processing and safe task performance.

to process and use information. Whereas the therapist often considers this factor with respect to disabled people, the human factors specialist is concerned with how an able-bodied population processes information on a day-to-day basis. It is in the area of information processing that attention must be given to the unique characteristics, capabilities, and limitations of the human machine, as compared with the robot or the computer.

The human factors specialist addresses the mental activities and skills required of workers. These include human information processing, storage and retrieval capacities, long- and short-term memory, rote tasks, vigilance, reaction times, anticipation, missed signals, and signal frequency (McCormick & Sanders, 1982). In addition, the experience and the age of the user, language standardization, familiarity with the job task, and the use of symbols (Grandjean, 1980) are considered in relation to different worker and ethnic groups. Generic to information-processing abilities are the visual capabilities of the user and the limitations of the human visual perception system. This applies to the design of computer screens and menus, displays, signs, scales and their subdivisions, fixed markers, and the size of letters, symbols, and numbers used to foster information processing and retention.

Clear messages enhance the user's information-processing capacities and contribute to less mental fatigue and fewer errors and accidents. Consideration must also be given to the psychological effects of shift work, the work schedule itself, pacing, breaks, the required degree of attention and concentration, fatigue (both mental and physical), and boredom, which can result from repetitious work.

Environmental factors in the total workplace also affect workers' performance, comfort, and productivity. These include lighting (direct and indirect), room color, noise levels, climatic conditions, air temperature, presence of fumes and exhausts, and indoor or outdoor location. It is beyond the scope of this chapter to deal with these factors. However, therapists working in industrial settings or with industrial clients should be aware of the factors and review their impact on worker health, safety, and productivity with other members of the industrial health team.

Implementing an Ergonomics Program

In recent years companies have slowly begun to understand the value of ergonomics. This pertains particularly to companies with high workers' compensation expenses, for whom long-term savings can be realized in both direct and indirect costs. The Occupational Safety and Health Administration (OSHA) has increased its role in citing and fining companies whose workplaces yield high existing rates of injury or pose potentially great risks in the future. In either of these cases ergonomics programs can help an industry deal with its health and safety concerns.

Ergonomics programs include musculoskeletal injury prevention, employee education, exercise, and workplace modifications. The introduction of an ergonomics program must be presented to management in such a manner that the bottom-line financial benefits—for example, cost savings with productivity gains—will be obvious. Cooperation among all levels of management is crucial to the success of any ergonomics program. Labor unions—among them, the United Auto Workers, the Amalgamated Textile Workers Union, the International Ladies Garment Workers Union and the United Food and Commercial Workers—have increased their interest in ergonomics as part of their health and safety programs. Joint task forces on ergonomics between labor and management are becoming more common, with health and safety often serving as the common link.

Proactive ergonomics programs have recently been used in the planning stages of some new facilities or job stations, in an attempt to minimize the potential development of ergonomic hazards and musculoskeletal injuries. During ergonomics program implementation (or before consideration of any large capital expenses), the first line of action should be how to use and improve existing resources.

Summary

The concerns of ergonomists parallel those of occupational therapists in industry. Both strive to reduce resultant and cumulative stress and strain on the human body, so that work can be performed safely and efficiently. Ergonomists concern themselves with fitting the demands of work to the efficiency of the human operator. They also address the issues of designing machines, equipment, and tools for the operator to perform with the greatest efficiency, accuracy, and safety while executing work tasks. Attention is given to proper body biomechanics and postural issues when designing and analyzing seated or standing work tasks, manual material handling, repetitive manipulation with the hands, use of tools, and reaching, bending, or lifting tasks.

The occupational therapist and the ergonomist can recommend modifications in the job process or the workplace itself to promote worker safety as part of larger rehabilitation, return-to-work, wellness, or injury prevention programs. The initial concerns of each professional may vary in relation to generic workplace issues; specific disability or worker groups; the job process or any of its component parts; or the equipment and the tools instrumental to complete a given job. Aimed at promoting worker health and safety, ergonomic interventions include, but are not limited to, training of workers in body mechanics, posture, and lifting techniques; basic methods of injury prevention; the introduction of exercise programs; task and workstation redesign; and general environmental changes in the workplace.

Successful industry programs require a collaborative and cooperative effort among the medical, safety, engineering, production, and workers' compensation departments, as well as between top management and labor. The end goal, worker health and safety with concurrent gains in efficiency and productivity, can be accomplished only by a team effort. This understanding is necessary to ensure the successful launching and implementation of an ergonomics program in industry. The occupational therapist who serves as a consultant to industry must realize that management needs, first, to be aware that a problem exists—for example, high workers' compensation costs—and second, to be committed to remedying the problem. It is hoped that proactive industry ergonomics programs that positively affect workers' health, safety, comfort, and ultimate productivity will become the rule rather than the exception as society moves into the 21st century.

Glossary

Adjustability—the ability to make changes in a workstation or a job design to meet the varied needs of the work force.

Anthropometry—the measurement of human body dimensions.

Cumulative trauma disorder—a condition affecting primarily the hands and the upper extremities that results from repetitive use or overuse.

Ergonomics—the study of work; the interaction and the fit between human capabilities and the demands of a job.

Manual material handling injury—a condition of the back and the body related to job tasks that involve lifting, loading, and carrying.

MODAPTs (Modular Arrangement of Predetermined Time Standards)—a systematic method of job analysis that describes motion and task components as an orderly series of performance elements.

Occupational biomechanics—the discipline within ergonomics concerned with matching human physical capacities to specific job demands for use of tools, machines, and materials.

References

Alexander, D., & Pulat, B. (1985). *Industrial ergonomics: A practitioner's guide.* Atlanta: Industrial Engineering and Management Press.

Armstrong, T. (1983). *An ergonomics guide to carpal tunnel syndrome* (Ergonomics Guides). Akron, OH: American Industrial Hygiene Association.

Armstrong, T., & Chaffin, D. (1979). Some biomechanical aspects of the carpal tunnel. *Journal of Biomechanics, 12,* 567–570.

Armstrong, T., Foulke, J., Goldstein, S., & Joseph, B. (1981). *Analysis of cumulative trauma disorders and work methods* (NIOSH Technical Report). Cincinnati, OH: U.S. Department of Health and Human Services.

Armstrong, T., Radwin, D., & Hansen, D. (1986). Repetitive trauma disorders: Job evaluation and design. *Human Factors, 28,* 325–336.

Armstrong, T., & Silverstein, B. (1987). Upper-extremity pain in the workplace—role of usage in causality. In N. Hadler (Ed.), *Clinical concepts in regional musculoskeletal illness* (pp. 333–354). New York: Grune & Stratton.

Botterbusch, K. F. (1987). *Vocational assessment and evaluation systems: A comparison.* Menomonie, WI: University of Wisconsin–Stout, Stout Vocational Rehabilitation Institute, Materials Development Center.

Brunnstrom, S. (1972). *Clinical kinesiology.* Philadelphia: F. A. Davis.

Buckle, P. (Ed.). (1987). *Musculoskeletal disorders at work.* Philadelphia: Taylor & Francis.

Cannon, L., Bernaacki, E., & Walter, S. (1981). Personal and occupational factors associated with carpal tunnel syndrome. *Journal of Occupational Medicine, 23,* 255–258.

Chaffin, D. (1987). Occupational biomechanics—a basis for workplace design to prevent musculoskeletal injuries. *Ergonomics, 30,* 321–329.

Chaffin, D., & Anderson, B. J. (1984). *Occupational biomechanics.* New York: John Wiley & Sons.

Chaffin, D., & Park, K. (1973). A longitudinal study of low-back pain as associated with occupational weight lifting factors. *American Industrial Hygiene Association Journal, 34,* 513–523.

Dimberg, L. (1987). The prevalence and causation of tennis elbow in a population of workers in an engineering industry. *Ergonomics, 30,* 573–580.

Dreyfuss, H. (1967). *Designing for people* (2nd ed.). New York: Grossman.

Eastman Kodak Co., Human Factors Section. (1983). *Ergonomics design for people at work* (Vol. 1). Belmont, CA: Lifetime Learning Publications.

Feldman, R., Goldman, R., & Keyserling, W. M. (1983). Peripheral nerve entrapment syndromes and ergonomic factors. *American Journal of Industrial Medicine, 4,* 661-681.

Field, T. F., & Field, J. E. (Eds.). (1988). *The classification of jobs according to worker trait factors.* Athens, GA: Elliot and Fitzpatrick.

Florida Occupational Information Coordinating Committee and Florida Association of Rehabilitation Facilities. (1984). *Job-related physical capacities system.* Tallahassee, FL: Florida Association of Rehabilitation Facilities.

Gelberman, R., Hergenroeder, P., Hargens, A., Lunborg, G., & Akeson, W. (1981). The carpal tunnel syndrome: A study of carpal canal pressures. *Journal of Bone and Joint Surgery, 63A,* 380–383.

Grandjean, E. (Ed.). (1976). *Sitting posture.* Philadelphia: Taylor & Francis.

Grandjean, E. (1980). *Fitting the task to the man: An ergonomic approach* (3rd ed.). Philadelphia: Taylor & Francis.

Hadler, N. (1977). Industrial rheumatology: Clinical investigations into the influence of the pattern of usage on the pattern of regional musculoskeletal disease. *Arthritis and Rheumatism, 20,* 1019–1024.

Heyde, C. (1978). *The sensible taskmaster.* Sydney, Australia: Heyde Dynamics.

Heyde, C. (1983). *MODAPTS PLUS.* Sydney, Australia: Heyde Dynamics.

Hoyt, W. (1984). Carpal tunnel syndrome: Analysis and prevention. *Professional Safety, 29*(11), 16–21.

Industrial Accident Prevention Association. (1982). *Industrial ergonomics.* Toronto, Ontario: Author.

Isernhagen, S. J. (1988). *Work injury: Management and prevention.* Rockville, MD: Aspen.

Kaplan, M. (1981). Task and tool design: "It's a man's world." *Occupational Health and Safety, 52*(2), 29–34.

Kelley, D. (1971). *Kinesiology: Fundamentals of motion description.* Englewood Cliffs, NJ: Prentice-Hall.

Kelsey, J. (1980). *Upper extremity disorders: A survey of their frequency and costs in the United States.* St. Louis, MO: C. V. Mosby.

Kelsey, J. (1982). *Epidemiology of musculoskeletal disorders.* New York: Oxford University Press.

Keyserling, M., Donoghue, J., Punnett, L., & Miller, A. (1982). *Repetitive trauma disorders in the garment industry.* Cincinnati, OH: National Institute for Occupational Safety and Health.

Kilbom, A., Perrson, J., & Jonsson, B. (1986). Disorders of the cervicobrachial region among female workers in the electronics industry. *International Journal of Ergonomics, 1,* 37–47.

Kroemer, K. (1978). Functional anthropometry. In *Proceedings of the Human Factors Society annual meeting* (pp. 680–683). Santa Monica, CA: Human Factors Society.

Kuorinka, I., & Koskinen, P. (1979). Occupational rheumatic diseases and upper limb strain in manual jobs in a light mechanical industry. *Scandinavian Journal of Work, Environment and Health, 5,* 39–47.

Luopajarvi, T., Kuorinka, I., Virolainen, M., & Homberg, M. (1979). Prevalence of tenosynovitis and other injuries of the upper extremities in repetitive work. *Scandinavian Journal of Work, Environment and Health, 5,* 48–55.

Lytel, R., & Botterbusch, K. (1981). *Physical demands job analysis: A new approach.* Menomonie, WI: University of Wisconsin–Stout, Stout Vocational Rehabilitation Institute, Materials Development Center.

Manuele, F. (1984). Back injury prevention: The significance of ergonomics. *Professional Safety, 29,* 33–37.

Maynard, H. B., Stegmerten, G. J, & Schwab, J. L. (1948). *Methods-time measurement.* New York: McGraw-Hill.

McCormick, E., & Sanders, M. (1982). *Human factors in engineering and design.* New York: McGraw-Hill.

National Institute for Occupational Safety and Health. (1981). *Work practices guide for manual lifting* (Technical Report No. 81-122). Cincinnati, OH: U.S. Department of Health and Human Services.

National Institute for Occupational Safety and Health. (1988). *Cumulative trauma disorders: A manual for musculoskeletal diseases of the upper limbs.* Philadelphia: Taylor & Francis.

National Safety Council. (1988). *Accident facts* (1988 ed.). Chicago: Author.

Rader, E. (1986). Ergonomics, occupational therapy, and computers. *Occupational Therapy in Health Care, 3,* 43–53.

Rodgers, S. (1984). *Working with backache.* Fairport, NY: Perinton Press.

Rodgers, S. H. (1988). Matching worker and worksite—ergonomic principles. In S. J. Isernhagen (Ed.), *Work injury: Management and prevention* (pp. 65–79). Rockville, MD: Aspen.

Rowe, M. (1983). Backache at work. Fairport, NY: Perinton Press.

Sahley, L. (1981). *Dimensions of the human figure.* Cleveland, OH: Cleveland Designers and Consultants.

Silverstein, B., Fine, L. J., & Armstrong, T. (1986). Hand wrist cumulative trauma disorders in industry. *British Journal of Industrial Medicine, 43,* 779–784.

Silverstein, B., Fine, L. J., & Armstrong, T. (1987). Occupational factors and carpal tunnel syndrome. *American Journal of Industrial Medicine, 11,* 343–358.

Snook, S. (1978). The design of manual material handling tasks. *Ergonomics, 21,* 963–985.

Snook, S. (1988). Approaches to the control of back pain in industry. *Professional Safety, 33,* 23–31.

Stroud, S. (1985, January). Hypothenar hammer syndrome: A commonly undetected occupational hazard. *Occupational Health Nursing,* pp. 31–32.

Tichauer, E. (1966). Some aspects of stresses on the forearm and hand in industry. *Journal of Occupational Medicine, 8,* 63–71.

Tichauer, E. (1977). *Ergonomic principles basic to hand tool design* (Ergonomics Guides). Akron, OH: American Industrial Hygiene Association.

Tichauer, E. (1978). *The biomechanical basis of ergonomics: Anatomy applied to the design of work situations.* New York: John Wiley & Sons.

U.S. Department of Labor. (1972). *Handbook for analyzing jobs.* Menomonie, WI: University of Wisconsin–Stout, Stout Vocational Rehabilitation Institute, Materials Development Center.

U.S. Department of Labor. (1977). *Dictionary of occupational titles* (4th ed.). Washington, DC: U.S. Government Printing Office.

U.S. Department of Labor, Employment and Training Administration. (1982). *A guide to job analysis.* Washington, DC: U.S. Government Printing Office.

Vihma, T. (1982). Sewing machine operators' work and musculoskeletal complaints. *Ergonomics, 25,* 295–298.

Waris, P., Kuorinka, I., Kurppa, K., Luopajarvi, T., Virolainen, M., Pesonen, K., Nummi, J., & Kukkonen, R. (1979). Epidemiologic screening of occupational neck and upper limb disorders. *Scandinavian Journal of Work, Environment and Health, 5,* 25–38.

Wehrle, J. (1976). *Chronic wrist injuries associated with repetitive hand motions in industry* (Occupational Health and Safety Technical Report, Department of Industrial and Operations Engineering). Ann Arbor, MI: University of Michigan.

Wells, J., Zipp, J., Schuette, P., & McEleney, J. (1983). Musculoskeletal disorders among letter carriers. *Journal of Occupational Medicine, 25,* 814–820.

Wells, K., & Luttgens, K. (1976). *Kinesiology: Scientific basis of human motion.* Philadelphia: Saunders College Publishing.

Woodson, W. (1981). *Human factors design handbook: Information and guidelines for design of systems, facilities, equipment and products for human use.* New York: McGraw-Hill.

Related Reading

Atlas Copco. (1986). *Ergonomic tools in our time.* Stockholm, Sweden: Author.

Biomechanics Corporation of America (for the Occupational Safety and Health Administration). (1986). *Principles of ergonomics* (2 vols.). Roslyn, NY: Author.

Botterbusch, K. (1978). *A guide to job site evaluation.* Menomonie, WI: University of Wisconsin–Stout, Stout Vocational Rehabilitation Institute, Materials Development Center.

Grandjean, E. (1987). *Ergonomics in computerized offices.* Philadelphia: Taylor & Francis.

Skovron, M., Mulvihill, M., Sterling, R., Nordin, M., Tougas, G., Gallagher, M., & Speedling, E. (1987). Work organization and low back pain in nursing personnel. *Ergonomics, 30,* 359–366.

Snook, S., Campanelli, R., & Hart, J. (1978). A study of three preventative approaches to low back injury. *Journal of Occupational Medicine, 20,* 478–481.

Chapter 4, Appendix A
Resources: Tool Manufacturers

Bennett's Bend, Inc.
Design Center
600 South County Road 18
Minneapolis, MN 55426

Chicago Cutlery
600 South County Road 18
Minneapolis, MN 55426

Cooper Tools
The Cooper Group
P.O. Box 249
Apex, NC 27502

Diamond Hand Tools
The Triangle Tool Group
Cameron Road
Orangeburg, SC 29115

Klein Tools, Inc.
7200 McCormick Road
Chicago, IL 60645

Randall-Midwest, Inc.
9741 James Avenue South
Bloomington, MN 55431

S/V Tool Company, Inc.
1450 North Spencer
Newton, KS 67114

Scandex Inc.
517 Commonwealth Avenue
Newton, MA 02159

Sorbothane, Inc.
2144 State Road 59
Kent, OH 44240

Swanstrom Tools USA
3300 James Day Avenue
Superior, WI 54880

5

The Transition from School to Adult Life

Karen Spencer, MA, OTR

Public education in the broadest sense presents children and youth with an opportunity to develop the knowledge, the skills, and the experience necessary to maximize their potential and to assume productive adult roles in society. Extensive legislation at the federal level has been largely responsible for securing the educational rights of Americans with disabilities. As a result, children and youth with disabilities are establishing a positive presence in public school programs that subsequently extends to a positive presence as adults in the workplace and the community. Americans of all ages are therefore provided with an opportunity to learn from, interact with, and value people with disabilities.

Each year an estimated 250,000 to 300,000 students with disabilities leave the public education system to assume adult roles in American society (Will, 1983). Upon graduation or upon completion of their public school career, these students have typically received between 12 and 16 years of public instruction. They are the beneficiaries of a free and appropriate education made possible in 1975 with passage of Public Law 94-142, the Education for All Handicapped Children Act.

However, despite the guarantees of Public Law 94-142 and the extensive education and related services provided to children and youth, individuals with disabilities continue to experience excessively high rates of unemployment and dependency following completion of their public school careers. Between 50 and 75 percent of adults with disabilities are unemployed, with many living at or below the poverty level (Halpern, Close, & Nelson, 1986; Wehman, Kregel, & Barcus, 1985). It has become clear that the protections provided in federal law do not fully translate into self-sufficiency and productivity for individuals with disabilities.

The failure of public education and human service systems to facilitate the successful transition of youth with disabilities from school to productive adult roles carries both human and economic costs. The human cost associated with unemployment and dependency is high in a society that values productivity, individual choice, and opportunity. The current status of people with disabilities is typified by poverty and limited opportunity for participation in the full spectrum of community activity (Bellamy, 1985; Hasazi, Gordon, & Roe, 1985; Wehman, Kregel, & Barcus, 1985). Nevertheless people challenged by mild, moderate, and severe disabilities have demonstrated their ability to produce goods and services, earn wages, and make valuable contributions to their communities (Falvey, 1986; Wehman, 1981; Wehman, Kregel, & Barcus, 1985; Will, 1983). These individuals are able and willing to become taxpayers, given the opportunity and the availability of effective and efficient support services.

The economic costs associated with the unsuccessful transition of students with disabilities from school to productive adult life are staggering and parallel the human costs of lost opportunity and productivity. Extensive resources are invested annually at local, state, and federal levels to support the basic needs of people with disabilities. Support is provided in the form of health care, disability income, and rehabilitative services through a multitude of agencies. Services for youth and adults with disabilities have traditionally emphasized extended and often indefinite readiness training with little accountability for outcomes in the form of employment and increased self-sufficiency. Society can no longer afford to pay for programs that perpetuate dependence on public entitlements.

The opportunity now exists to maximize the return on the public investment by designing and implementing outcome-oriented transition programs that enable youth with disabilities to engage in paid employment, community living, and a full range of community-integrated activities. In American society a job and an earned income are central to achieving a desired quality of life. When employment opportunities are limited or nonexistent, the quality of life is compromised. A job influences to a large extent where people live, what activities they engage in, and what relationships they develop. Employment therefore becomes a critical focus of the transition process for youth with disabilities.

The Transition Initiative

The increasingly apparent need for youth with disabilities to make the transition from school to productive adult life has led to a multifaceted transition initiative at the federal level (Will, 1983, 1987a, 1987b). This initiative signals a major shift in the design and the delivery of services. Professionals in education, related services, and adult services are now increasingly accountable for positive outcomes for students, which include jobs, community integration, and participation. This is in sharp contrast to the historical emphasis by professionals and human service agencies on indefinite and often lifelong readiness training programs in segregated environments.

The U.S. Department of Education, Office of Special Education and Rehabilitative Services (OSERS), has assumed a major role in the transition initiative of the 1980s. OSERS has identified transition as a federal priority and has allocated extensive resources to research, demonstration projects, and personnel preparation (Will, 1983, 1987a, 1987b).

In the wake of federal initiatives, states have begun the process of developing and implementing comprehensive transition programs (Idaho State Department of Education, Special Education Section, 1976; San Diego County Supported Employment Task Force, 1987; Spencer, Bean, & Sample, 1988; Transition Ad Hoc Committee, 1986). Colorado and North Dakota serve as two fine examples of states that have provided leadership in addressing transition-related issues and facilitating positive action at state and local levels. A state-level committee of Colorado's human service agencies has defined transition from school to adult life as

> a carefully planned, outcome-oriented process, initiated at the local education agency or primary service provider that establishes and implements a multi-agency service plan for each youth with special transition needs. Transition planning focuses on a broad array of functional life skills (including but not limited to vocational, academic, social, and residential) that result in maximum independent functioning within the community. (Statewide Transition Policy Committee, 1987, p. 1)

North Dakota has adopted a similar definition of transition to guide planning and services in that state:

> The transition from school to adult life is an outcome-oriented process encompassing a broad array of services and experiences. Transition is a period that includes high school, the point of graduation, additional post-secondary education or adult services, and the initial years in employment. Transition is a bridge between the security of and structure of the school and the opportunities and risks of adult life. Any bridge requires both a solid span and a secure foundation at either end. The transition from school to work and adult life requires sound prepa-

ration in the secondary school, adequate support at the point of leaving school, and secure opportunities and services, if needed, in adult situations. (Transition Ad Hoc Committee, 1986, p. 7)

A growing body of knowledge and experience related to the abilities and the needs of citizens with disabilities has resulted in over 20 years of federal legislation and innovative programming, which in turn have led to the present emphasis on transition. The legislative effort at the federal level reflects the nation's growing awareness of the capabilities and the often untapped potential of individuals who are disabled. Federal, state, and local human service systems, with legislative support, are now challenged to design and implement effective outcome-oriented transition services that increase productivity, independence, and the quality of life for Americans with disabilities.

Transition: An Interdisciplinary and Interagency Process

The transition of students from school to a variety of productive adult roles requires the efforts and the contributions of the family, multiple professions, and a range of human service agencies. Transition planning and implementation, when done well, allows for continuity of services and support systems as the student exits public school and enters adult services. Comprehensive and effective transition planning and service therefore cannot be carried out by one individual or one agency. Teamwork, coordination, and cooperation across disciplines and agencies become essential in addressing the often complex and diverse needs of youth making the transition to adult roles and to the services of myriad adult support agencies.

The agencies that most frequently assume an active role in transition planning and services include, as appropriate, the local education agency, the state vocational rehabilitation office, the local and state departments of mental retardation, the local and state departments of mental health, various social services, and the Social Security Administration. Professionals who frequently participate along with the student and his or her family in transition planning and service implementation may include, but are not limited to, special educators, vocational educators, occupational therapists, speech pathologists, physical therapists, psychologists, social workers, vocational rehabilitation counselors, case managers, and residential counselors. The role assumed by each professional is determined by the needs of the student, the goals established by the team, and the knowledge and the expertise that reside within that individual team member.

Occupational Therapy and the Transition Process

Occupational therapists have a vital and emerging role in the transition process, particularly for students with severe disabilities. Occupational therapy's focus on each individual's ability and his or her need to meet environmental demands and role expectations greatly enhances team efforts. Occupational therapists share responsibility with other team members for student outcomes that include community living, employment, and recreation.

Assessment

As a transition team member, the occupational therapist is able to contribute vital information related to a student's performance abilities and needs in four major performance domains: home, work/school, recreation, and the community. It is recommended that occupational therapy assessments be organized and systematically carried out to address each domain. Effective transition-related assessment relies in large part on the use of nonstandardized, observational approaches in contrast to standardized and norm-referenced methods. The use of developmental scales to determine a student's transition-related needs has been shown to be largely ineffective (Falvey, 1986; Idaho State Department of Education, Special Education Section, 1976; San Diego County Supported Employment Task Force, 1987; Transition Ad Hoc Committee, 1986; Wehman, Moon, Everson, Wood, & Barcus, 1988).

The occupational therapist conducting transition-related assessments seeks to identify the student's current abilities and interests, any supports that are needed, and any barriers that may interfere with transition. Assessment activities may include the following:

1. Interviews with the student, his or her family, and other individuals who know the student well. The purpose of interviews is to determine the student's current abilities and interests related to home, work/school, recreation, and community environments. Interviews also allow for discussion of the family's long-term goals and expectations for the student.
2. Situational observations of student performance in home, work/school, recreation, and community environments. Situational observations allow the occupational therapist to observe student performance directly and to identify areas in which additional support, training, adaptation, or compensation are needed. Observations may

take place at the student's home, in a city park, at a local restaurant, on a city bus, at a work-study site, at the school, or at a grocery store. The possibilities for observation are endless; team involvement is required to determine the most critical environments for observation. At a minimum, observations are needed in each of the four performance domains.

3. Activity analyses and ecological inventories to identify systematically the demands of a given activity or environment. Discrepancies that exist between demands and a student's ability to meet them are then identifiable. When discrepancies exist, strategies are formulated to minimize the discrepancy either through direct training of the student or through adaptation of the activity or the environment.

An *activity analysis* is generally completed for a specific activity or task such as preparing baked chicken, folding towels at a work site, or identifying and boarding the correct bus. An *ecological inventory* provides more information than an activity analysis because it considers the total context within which activities and tasks occur. As an example, an ecological inventory at a job site may involve systematic observation and recording of the supervisor's communication approach, existing environmental cues (bells, lights, etc.) that signal the start of the work day, interaction patterns among co-workers, and interaction patterns among workers on break. The ecological inventory would also record in detail the steps involved in specific job tasks.

The use of interviews, situational observations, activity analyses, and ecological inventories provides the occupational therapist and therefore the team with vital information regarding a student's abilities, interests, current performance environments, learning and communication styles, and needs related to the transition from school to adult life. The information is then used by the team to conduct individualized program planning for each student.

Program Planning

The shift away from standardized and development-referenced assessment parallels a shift away from discipline-specific program planning and goal setting toward team planning and goal setting (Falvey, 1986; Rainforth & York, 1987). The ability of a multidisciplinary and multiagency team to meet the unique transition needs of students with disabilities depends on a thoughtful and strategic combination of resources and expertise to achieve common goals. Discipline-specific goals are replaced by team goals, and responsibility for achievement of goals rests with all team members. Teamwork, therefore, is the key to achieving desired transition outcomes for youth with disabilities.

Transition planning for students with disabilities must be done on a highly individualized basis. Transition from school to adult life realistically begins early in a student's educational career. The elementary years allow for the acquisition and the practice of essential skills that will be needed in later years. Young students gain a gradual awareness of adult roles and begin to establish individual interests and abilities that will carry into adult life. When students reach the secondary education level at the approximate age of 14, a formal transition plan becomes necessary to guide the design and the implementation of transition activities leading to postschool employment, community living, and community recreation. For students with severe disabilities, early and comprehensive transition planning is especially critical.

Transition planning at the secondary level is guided by a holistic and positive view of the student. It is essential that the student and the student's family participate in all aspects of planning and decision making. As transition becomes a major focus of a student's education program at the secondary level, a written Individualized Transition Plan (ITP) is needed to complement and expand the Individualized Education Program (IEP). ITP and IEP processes may be combined at the secondary level to maximize efficiency and to minimize the number of team meetings. Whether a school district integrates or separates them, critical transition issues must be addressed, outcome-oriented goals established, and responsibility for service provision assigned. A written transition plan is necessary and will increase professional and system accountability for transition outcomes.

Many transition-planning formats exist to facilitate and record planning activities. Whatever format is used, it must assist team members in establishing outcome-oriented goals in critical areas of adult functioning:

1. Employment
2. Housing and community living
3. Recreation and socialization
4. Health care
5. Disability benefits and/or income
6. Guardianship
7. Transportation and community access.

Sample transition-planning formats are included in Appendixes 5-A through 5-D.

When the transition from school to productive adult life becomes a major focus of educational programming for a given student, the team gathers assessment information, sets

Table 5-1
An Example of Objectives in the Home Domain

Team Goal 1.0 (Home Domain): Following completion of high school, the student will live in an apartment within one-fourth mile of shopping areas.

Objectives	Responsible Party(ies)
1.1 Student will independently drive electric wheelchair over uneven sidewalks and up and down curb cuts.	Occupational therapist and occupational therapy assistant
1.2 Student will independently open and heat store-bought microwave meals for lunch three days a week.	Teacher with occupational therapist consulting
1.3 Student will independently grocery-shop weekly, using a picture list and the assistance of the store's courtesy clerk.	Teacher with occupational therapist consulting
1.4 Student will search for, visit, and select an apartment that is barrier-free and within one-fourth mile of shopping areas.	Occupational therapist, occupational therapy assistant, and family

goals, and plans services around the same performance domains that have guided assessment: home, work/school, recreation, and the community. Examples of goals that may be set by the team include the following:

1. Home domain: Following completion of high school, the student will live in an apartment within one-fourth mile of shopping areas.
2. Work domain: The student will obtain a paid, community job that matches her abilities and interests and is accessible via public transportation.
3. Recreation domain: The student will independently use public transportation to travel on a regular basis to the community pool.
4. Community domain: The student will deposit or withdraw funds from her bank account weekly with the support of bank personnel.

All team members, including student and family, work to attain the transition goals. Individual team members, as appropriate, establish specific objectives and training methodologies that represent the many small steps needed to reach the larger goal. Table 5-1 illustrates specific objectives that an occupational therapist might address in cooperation with other team members to achieve a larger team goal.

The transition of youth with disabilities from school to adult life represents a complex process involving the family, professionals, and multiple service agencies. The outcome of individualized program planning is implementation within a variety of school and community environments.

Program Implementation

Comprehensive transition services address students' needs in four critical performance domains: home, work/school, recreation, and the community (Falvey, 1986; Wehman, Moon, Everson, Wood, & Barcus, 1988). As an outcome-oriented process, transition considers students' abilities, interests, and needs within the context of current and anticipated performance environments. The final measure of transition effectiveness is the degree to which students with disabilities are able to choose, gain access to, and participate in meaningful, community-integrated activities that are appropriate to their chronological age. This includes employment, postsecondary education programs, community living, use of community services, and recreation.

Occupational therapy services within a transition framework require a highly functional, outcome-oriented approach. No longer can the occupational therapist afford to focus primarily on remediating or mitigating deficit skills. The focus of intervention therefore becomes one of identifying (through ecological inventories and activity analyses) critical activities that the individual needs to perform in a range of natural environments including, for example, the home, the school bus, the classroom, local restaurants, and the workplace. Intervention is guided by the individual student's goals and objectives and often occurs within real-life settings in collaboration with teachers, parents, employers, community members, and others. Through a variety of intervention approaches (direct service, consultation, etc.), the occupational therapist seeks to minimize discrepancies between students' abilities and environmental demands. Outcome measures used to evaluate the effectiveness of occupational therapy services may include evaluation of the extent to which the student is able to gain access to a variety of community environments and engage in paid employment, community living, and integrated recreation and leisure activities.

Summary

Public services for youth and adults with disabilities have traditionally emphasized extended and often indefinite readiness training. There has been little accountability for outcomes in the form of employment and increased self-sufficiency. A multifaceted program initiated by the federal government enables service providers to maximize the return on the public investment by designing and implementing outcome-oriented transition programs that make it possible for youth with disabilities to engage in paid employment, community living, and a full range of community-integrated activities. States too have begun developing and implementing comprehensive transition programs. Transition planning and implementation, when done well, allows for continuity of services and support systems as the student exits public school and enters adult services.

Occupational therapists have a vital and emerging role to play in the transition process, particularly for students with severe disabilities. The profession's focus on individuals' ability and need to meet environmental demands and role expectations greatly enhances team efforts.

Glossary

Activity analysis—a detailed analysis of the specific steps and actions involved in completing an activity, such as preparing baked chicken, folding towels at a work site, or identifying and boarding the correct bus. The activity analysis provides a guide for training and intervention. Compare **Ecological inventory.**

Ecological inventory—an analysis considering the total context within which activities and tasks occur. It provides more information than an activity analysis because it takes the setting of activities and tasks into account. Compare **Activity analysis.**

Individualized Education Program (IEP)—the written result of an interdisciplinary planning process mandated by the Education for All Handicapped Children Act of 1975, Public Law 94-142.

Individualized Education Program/Individualized Transition Plan (IEP/ITP)—a written plan that integrates the Individualized Education Program (IEP) and the Individualized Transition Plan (ITP) to maximize efficiency and to minimize the number of team meetings.

Individualized Transition Plan (ITP)—a written plan to complement and expand the Individualized Education Program (IEP). Critical transition issues must be addressed, outcome-oriented goals established, and responsibility for service provision assigned.

Transition (from school to adult life)—"a carefully planned, outcome-oriented process, initiated at the local education agency or primary service provider that establishes and implements a multiagency service plan for each youth with special transition needs.

Transition planning focuses on a broad array of functional life skills (including but not limited to vocational, academic, social, and residential) that result in maximum independent functioning within the community" (Statewide Transition Policy Committee, 1987, p. 1).

References

Bellamy, G. T. (1985). Transition progress: Comments on Hasazi, Gordon and Roe. *Exceptional Children, 51,* 474–477.

Education for All Handicapped Children Act of 1975, Pub. L. 94-142, 89 Stat. 773 (1975).

Falvey, M. (1986). *Community-based curriculum: Instructional strategies for students with severe handicaps.* Baltimore: Paul Brookes.

Halpern, A. S., Close, D. W., & Nelson, D. J. (1986). *On my own: The impact of semi-independent living programs for adults with mental retardation.* Baltimore: Paul Brookes.

Hasazi, S. B., Gordon, L. R., & Roe, C. A. (1985). Factors associated with the employment status of handicapped youth exiting high school from 1979 to 1983. *Exceptional Children, 51,* 455–469.

Idaho State Department of Education, Special Education Section (1976). *School to community transition: A guide for transition planning.* Boise, ID: Author.

Rainforth, B., & York, J. (1987). Integrating related services in community instruction. *Journal of the Association for Persons with Severe Handicaps, 12,* 190–198.

San Diego County Supported Employment Task Force. (1987). *Transition of individuals with developmental disabilities from school to adult services: A procedural handbook for parents and teachers* (Draft). San Diego, CA: Author.

Spencer, K., Bean, G., & Sample, P. (1988). *Transition from school to adult life: A process and procedural handbook* (Draft). Fort Collins, CO: Colorado State University, Department of Occupational Therapy.

Statewide Transition Policy Committee. (1987). *Transition: Policy statement.* Denver: Colorado Department of Education, State Board for Community Colleges and Occupational Education, Division for Developmental Disabilities, Division for Mental Health, Division for Youth Services, Department of Labor and Employment, Colorado Developmental Disabilities Planning Council, Division of Rehabilitation, and Rocky Mountain Resource and Training Institute.

Transition Ad Hoc Committee (1986). *Transition: A team approach. A process handbook.* Bismarck, ND: Department of Public Instruction, Department of Human Services, and State Board for Vocational Education.

Wehman, P. (1981). *Competitive employment: New horizons for severely disabled individuals.* Baltimore: Paul Brookes.

Wehman, P., Kregel, J., & Barcus, M. (1985). From school to work: A vocational transition model for handicapped students. *Exceptional Children, 52,* 25–37.

Wehman, P., Moon, M. S., Everson, J. M., Wood, W., & Barcus, M. (1988). *Transition from school to work: New challenges for youth with severe disabilities.* Baltimore: Paul Brookes.

Will, M. (1983). *Bridges from school to working life.* Washington, DC: Office of Special Education and Rehabilitative Services.

Will, M. (1987a). Supported employment: The Federal perspective. *American Rehabilitation, 13*(4), 2–3.

Will, M. (1987b). Turning possibilities into realities. *Exceptional Parent, 17*(1), 62–63.

Related Reading

Everson, J., Barcus, M., Moon, M. S., & Morton, M. V. (Eds.). (1987). *Achieving outcomes: A guide to interagency training in transition and supported employment.* Richmond, VA: Virginia Commonwealth University, School of Education, Rehabilitation Research and Training Center, Project Transition into Employment.

Chapter 5, Appendix A

Transition Services
Department of Occupational Therapy
Colorado State University
Fort Collins, Colorado 80523

Transition-Planning Time Line

Student Age	Action	Person Responsible	Completion Date
14	Assign transition co-coordinators (parent plus school staff member).		
14	Give transition information to student and parent(s)/guardian.		
14	Review student's cumulative file and assemble IEP/ITP team.		
14	Obtain or verify Social Security Number.		
14	Hold initial meeting to develop IEP/ITP, to be reviewed and updated annually.		
14	Arrange access to public transportation.		
14	Commence transition-related assessment processes: • Identify vocational interests/abilities. • Identify residential needs, interests, and abilities. • Identify recreational interests and abilities. • Identify types of support and training needed.		
14	Provide training in variety of school sites (e.g., grounds, cafeteria, and office).		
14	Provide training in communication, self-care, mobility, independent living, and recreation within natural environments whenever possible.		
16–18	Establish linkages to postsecondary service options: • Education and training • Social Security disability programs (including Medicare and Medicaid) • Residential services • Vocational services • Recreational services.		
16	Evaluate transition-related assessments: Are they up-to-date?		
16+	Investigate need for driver's license.		
16–17	Establish graduation date.		

Developed by the Office of Transition Services, Department of Occupational Therapy, Colorado State University, with support from Office of Special Education and Rehabilitative Services grant number G00873015088.

Student Age	Transition-Planning Time Line (cont.) Action	Person Responsible	Completion Date
16–18	Provide training in community job sites and in several job types that are realistic, permanent job possibilities.		
16	Prepare job-placement file with references, descriptions of acquired skills, work history, and community-assessment information.		
17	Consider guardianship if appropriate.		
16–18	Complete eligibility/application process for needed adult services.		
18	Evaluate transition-related assessments: Are they up-to-date?		
18	Establish needed health benefits.		
18	Develop long-term financial support plan.		
18–21	Establish part-time community employment while student is still in school.		
18	Develop postsecondary plan in cooperation with adult service agencies.		

Chapter 5, Appendix B

**Transition Services
Department of Occupational Therapy
Colorado State University
Fort Collins, Colorado 80523**

Current Levels of Functioning/Needs

Strengths/Interests	Supports Needed/Barriers	Needs
Home Domain		
Work/School Domain		
Recreation/Leisure Domain		
Community Domain		

Developed by the Office of Transition Services, Department of Occupational Therapy, Colorado State University, with support from Office of Special Education and Rehabilitative Services grant number G00873015088.

Chapter 5, Appendix C

Transition Services
Department of Occupational Therapy
Colorado State University
Fort Collins, Colorado 80523

**A Guide for Transition Planning:
Topics for Discussion**

Home Domain
1. Living Arrangement
   - ____ With family
   - ____ Foster care (child/adult)
   - ____ Supervised group living
   - ____ Semi-independent (supported) living
   - ____ Share living (roommate)
   - ____ Independent living (own house/apartment)
   - ____ Host home
   - ____ Out-of-community residential placement
   - ____ Other

2. Personal/Family Relationships
   - ____ Counseling
     - ____ Genetic
     - ____ Family
     - ____ Individual
     - ____ Marriage
     - ____ Crisis
   - ____ Support group
   - ____ Respite care
   - ____ Visiting arrangements with family
   - ____ Churches
   - ____ Sexuality
   - ____ Caring for others (e.g., children, pets, spouse, and siblings)
   - ____ Guardianship/conservatorship
   - ____ Wills/trusts
   - ____ Other

3. Self-Care
   - ____ Household management/maintenance
   - ____ Money management
   - ____ Social skills
   - ____ Drugs and alcohol counseling
   - ____ Family planning and sex education
   - ____ Personal care (attendant) services
   - ____ Fitness
   - ____ Time management
   - ____ Eating

Developed by the Office of Transition Services, Department of Occupational Therapy, Colorado State University, with support from Office of Special Education and Rehabilitative Services grant number G00873015088.

Self-Care (cont.)
- ____ Meal planning and food preparation
- ____ Clothing care and selection
- ____ Dressing and grooming
- ____ Personal hygiene and toileting
- ____ Safety and health
- ____ Medication use
- ____ Other

Work/School Domain

1. Vocational Training/Postsecondary Education
   - ____ Career awareness
   - ____ Career exploration (shadowing, work-study, volunteering, etc.)
   - ____ Work experience
   - ____ On-the-job training (OJT)
   - ____ Community colleges/universities
   - ____ Postsecondary vocational/technical training
   - ____ Vocational rehabilitation
   - ____ Other

2. Placement/Employment
   - ____ Competitive employment
   - ____ Supported employment
   - ____ Volunteer work
   - ____ Sheltered employment
   - ____ Other

3. Income and Financial Support
   - ____ Earned income
   - ____ Unearned income (gifts, dividends, etc.)
   - ____ Insurance (life insurance, annuities, etc.)
   - ____ General public assistance
   - ____ Food stamps
   - ____ Social Security benefits
   - ____ Trust/will or similar income
   - ____ Tax deductions for developmentally disabled people who reside at home
   - ____ Other

4. Communication
   - ____ Expression of needs, wants, and desires
   - ____ Understanding of directions and feedback
   - ____ Assertiveness
   - ____ Use of communication devices: telephone, computer, etc.
   - ____ Interactions with co-workers and supervisor
   - ____ Other

Recreation/Leisure Domain

1. Socialization/Friendship
   - ____ Friendships with peers
   - ____ Reciprocal relationships

Socialization/Friendship (cont.)
____ Different levels of friendships
    ____ Acquaintances
    ____ Close friends
    ____ Intimate friends
____ Friendships that carry outside the school
____ Other

2. Leisure
   ____ Continuing or noncredit education (craft classes, art, music, etc.)
   ____ Hobbies
   ____ Church groups
   ____ Social clubs
   ____ Community parks and recreation programs
   ____ Self-initiated recreation
       ____ Individual hobbies and activities
       ____ With others
   ____ School clubs and activities
   ____ Scouting
   ____ Other

3. Fitness
   ____ Sporting clubs
   ____ Team sports
   ____ Individual sports (walking, swimming, bicycling, etc.)
   ____ Health clubs or YMCA/YWCA
   ____ Other

Community Domain
1. Community Mobility/Accessibility/Transportation
   ____ Independence (own car, bicycle, walking, skateboard, or wheelchair)
   ____ Public transportation (bus, taxi, or trolley)
   ____ Transportation service for handicapped
   ____ Specialized equipment (vehicle modifications, adaptive equipment, etc.)
   ____ Mobility with service dog
   ____ Efficient planning of transportation needs and services
   ____ Family car and driver
   ____ Carpooling
   ____ Reimbursement to others for travel costs
   ____ Other

2. Consumerism
   ____ Health and beauty services
   ____ Grocery store
   ____ Retail stores
   ____ Restaurants
   ____ Bank
   ____ Post office
   ____ Other

3. Citizenship
   ____ Service organizations/volunteerism
   ____ Voting
   ____ Homeowners/neighborhood associations
   ____ Selective Service
   ____ Identification card
   ____ Courtesy toward others
   ____ Reciprocal relationships (give-and-take)
   ____ Interaction appropriate to chronological age
   ____ Interactive communication
   ____ Other

4. Advocacy/Legal Services
   ____ Ability to advocate for self
   ____ Ability to gain access to community resources
   ____ Other

5. Medical Services
   ____ Access to general medical offices and services
   ____ Financial resources for medical services: group or individual insurance policy, Medicaid, other
   ____ Use of specialized medical care (for eye, ear, or throat conditions, seizures, etc.)
   ____ Dentist
   ____ Equipment purchase and maintenance (wheelchair, lift, etc.)
   ____ Other

Chapter 5, Appendix D

Transition Services, Department of Occupational Therapy
Colorado State University
Fort Collins, Colorado 80523

Transition Plan
Home Domain

Student's Name _____ Date _____ Age _____ Grade _____

	Service Providers	Time Line (Dates) Initiated	Time Line (Dates) Completed	Time Involved	Criteria for Evaluation
Life Goals					
Annual Goals Living arrangements					
Personal/family relationships					
Self-care					

Developed by the Office of Transition Services, Department of Occupational Therapy, Colorado State University, with support from Office of Special Education and Rehabilitative Services grant number G0087301508B.

Community Domain

Student's Name _____ Date _____ Age _____ Grade _____

	Service Providers	Time Line (Dates) Initiated	Time Line (Dates) Completed	Time Involved	Criteria for Evaluation
Life Goals					
Annual Goals Community mobility/accessibility/ transportation					
Consumerism					
Citizenship					
Advocacy/legal services					
Medical services					

Recreation/Leisure Domain

Student's Name _____ Date _____ Age _____ Grade _____

	Service Providers	Time Line (Dates) Initiated	Time Line (Dates) Completed	Time Involved	Criteria for Evaluation
Life Goals					
Annual Goals Socialization/friendship					
Leisure					
Fitness					

Work/School Domain

Student's Name _____ Date _____ Age _____ Grade _____

	Service Providers	Time Line (Dates) Initiated	Time Line (Dates) Completed	Time Involved	Criteria for Evaluation
Life Goals					
Annual Goals Vocational training/postsecondary education					
Placement/employment					
Income and financial support					
Communication					

6
Overview of Supported Employment

Karen Spencer, MA, OTR

Supported employment is a strategy for securing and maintaining community employment for individuals with severe disabilities. These individuals have historically experienced extremely limited employment opportunities resulting in insufficient income, dependence on public entitlement programs, and limited options for participation in the full array of community life.

People who are likely to benefit from supported employment include those whose disabilities pose a significant barrier to securing and maintaining paid community employment. Severe disabilities may include one or more of the following: physical or neurological dysfunction, mental retardation, cerebral palsy, epilepsy, mental illness, or other conditions that impair a person's ability to obtain or maintain employment.

Supported employment provides highly individualized training and support at community-integrated job sites for people previously deemed too disabled to work. It is emerging as an effective alternative to segregated or restrictive vocational training or day activity programs that do not consistently lead to individual placement in community jobs. Supported employment can be described as a "place, then train" approach, in contrast to more traditional readiness approaches ("train, then place").

Supported Employment: A National Priority

The U.S. Department of Education, Office of Special Education and Rehabilitative Services (OSERS), has provided leadership in conceptualizing and promoting supported employment as a national priority (Will, 1983, 1987a, 1987b). Extensive resources have been allocated to supported employment research, demonstration projects, and personnel training. Former Assistant Secretary for Special Education and Rehabilitative Services Madeleine Will worked to turn a vision of employment for all individuals challenged by disabilities into reality:

> The cornerstone of many activities currently underway in the Office of Special Education and Rehabilitative Services (OSERS) to improve the quality of life for individuals with severe physical and mental disabilities is the Supported Employment initiative.
>
> OSERS is committed to the development and expansion of supported employment programming at the State and local levels, for it offers a cost-effective and viable means for enabling individuals with severe physical and mental disabilities to assume their rightful place as productive, contributing members of communities in which they live. (as quoted in OSERS, 1987, p. 1)

Supported employment is emerging as the method of choice in meeting the employment needs of individuals with severe disabilities. It presents an effective alternative to services that have historically focused on readiness training within segregated or sheltered environments. Federal supported employment initiatives have prompted state and local human service agencies to reevaluate the effectiveness of extended skill building and vocational readiness training. A 50 to 75 percent unemployment rate for individuals with disabilities reflects the ineffectiveness of past and existing vocational service options (U.S. Commission on Civil Rights, 1983). Accountability for paid employment outcomes and increased self-sufficiency has not been required of service providers until very recently. The need for a major reevaluation and redesign of vocational services is therefore apparent.

Supported employment was first given the authority of law by the Developmental Disabilities Act of 1984, Public Law 98-527 (an amendment to the Developmental Disabilities Assistance and Bill of Rights Act of 1975, Public Law 94-103). In 1986 supported employment became included as a habilitation service under Medicaid because it was perceived to reduce the risk of institutionalization for people with severe disabilities (Omnibus Budget Reconciliation Act of 1986, Public Law 99-509).

Supported employment gained additional support through the 1986 Amendments to the Rehabilitation Act (Public Law 99-506). New language authorized funds to assist states in establishing supported employment as an alternative to more traditional training and time-limited services. The amendments strongly promoted collaboration and resource sharing among agencies to meet the complex supported employment needs of people with severe handicaps.

The 1986 amendments define supported employment as competitive work in an integrated work setting for individuals who, because of their disability, need continuing support services to perform that work. Supported employment is targeted at people with severe disabilities for whom competitive employment has not traditionally occurred or for whom competitive employment has been interrupted or intermittent as the result of their disability. In addition, supported employment may include transitional job placement for individuals with chronic mental illness.

Characteristics of Supported Employment Service

Supported employment, as defined by OSERS and by statute, has three essential characteristics:
1. Paid work that is performed on a full-time or part-time basis, for which the individual is compensated in accordance with the Fair Labor Standards Act.
2. Employment in an integrated work setting where most co-workers are not disabled and regular opportunities exist for interaction and contact with them. Contact solely with personnel providing training or support does not constitute integration.
3. Ongoing support services available to meet continuous or periodic training needs of the individual at the work site or away from the work site, to maximize work performance. Ongoing support services, by definition, are not time limited, the assumption being that many people with severe disabilities may always require some type of support to function within community environments.

Supported employment may take many forms as long as the conditions for paid work, integration, and continuing support are met. Within these parameters human service agencies may be creative in designing, individualizing, and implementing supported employment services. It has been clearly demonstrated that supported employment allows adults with severe and profound disabilities successfully to obtain and maintain paid community employment (Falvey, 1986; Wehman, 1981; Will, 1983, 1987b). An individual's inability to make a clear job choice or to demonstrate specific job skills does not prevent a supported job placement, but requires the supported employment team to identify and present job opportunities that reflect, to the best of its ability, the observed interests and abilities of the individual.

When supported employment is identified as the approach needed to meet the needs of an individual, a supported employment service team is assembled. The team may have representation from multiple agencies and include an interdisciplinary group of professionals. Occupational therapists or occupational therapy assistants may assume important roles on the team in the areas of assessment, program planning, and service implementation.

A lead agency is generally needed to oversee and direct supported employment services for a given individual. The lead agency may differ depending on the needs or the characteristics of the referred person and the capabilities of the agency. For instance, when the person has disabilities that include mental retardation, the local or state developmental disability provider may assume a lead role. For the individual with traumatic brain injuries, the state vocational rehabilitation agency may serve as the coordinator. When the person targeted for services is of school age, the public school district may assume the lead role.

Occupational Therapy and Supported Employment

Occupational therapists and occupational therapy assistants working in agencies that provide supported employment services are valuable members of the team. Occupational therapy's focus on a person's functioning within the context of everyday environments, including the home, the community, and the job site, enhances the team's ability to plan and implement effective services.

Assessment

Within a supported employment framework, the focus of assessment is on the individual's ability to function both in the community (e.g., mobility and use of transportation) and in the context of a prospective or an existing job. During assessment, occupational therapists identify the requirements of prospective jobs through the use of environmental and activity analyses. Sample formats appear in Appendix 6-A. Job demands are then related to individual workers' abilities, interests, and needs. When assessment reveals a discrepancy between a job's demands and a worker's abilities, the occupational therapist may recommend individualized training strategies or job adaptations/accommodations that will facilitate successful job performance.

Singular assessment of job-specific abilities, however, does not constitute a comprehensive supported employment assessment. The occupational therapist, in cooperation with other team members, must also assess the individual's home situation to identify abilities and needed supports that will contribute to eventual job success. Direct assessment of the individual's ability to gain access to and use available transportation is critical in determining if the person will be able to travel to and from the job in a timely fashion. Occupational therapy's involvement in these functional assessment processes greatly enhances team planning and provides guidance for needed adaptations or accommodations related to a job.

The use of prevocational development-referenced checklists and standardized assessments has been found to be largely ineffective in predicting supported employment needs and subsequent job success for individuals with severe disabilities (Albright & Cobb, 1987; Wehman, 1981; Wilcox & Bellamy, 1982). Reliance on these approaches in a supported employment context is not recommended. Situational observation of individual performance in a variety of community and work environments, and activity and environmental analysis, are the assessment methods of choice.

Individualized Program Planning

Assessment information gathered by the occupational therapist and other team members is shared and discussed with the entire supported employment team during program planning. The outcome of program planning is an action plan that specifies the following:

1. Critical job conditions to match the assessed abilities and interests of the individual. For example:
   a. The job must be located on a public bus route.
   b. The job must be part-time, preferably mornings.
   c. The job must have direct and frequent supervision available from co-workers or supervisors.
   d. The job site must be on one level and accessible by wheelchair.
   e. The job must have minimum speed requirements.
   f. The job will ideally require a uniform.
   g. The job will ideally relate to the individual's interest in animals.
2. A job development approach, with assignment of appropriate responsibilities to various team members. The occupational therapist or some other team members will be made responsible for seeking job opportunities that match the individual's abilities, interests, and "critical conditions." This requires skill in direct marketing and negotiation with prospective employers. Before a job placement is finalized, the occupational therapist or the occupational therapy assistant may be invaluable in completing a job analysis to determine if a good match exists between the individual and the targeted job.
3. Training objectives for the individual. These are developed by the team and specifically address the behaviors

and the skills that are needed by the individual in relation to the targeted job. Examples include the following:
  a. The individual will independently travel to and from the job site by taxi on a daily basis.
  b. The individual will accurately package surgical trays with only gestural prompts from a job coach at a rate of 20 trays per hour.
  c. The individual will independently select and don a clean uniform each work day.
  d. The individual will independently greet co-workers by name each morning at the job site.
4. Training methodologies to be used by team members to teach the desired skills and behaviors specified in the objectives. Training methodologies will typically specify teaching and cuing strategies, job adaptations or accommodations, and consequences for correct and incorrect performance. Nonintrusive and discreet training methodologies are essential at a community job site and must be used by all team members to prevent negative stigmatization of the individual.

Program Implementation

When the job placement is made, the occupational therapist, the occupational therapy assistant, and others may provide services both on and off the job site in accordance with the objectives established by the team. For example, occupational therapy personnel may be involved in helping the individual manage personal care at home as it relates to the job. At the job site the occupational therapist may work in a consultative role with direct-training staff or job coaches to identify additional supports that are needed and to address problems that may arise. Occupational therapy assistants are well qualified to provide direct, on-the-job, or community-based (e.g., bus travel) training to enhance an individual worker's job performance and satisfaction. Maximum consideration at this stage must be given to the culture of the workplace and the ability and the willingness of the workplace to accept the presence and the intervention of supported employment team members. Great care is needed to minimize adaptations and changes in work routines in the disabled worker's behalf. Inadvertent and negative stigmatization of the worker may result when significant disruptions in the day-to-day operation of a community business occur.

Supported Employment Approaches in Common Use

Three supported employment approaches that are in common use are described here to illustrate the variability of service options that have been designed to meet the unique employment, training, and supervision needs of workers with severe disabilities. Occupational therapists and occupational therapy assistants have a role regardless of the approach being used. The role will vary, however, depending on the individuals being served and the environment within which the service is provided.

Individual Job Placement

The individual job placement approach directly matches the individual who has a disability with a community job opportunity. Before placement a team effort is used to identify and evaluate job opportunities in light of individual interests and abilities. Wages are paid to the worker by the employer. In the event that a worker is unable to maintain the necessary productivity levels, a minimum-wage waiver can be negotiated in accordance with the Fair Labor Standards Act.

Job placement is followed by direct, on-the-job, one-to-one training at the job site by a *job coach*. The job coach systematically teaches the individual how to perform specific job tasks (e.g., clocking in, setting up his or her work area, and completing job activities) and job-related activities (e.g., socialization during breaks and transportation to and from the job site). The job coach may at times actually perform job tasks in conjunction with the individual, especially during initial training phases. This assures the employer that the job will be done because the job coach completes or monitors tasks that the worker has not yet mastered.

Direct on-the-job training by a job coach is gradually decreased as the individual assumes greater responsibility for job performance and demonstrates competence and confidence as a worker. Support continues on an intermittent, as-needed basis. It can be varied in amount and intensity depending upon the needs of the individual, the employer, or co-workers. The individual job placement approach allows for a high degree of integration within the job setting because opportunities to meet and interact with co-workers are generally present throughout the day.

Enclave

An enclave is a small group of individuals (typically eight or fewer) who are trained and supervised together at a community work site. An enclave generally exists within a larger "host" environment (e.g., a manufacturing company). A trainer who is not an employee of the host company is typically provided and funded by a nonprofit supported employment agency. The direct training and the monitoring of enclave workers constitute the trainer's responsibilities. The host company receives a guarantee from the supported employment agency that a certain level of productivity and quality will be maintained by the enclave. Workers are typically evaluated and compensated by the host company on a piecework basis. Minimum-wage waivers are often involved. These allow the employer to pay less than minimum wage, thereby accommodating individual discrepancies in productivity.

Opportunities to be integrated with nondisabled co-workers are somewhat fewer than in the individual job placement approach. They may exist during the work shift, before and after work, and during breaks and lunch periods.

Mobile Work Crew

A mobile work crew may be established by a supported employment agency to meet the employment needs of individuals with disabilities. A mobile work crew operates as a business, soliciting and bidding on work contracts and then carrying out the work in a variety of community environments. Work contracts are often secured in janitorial, maintenance, or landscaping areas. When a contract is obtained, it generally covers wages for the trainer and the workers with disabilities and some overhead expenses (equipment purchase and maintenance, mileage, etc.). Crew workers who have disabilities are often paid less than minimum wage in accordance with the Fair Labor Standards Act.

A mobile work crew may comprise at least one supported employment trainer and between two and five workers who have disabilities. Supervision and training is available on a continuous basis because the trainer transports the workers and works alongside them. Fading of support is more difficult in this approach because the crew depends on the trainer to obtain contracts and manage transportation.

A crew frequently operates from a van and often has its own equipment. As a consequence, workers have infrequent opportunities for integration except during lunch breaks, or before and after work. This approach has particular benefits when consistency in worker attendance is a problem. If a critical mass of workers is always available, absences do not adversely affect the crew's ability to complete a job. Frequent substitution of workers to fulfill contracts may, however, compromise the concept of individualized job matching, placements being made on the basis of job availability rather than individual workers' needs or desires.

Summary

Human service personnel are rapidly gaining the knowledge, the skills, and the experience to effectively support and train people with severe disabilities in community jobs. Supported employment represents one strategy that has been demonstrated to be effective for people previously deemed not ready or too disabled to work.

Supported employment requires a significant, up-front investment of staff time and resources. The initial investment is necessary to complete functional assessments, identify appropriate job opportunities, and provide highly individualized training at community job sites. In spite of the initial up-front investment, an increasing body of research is revealing that supported employment brings significant savings over time as the worker gradually requires less support, earns wages, and becomes a taxpayer (Hill, Wehman, Kregel, Banks, & Metzler, 1987; Noble & Conley, 1987; Rhodes, Ramsing, & Hill, 1987).

The personnel needed to implement supported employment services vary in their training and experience. Supported employment teams are ideally configured based on the needs of the targeted individual and the expertise that resides within each team member. A supported employment team may consist of representatives from several disciplines and multiple human service agencies. The agencies most frequently involved in the delivery of supported employment services are public schools, state vocational rehabilitation agencies, developmental disability providers, mental health agencies, independent living centers, and private, not-for-profit supported employment agencies. The delivery of supported employment services is ideally overseen by an interdisciplinary, interagency team. The team includes the individual with a disability along with vocational rehabilitation counselors; developmental disability providers; mental health providers; special educators; parents (when appropriate); case managers; occupational, physical, and speech-language therapists; employers; psychologists; and others as needed. Responsibility for assessment, job development, placement, on-the-job training, and continuing support rests with the supported employment team. The team is accountable for positive employment outcomes, including increased self-sufficiency and quality of life for the individuals served.

Glossary

Enclave approach—an approach to supported employment in which an enclave, or a small group, of individuals (typically eight or fewer) is trained and supervised as a group at a community work site.

Individual job placement approach—an approach to supported employment in which an individual with disabilities is directly matched with a community job opportunity and provided with support on a one-to-one basis at the job site.

Job coach—a person who systematically teaches a worker with disabilities how to perform specific job tasks (e.g., clocking in, setting up his or her work area, and completing job activities) and job-related activities (e.g., socialization during breaks and transportation to and from the job site).

Lead agency—the agency designated to oversee and direct supported employment services for a given individual.

Mobile work crew—an approach to supported employment in which a group of people with disabilities, under the supervision of a trainer, operates as a business, soliciting and bidding on work contracts and then carrying out the work in a variety of community environments.

Supported employment—paid work in an integrated work setting for individuals who, because of their disability, need continuing support services to perform that work.

References

Albright, L., & Cobb, B. (1987). A model to prepare vocational educators and support services personnel in curriculum-based assessment. *Interchange* (newsletter of the University of Illinois at Urbana, College of Education, Secondary Transition Intervention Effectiveness Institute), 7(4), 2-6.

Amendments to the Rehabilitation Act of 1986, Pub. L. 99-506, 100 Stat. 1807 (1986).

Developmental Disabilities Act of 1984, Pub. L. 98-527, 98 Stat. 2662 (1984).

Developmental Disabilities Assistance and Bill of Rights Act of 1975, Pub. L. 94-103, 89 Stat. 486 (1975).

Falvey, M. (1986). *Community-based curriculum: Instructional strategies for students with severe handicaps.* Baltimore: Paul Brookes.

Hill, M. L., Wehman, P. H., Kregel, J., Banks, P. D., & Metzler, H. M. D. (1987). Employment outcomes for people with moderate and severe disabilities: An eight-year longitudinal analysis of supported competitive employment. *Journal of the Association for Persons with Severe Handicaps, 12,* 182–189.

Noble, J. H., & Conley, R. W. (1987). Accumulating evidence on the benefits and costs of supported and transitional employment for persons with severe disabilities. *Journal of the Association for Persons with Severe Handicaps, 12,* 163–174.

Office of Special Education and Rehabilitative Services, National Institute on Disability and Rehabilitation Research. (1987). Supported employment. *Rehab Brief: Bringing Research into Effective Focus, 10*(1), 1–4.

Omnibus Budget Reconciliation Act of 1986, Pub. L. 99-509, 100 Stat. 1874 (1986).

Rhodes, L., Ramsing, K., & Hill, M. (1987). Economic evaluation of employment services: A review of applications. *Journal of the Association for Persons with Severe Handicaps, 12,* 175–181.

U.S. Commission on Civil Rights. (1983). *Accommodating the spectrum of human difference.* Washington, DC: Author.

Wehman, P. (1981). *Competitive employment: New horizons for severely disabled individuals.* Baltimore: Paul Brookes.

Wilcox, B., & Bellamy, G. T. (1982). *Design of high school programs for severely handicapped students.* Baltimore: Paul Brookes.

Will, M. (1983). *Bridges from school to working life.* Washington, DC: Office of Special Education and Rehabilitative Services.

Will, M. (1987a). Supported employment: The Federal perspective. *American Rehabilitation, 13*(4), 2-3.

Will, M. (1987b). Turning possibilities into realities. *Exceptional Parent, 17*(1), 62-63.

Related Reading

Braddock, D. (1987). *Federal policies toward mental retardation and developmental disabilities.* Baltimore: Paul Brookes.

Heal, L., Haney, J., & Novak-Amado, R. (1988). *Integration of developmentally disabled individuals into the community* (2nd ed.). Baltimore: Paul Brookes.

Wehman, P., Kregel, J., & Barcus, M. (1985). From school to work: A vocational transition model for handicapped students. *Exceptional Children, 52,* 25-37.

Chapter 6, Appendix A

**Transition Services
Department of Occupational Therapy
Colorado State University
Fort Collins, Colorado 80523**

Job Analysis Terminology and Forms

A thorough job analysis must be conducted by a member of the supported employment service team before a person with a disability can be placed in a job. A full job analysis includes the careful completion of a job analysis cover sheet and more detailed job routine analysis work sheets. Attached are examples of such forms. Following are explanations of the terminology of job analysis:

Routine: an activity that is performed by the worker. Multiple skills and tasks are grouped into a single routine. Three types of routines are core, episodic, and job related.

    Examples of routines: Restock salad bar.
             Clean animal cages.
             Mop floor.

Core work routines: job routines that occur on a repeating and regular basis. These are the routines performed most frequently by the worker.

The employer identifies the core work routines. The job developer and/or the job trainer (the job coach) may negotiate modifications or adaptations of core work routines when it appears necessary.

    Examples of core work routines: Bus tables.
                 Set tables.
                 Phone customers.

Episodic work routines: job routines that occur infrequently—once or twice a shift, once a week, etc.

The employer identifies episodic work routines. The job developer and/or the job trainer may negotiate modifications or adaptations of episodic work routines when it appears necessary.

    Examples of episodic work routines: Punch time clock.
                   Restock supplies.
                   Change mop water.

Job-related routines: routines that are not the direct responsibility of the employer. They include transportation to and from work, dress and personal appearance on the job, taking of lunch or midday breaks, etc.

The job trainer is responsible for identifying job-related routines and providing necessary supports or training. The job trainer may identify "natural" supports, that is, co-workers who can assist with transportation, family that can assist with laundering of uniforms, etc.

Adapted from material developed by Marc Gold & Associates, Inc., Syracuse, NY.

Transition Services
Department of Occupational Therapy
Colorado State University
Fort Collins, Colorado 80523

Job Analysis Cover Sheet

Worker _____

Employer _____

    Address _____

    Phone _____ Contact person _____

    Job title _____

Schedule _____ Wages _____

Job analysis completed by _____

Core Work Routines (identified by employer)

Episodic Work Routines and Frequency (identified by employer)

Job-Related Routines (identified during job analysis)

Chapter 6, Appendix A: Job Analysis Terminology and Forms

Job Analysis Cover Sheet (cont.)

Accommodations Required (modifications of routines, schedule, etc.)

Critical Job-Related Policies (regarding uniforms, paychecks, safety, etc.)

Key Co-Workers and Titles

Emergency Procedures

Miscellaneous

**Transition Services
Department of Occupational Therapy
Colorado State University
Fort Collins, Colorado 80523**

Job Routine Analysis Work Sheet

Worker _____ Date _____

Routine _____

Type of routine _____
(core, episodic, job related)

How often performed (number/hour, number/day, etc.) _____
_____

Routine analysis completed by _____

Content Analysis Worker actions, specific job steps/skills: "What does worker do?"	**Informing Strategies** Trainer actions, including instructional cues, use of natural cues, and adaptation: "What does trainer do?"

Chapter 6, Appendix A: Job Analysis Terminology and Forms

Job Routine Analysis Work Sheet
Page _____ of _____

Worker _____

Content Analysis Worker actions, specific job steps/skills: "What does worker do?"	**Informing Strategies** Trainer actions, including instructional cues, use of natural cues, and adaptation: "What does trainer do?"

7
Intervention in Traumatic Head Injury: Learning Style Assessment

Carol J. Wheatley, MS, OTR/L
Judy J. Rein, MS, OTR/L

Rehabilitation of clients with traumatic head injury presents an opportunity as well as a challenge for occupational therapy. The profession is unique for its emphasis on function and its use of everyday tasks as both treatment modalities and measures of outcome. Rehabilitation professionals are beginning to recognize the validity of functional task performance as a measure of a client's capacities and limitations, particularly when employed in combination with formal, clinical tests (Acker, 1986).

This chapter describes the Learning Style Assessment, a method to identify the environmental and interpersonal characteristics that support optimal functioning in the client with traumatic head injury. The chapter also discusses the value of microcomputers in assessment. Further, it illustrates the use of information from the Learning Style Assessment in treatment both at home and on the job. A suggested reading list appears at the end of the chapter, providing the reader with additional resources on the subjects addressed here.

Learning Style Assessment

The purpose of assessment in a vocational rehabilitation program differs somewhat from that in acute health care settings. Early in rehabilitation, evaluation is employed to determine assets and deficits in daily function, preliminary to setting useful treatment goals. As the program continues, reevaluation is used to determine the efficacy of the intervention. In a vocational setting, the purpose of assessment is to identify specific job-related capacities as well as limitations, to determine potential for change, and to relate current characteristics to employment possibilities.

The occupational therapy assessment battery in any setting usually consists of a combination of standardized tests and functional activities. Use of standardized tests of a client's status is essential to obtain reliable and valid measures of treatment effects. Several authors have described assessment batteries for specific purposes (Abreu, 1987; Siev, Freishtat, & Zoltan, 1986). Lezak (1983) has published a comprehensive review of measurement tools commonly available.

The Learning Style Assessment, developed at the Maryland Rehabilitation Center, can be used in conjunction with any battery of tests, as appropriate for a given population—in this case, people with traumatic head injury. The Learning Style Assessment is not itself a standardized instrument, but a way of interpreting the quantitative and qualitative results of tests to provide more effective treatment and to plan the optimal environment for a client.

For example, a person who was a verbal learner but is now aphasic as a result of a head injury must rely more heavily on his or her visual processing system, which is relatively less impaired. Although the person may perform in the average range on tests of visual perception, a therapist might still choose as a valid treatment goal the development of more skill in visual processing to compensate for the language deficits. Such a choice could result from use of the Learning Style Assessment.

The Learning Style Assessment involves identifying the kinds of information outlined in Table 7-1. Each of these areas of the assessment is explained in the following sections.

Determining the Optimal Method of Presentation

New information can be presented in a variety of ways, used singly or in combination. Visual presentation may involve demonstration of a task using the actual materials for which the task calls, or it may take the form of written or illustrated instructions for performing the task. Verbal (oral) information may accompany the visual display. It may be provided on tape (video, audio, or a combination of the two) or live. A tape allows for multiple repetitions without the instructor's having to be present. An additional advantage of a tape is the control that it gives to the learner over the rate of presentation and the number of repetitions. In a live teaching situation an instructor must be sensitive to the pace at which he or she presents information and to the schedule and the frequency of repetition. Feedback from the learner is essential to identify problems. However, the signs of response may be quite subtle, particularly with lower-functioning individuals. For example, an increase in a client's distractibility or agitation may be a cue that the information is not being presented in an effective way.

Table 7-1
Information to Be Identified in the Learning Style Assessment

I. Optimal method of presentation
   A. Modality
      1. Visual
      2. Verbal
      3. Motor
   B. Rate of presentation
   C. Repetition required

II. Retention strategy
   A. Internal
   B. External

III. Optimal environment
   A. Physical characteristics
   B. Psychological characteristics
   C. Distraction
   D. Stimulation

IV. Metacognitive capacity
   A. Level of dependence on structure
   B. Capacity to generalize
   C. Capacity to respond to unanticipated events
   D. Level of awareness of cognitive characteristics
   E. Ability to resist distractors
   F. Level of self-control
   G. Motivation to maximize capacity
   H. Self-hindering characteristics

Note: © 1989 by Carol J. Wheatley. Reprinted by permission.

Learning situations typically involve a multisensory approach. However, a person who has difficulty attending to multiple sources of input may be overloaded in such circumstances. Exploration of various combinations of approaches may be required to isolate the best methods to use with a given client.

Identifying the Best Retention Strategies

Considerable work is in progress to develop mnemonic strategies for use with clients who have sustained traumatic head injuries (Parente, in press; Wilson, 1987). Mnemonic strategies are techniques of compensation or substitution for memory deficits. They may be internal, such as silent rehearsal of verbal information, or external, such as a written reminder. The internal strategies require a higher level of cognitive functioning and control. The external methods can be provided by therapists initially, with the goal of instructing clients to generate their own strategies when and if they become capable of doing so.

Ascertaining the Optimal Environment

Surroundings can be manipulated to support the maximum functioning of a client with head injury. A work setting can be assessed as part of a job analysis, based on a job-site visit. Given the details of a particular client's optimal environment, a therapist can evaluate future employment settings for their capacity to meet that client's needs.

The detrimental effects of environmental distractions are well recognized. Such distractions are frequently minimized in occupational therapy clinics by the use of quiet rooms. However, because people normally must cope with a variety of environments in the home and the community, it is important that the person with attention deficits be gradually acclimated to settings with various levels of stimulation. The different kinds of stimulation needed to supplement a person's mnemonic efforts must also be identified, and they must be provided when possible. Although a long-term goal of rehabilitation may be to improve a person's memory to a level that enables him or her to be self-sufficient, continuing support may be necessary to maximize his or her functioning.

Assessing Metacognitive Capacity

Metacognition may be defined as "an individual's access to and control over [his or her] own beliefs, cognitive skills and strategies, and executive processes" (Cicerone & Tupper, 1986, p. 75). People with head injuries frequently exhibit decreased capability in this area because their capacity for self-awareness is impaired. They need to adjust their prior concepts of their cognitive abilities to reflect their diminished capacities.

Lessened awareness of self can significantly affect level of motivation and potential independence. A person who is incapable of recognizing the characteristics of his or her cognitive style may be unwilling or unable to employ various strategies in compensation. Peer group sessions can be of value in building a client's perception of his or her capabilities and deficits.

Conducting a Learning Style Assessment

A person with unimpaired cognitive functioning may prefer certain learning styles over others, but be adaptable to a wide range of situations as needed. For example, a student with a preference for visual learning through diagrams, charts, etc., may respond well in a classroom setting with an instructor who provides such stimuli. However, with a topic that does not lend itself to this kind of presentation or with an instructor who employs a different teaching style, the student needs to adapt. Although this requires more effort on the part of the student, he or she has the flexibility to learn by a variety of methods.

The person with a head injury, on the other hand, may have lost some of this adaptability and be unable to learn information presented by any other approach than the optimal one for him or her. If the characteristics of the person's best learning style can be identified, teaching efforts can be adjusted accordingly, and unnecessary frustration can be avoided.

Standardized tests can be used to identify the relative strengths and weaknesses of a client with head injury. For example, the client's speed of visual and auditory processing can be evaluated to determine the best way to present new information to be learned. Tests can also be used to evaluate the effectiveness of a compensatory strategy. If the auditory or language processing of a client with a deficient memory is superior to his or her visual processing, verbal rehearsal may be effective as a mnemonic technique. A formal memory assessment can be administered to determine the effectiveness of the rehearsal strategy.

The use of microcomputers to administer, respond to, and score evaluations is a cost-effective approach. Presentation of test items via computer screen ensures that administrative procedures are standardized (Collins & Odell, 1986). Recording responses on a computer disk allows immediate, precise analyses of data. By freeing professionals from the tedium of administering and scoring tests, computers can provide them with time for other professional responsibilities. However, people with head trauma may require considerable orientation to be able to respond to computer-based assessments. Accordingly, computer-based assessments should comprise only a small part of a battery (Skilbeck, 1984).

Testing a client's performance in functional activities is also important in overall evaluation. The occupational therapist should observe performance in various everyday situations, some structured as timed tests, to identify the problem-solving strategies used spontaneously by the client, determine their practical value, and isolate the environmental characteristics apparently conducive to either successful or poor performance.

The findings from a Learning Style Assessment of a male client with aphasia and memory and cognitive deficits might be reported as follows:

> J.B. demonstrated in his responses to testing materials that he learned best when directions were given orally with time allowed for discussion. He was aware when he was confused and sought help as necessary. He could follow written directions, but first required that they be

discussed. He tended not to refer to them because of his reading deficit.

J.B.'s memory for oral instructions was satisfactory once he understood them. He was able to work on a complex project for several days without recall difficulties. Over the several months of therapy, he developed the ability to perform several tasks simultaneously, working on each in turn. Further, he was able to work in environments of both high and low distraction, though he preferred the latter when a choice was available.

J.B. could independently structure a task once its goals were identified. In general, he used an organized, comprehensive approach. However, he occasionally chose a problem-solving strategy that was somewhat less efficient, though still effective. He was responsive to suggestions for increasing his efficiency at a task and could continue the task without error.

J.B. occasionally needed reminders to double-check his work before presenting the finished product. He became so capable of working in a busy environment without being distracted that infrequently he became engrossed in his work and forgot appointments. This problem was resolved by the use of an alarm watch, which he could set independently.

Applying the Findings from a Learning Style Assessment

Management Strategies

A therapist must develop evaluation and treatment strategies unique to each client's needs. Arriving at an effective clinical approach is frequently a trial-and-error process as the therapist attempts various styles of relating to a client and adjusts his or her own behavior in response to the client's. The process can be streamlined by using a standardized assessment battery, the results of which can aid the therapist in selecting and sequencing techniques.

The interpersonal sensitivity of a therapist is of primary importance in building a therapeutic relationship, particularly with a client who has sustained a traumatic head injury. Knowledge of a client's characteristics must guide the timing, the intensity, and the phrasing used to shape his or her behavior in a given situation.

Under the guidance of a skillful therapist, a client may exhibit performance in the occupational therapy clinic that he or she may not display in different environments or with other staff members. For example, therapists frequently report that a client performs better "with structure." However, the details of this structure are seldom communicated meaningfully to those who could use the knowledge. Unless successful methods are shared with others who work with a client, generalization to different settings and tasks will be poor.

In identifying the structure in which people with head injury function best, baseline and follow-up data on performance are important. Microcomputers become key assets. Depending on the type of software used, they can gauge and analyze responses within controlled conditions (Skilbeck, 1984). Parameters that can be measured include correctness of response, response latency, frequency of response, and the number of responses required to achieve a specific criterion.

Communication among team and family members regarding strategies that help clients function best is important throughout evaluation and treatment but particularly so when a client is preparing to leave a rehabilitation facility. Many of the gains noted in the facility may fade if they are unsupported when the client returns home, reenters school, or attempts to work. Aiding the client's transition to the new environment requires considerable planning by the rehabilitation team. Visits to the home, the school, and/or the job site can yield invaluable guidance.

Environmental Restructuring

Occupational therapists are frequently called upon to improve clients' work performance. The characteristics of the environment that will support a client's best performance need to be identified and matched to the job site as closely as possible. Components of the environment are the physical surroundings, including visual distractions, and the interpersonal aspects, such as the therapist's phrasing and timing of verbal interactions. A typical occupational therapy clinic offers many options for simulating work situations. Thus for a person with traumatic head injury, a clinic can provide a variety of environmental conditions: high- and low-stimulus areas, adjustable work settings, and diverse activities through which the person can be guided to achieve any single goal. Indeed, the environment can be manipulated to maximize independent functioning.

Microcomputer programs offer specific methods of restructuring the environment in precise and consistent ways (Skilbeck, 1984). Well-designed software allows a therapist, choosing from various environmental parameters, to (a) control the intended stimulus, (b) reduce extraneous stimuli, (c) grade a new stimulus based on a client's performance, and (d) provide feedback to enhance performance (Hollander, 1988).

Environmental restructuring was used effectively in the following case of a female client with severe memory loss. Much prior rehabilitation effort had been expended to remediate her memory capacity. Conditions necessary for her optimum learning had been identified, and they had been integrated into the work environment.

M.G. worked effectively on her assigned task, and environmental cues enabled her to maintain sequence in the activity. However, when she returned to her task from a break, she could not recall where she had been sitting, what she had been doing, or what her next step in the project was. To help her compensate, the therapist assigned M.G. to her own work table, and she developed the habit of leaving a personal item positioned on the table as an additional cue. She was trained to take notes on the next step of her activity's process just before leaving on her break. Thereafter, using the notes, she could resume her activity independently upon her return.

Creating an optimal environment in the real world is more difficult and presents many hazards. Although a therapist may be willing and prepared to adapt his or her approach to a client's needs, a family member, a teacher, or a supervisor may be less willing or less able to comply. The characteristics of interaction between these people and the client may have been established over many years and be resistant to change. Consider a family with numerous siblings who have always shared personal items and not routinely returned them promptly. A son with a memory deficit now comes home from a rehabilitation facility. He has a tendency to misplace things, but has learned through treatment to minimize the problem by organizing his surroundings. His siblings continue their habit of borrowing items and sometimes not returning them. This results in an extremely stressful environment for the son. People with head injury may adjust more successfully and retain adaptive habits better in living quarters of their own, even though family may want to keep them at home, closely supervised. Family must be helped to realize that an unchanged home environment can contribute to regression to undesired behaviors.

Another example of environmental influence is a supervisor whose decision-making style is impulsive, resulting in frequent revision of previous orders. A female employee who has sustained a head injury returns to work with significant memory deficits, but with an effective mnemonic strategy of recording information to compensate for possible memory lapse. The supervisor's frequent changes of orders place considerable demand on the employee to keep her notes updated.

The supervisor does not recognize that consistency and stability in the work environment are imperative for the worker to use her mnemonic strategy effectively.

Vocational Rehabilitation

The traditional sequence of services in vocational rehabilitation is evaluation, training, job placement—the "train, then place" model. Fawber and Wachter (1987) present several criticisms of the use of this model with clients who have sustained head injuries. For one, the model requires that a client be able to generalize, that is, to demonstrate carryover of learning, such as new skills, from a training program to a job site. The problems of generalization are well documented (Schacter & Glisky, 1986). Diller and Gordon (1981) have expanded the concept of generalization, dividing it into three levels:

Level I	Within-task learning, with generalization to an alternate version of the same task
Level II	Generalization from task performance to test performance
Level III	Carryover of learning to everyday activities, with the capacity for modification in response to variations in the everyday situation.

The traditional approach to vocational rehabilitation presumes that a client has the capacity for Level III generalization, a skill of which many clients with traumatic head injury are incapable. However, with the use of domain-specific learning, described by Schacter and Glisky (1986), clients with severe memory impairments have been able to acquire sufficient skills for productive employment. By *domain-specific learning,* Schacter and Glisky mean the learning of skills particular to a task—for example, word processing with a certain program on a given type of computer. The types of jobs that appear suitable for clients capable of only Level I generalization are "those that require a set of relatively invariant procedures" (Glisky, 1988, p. 557). Jobs involving data entry and similar computer-based tasks may be particularly appropriate. One single-subject study found that direct, explicit training in all components of a data-entry job, combined with extensive opportunity for repetition, supported transfer of skills from the laboratory to employment (Glisky & Schacter, 1987). The function of microcomputer technology in this context is similar to an assistive device that compensates for memory problems by providing a highly structured work environment.

Alternatives to Traditional Vocational Rehabilitation

Supported employment offers a fresh approach to vocational placement of disabled individuals (NARF, 1985). It provides people with assistance in making the transition from the habilitation or rehabilitation setting to the workplace. Chapter 6 describes supported employment at length. Originally designed for people who have severe and profound developmental disabilities (Wehman, 1981), with minimal modification it has proven successful with people who have sustained head injuries (Fawber & Wachter, 1987). The model consists of four essential components: (a) a person with a severe level of disability, (b) the availability of a salaried position, (c) a real-life work environment, and (d) lifetime support.

The job coach is a key ingredient of supported employment. After learning the requirements of a particular job, the job coach accompanies the client to the job site, trains him or her to do the tasks required, and sets up the physical and interpersonal environment to support his or her independence. Over time, the job coach withdraws, replacing his or her presence with support mechanisms. In the traditional supported employment model, the services of the job coach and the rehabilitation team remain available for the lifetime of the client.

Occupational therapists can function as job coaches or in supportive roles in the supported employment model. They can help assess the capacities and the limitations of a person with head injury and determine his or her best learning style. Using job analysis, they can identify the requisite skills for a job and either provide simulated work tasks to train the client or conduct the training on the actual job site, following the "place, then train" approach of the classic supported employment model (NARF, 1985). Under the latter approach a client may initially attend the workplace on a volunteer or part-time basis.

Following is an example of the successful use of this model to place a female client in a competitive job:

> C.M. had minimal physical, visual-perceptual, and language deficits, but profound loss of memory for recent information. This combination resulted in severely diminished learning capacity. A period of treatment produced improved attention and concentration skills and ability to record and follow written directions. C.M. then underwent a vocational evaluation. The specific mnemonic strategies developed in occupational therapy were continued in the vocational evaluation. These included

control of the physical aspects of her low-stimulus work station and the evaluator's use of oral and written directions. C.M. demonstrated an aptitude for clerical tasks, her work speed and accuracy being satisfactory. The job placement department found a part-time position for her as a receptionist at a small driving school.

Job analysis by the occupational therapist revealed several responsibilities that were required: (a) opening the office each day, (b) answering phone calls regarding the classes offered, and (c) registering new students. A job simulation was developed in the occupational therapy clinic. It involved C.M.'s using a script for the pertinent information such as time, length, and cost of classes, and it offered her practice in filling out the appropriate forms. C.M. was given the responsibility of answering the department phone and taking messages accurately. She possessed a pleasant telephone personality, exhibited good social skills, and demonstrated a polite manner of requesting repetition when needed.

Once C.M. performed satisfactorily in this setting, she went to the job with the job coach. The occupational therapist and the job coach devised a checklist of the tasks for opening the office each day. A variety of written cues were developed for the details of the costs of the various services. A large blackboard in easy view of the reception desk proved most effective. During quiet times the job coach provided role-playing experiences, which covered typical scenarios of requests for information.

The job coach kept detailed records of C.M.'s accuracy. When C.M. reached a set criterion of performance, the job coach began to phase out her influence by shortening her hours of supervision at the job site. This left C.M. on her own resources, for no other workers kept regular hours at that office until the evening classes began. During the first few days of this weaning, various members of the rehabilitation team telephoned C.M. with typical questions about the services. The team members rated her accuracy, her social skills, and her ability to handle inquiries beyond her scope of knowledge. C.M.'s performance in this situation was found to be actually superior to that in the presence of the job coach. She had developed dependencies on the coach because she did not trust her own memory capacity.

The employer was impressed with C.M.'s willingness to work and her strong efforts to learn the job. She was eventually provided with a pay increase and permanent employment. The services of the job coach remained available to her as needed, but reports continued to be satisfactory. A few months later, fees for the driving services were raised. C.M. independently changed the information on the reference blackboard and accommodated to the change without a problem. She evidenced considerable pride in her accomplishment. Complimented on her progress, she responded, "My memory improved because it had to."

Summary

Knowledge of the impact of the subtle sequelae of traumatic head injury is expanding rapidly. Rehabilitation techniques are now being developed that can maximize a survivor's capacity to reestablish a satisfactory life-style. Appreciation of the complexity of human cognitive capacity is expanding; consequently techniques to compensate for impaired ability can be further refined. The Learning Style Assessment represents a refinement in evaluation, offering a means of interpreting the results of tests and observations to provide more effective treatment and to plan the optimal environment for a client.

A role for microcomputers is emerging in rehabilitation. Potential applications can be seen in cuing, collecting data, facilitating learning, and providing a framework for returning people with traumatic head injury to work. A smooth transition from the rehabilitation facility to the workplace is acknowledged to be an important facet of return to work, one to which occupational therapy has much to contribute.

Glossary

Aphasia—an impairment in expression or comprehension of speech, writing, and/or other related communication behaviors because of an injury to or a disease of the brain.

Assistive device—adaptive equipment applied with compensatory strategies to improve a person's functional capabilities in educational, vocational, and daily-living activities.

Cognition—the process of thinking, by which a person perceives and responds to internal and external stimuli.

Cognitive rehabilitation—"the diversity of interventions intended to improve physical and mental functioning offered by a variety of disciplines including physical therapy, physiatry, occupational therapy, neuropsychology, and speech pathology" (Kreutzer, Gordon, & Wehman, 1989, p. 118).

Cognitive remediation—"a set of strategies intended to improve the intellectual, perceptual, cognitive, and behavioral skills of persons with brain dysfunction" (Kreutzer, Gordon, & Wehman, 1989, p. 118).

Compensation—a reorganization of functional responsibilities so that an area of capacity minimizes an area of liability.

Generalization of skills—carryover of skills learned in one setting to a similar situation.

Independent living—a state of existence in which the need for physical, emotional, and cognitive assistance from others has been minimized.

Job analysis—an investigation of the physical and cognitive factors required to perform a given job.

Job coach—a rehabilitation professional who accompanies a client to the workplace and is responsible for teaching him or her the skills needed to perform the job.

Metacognition—"an individual's access to and control over [his or her] own beliefs, cognitive skills and strategies, and executive processes" (Cicerone & Tupper, 1986, p. 75).

Microcomputer—a device that processes information electronically at extremely rapid rates.

Mnemonic strategies—a variety of techniques to compensate or substitute for memory deficits. The term includes internal methods such as rehearsal, imagery, and association, and external strategies such as notebooks, calendars, and watches.

Software—the set of instructions or the program by which a computer operates, usually stored on silicon chips, magnetic disks, or magnetic tape.

Substitution—the exchange of an alternative approach for a lost function.

Supported employment—"direct placement in competitive employment with a job coach who gradually fades out supervision as the client achieves work proficiency" (NARF, 1985, p. xi)

Traumatic head injury—"an insult to the brain, not of a degenerative or congenital nature but caused by an external physical force, that may produce a diminished or altered state of consciousness, which results in impairment of cognitive abilities or physical functioning. These impairments may be either temporary or permanent and cause partial or total functional disability or psychosocial maladjustment" (official definition adopted by the National Head Injury Foundation, February 22, 1986).

References

Abreu, B. C. (1987, October 30–November 1). *Rehabilitation of perceptual cognitive dysfunction*. Unpublished manual distributed at a workshop, Baltimore.

Acker, M. B. (1986). Relationships between test scores and everyday life functioning. In B. P. Uzzell & Y. Gross (Eds.), *Clinical neuropsychology of intervention* (pp. 85–117). Boston: Martinus Nijihoff.

Cicerone, K. D., & Tupper, D. E. (1986). Cognitive assessment in the neuropsychological rehabilitation of head injured adults. In B. P. Uzzell & Y. Gross (Eds.), *Clinical neuropsychology of intervention* (pp. 59–83). Boston: Martinus Nijihoff.

Collins, M., & Odell, K. (1986). Computerization of a traditional test of nonverbal visual problem solving. *Cognitive Rehabilitation, 4*(5), 16–18.

Diller, L., & Gordon, W. A. (1981). Rehabilitation and clinical neuropsychology. In S. Filskov & T. Boll (Eds.), *Handbook of clinical neuropsychology* (pp. 702–733). New York: John Wiley & Sons.

Fawber, H. L., & Wachter, J. F. (1987). Job placement as a treatment component of the vocational rehabilitation process. *Journal of Head Trauma Rehabilitation, 2*(1), 27–33.

Glisky, E. L. (1988). The use of microcomputers in the rehabilitation of organic memory disorders. In *Proceedings of the International Conference of the Association for the Advancement of Rehabilitation Technology* (pp. 556–558). Washington, DC: RESNA.

Glisky, E. L., & Schacter, D. L. (1987). Acquisition of domain-specific knowledge in organic amnesia: Training for computer related work. *Neuropsychologica, 25,* 893–906.

Hollander, R. (1988). Computer use for the remediation of cognitive, perceptual, and fine motor deficits. In K. M. Kovich & D. E. Berman (Eds.), *Head injury: A guide to clinical functional outcomes in occupational therapy* (pp. 191–194). Rockville, MD: Aspen.

Kreutzer, J. S., Gordon, W. A., & Wehman, P. (1989). Cognitive remediation following traumatic brain injury. *Rehabilitation Psychology, 34,* 117–133.

Lezak, M. D. (1983). *Neuropsychological assessment.* New York: Oxford University Press.

National Association of Rehabilitation Facilities. (1985). *From theory to implementation: A guide to supported employment for rehabilitation facilities.* Washington, DC: Author.

Parente, F. J. (in press). *Retraining of memory.* Rockville, MD: American Occupational Therapy Association.

Schacter, D. L., & Glisky, E. L. (1986) Memory remediation: Restoration, alleviation, and the acquisition of domain-specific knowledge. In B. P. Uzzell & Y. Gross (Eds.), *Clinical neuropsychology of intervention* (pp. 257–282). Boston: Martinus Nijihoff.

Siev, E., Freishtat, B., & Zoltan, B. (1986). *Perceptual and cognitive dysfunction in the adult stroke patient.* Thorofare, NJ: Charles B. Slack.

Skilbeck, C. (1984). Computer assistance in the management of memory and cognitive impairment. In B. A. Wilson & N. Moffat (Eds.), *Clinical management of memory problems* (pp. 112–131). Rockville, MD: Aspen.

Wehman, P. (1981). *New horizons for severely disabled individuals.* Baltimore: Paul Brookes.

Wilson, B. A. (1987). *Rehabilitation of memory.* New York: Guilford Press.

Related Reading
General Information

Bransford, J. D. (1979). *Human cognition.* Belmont, CA: Wadsworth.

Corthell, D. W., & Tooman, M. (1985). *Rehabilitation of TBI.* Menomonie, WI: Research and Training Center, Stout Vocational Rehabilitation Institute.

Filskov, S. B., & Boll, T. J. (Eds.). (1981). *Handbook of clinical neuropsychology.* New York: John Wiley & Sons.

Heilman, K. M., & Valenstein, E. (Eds.). (1979). *Clinical neuropsychology.* New York: Oxford University Press.

Kolb, B., & Whishaw, I. Q. (1980). *Fundamentals of human neuropsychology.* San Francisco: W. H. Freeman.

Kovich, K. M., & Berman, D. E. (1988). *Head injury: A guide to clinical functional outcomes in occupational therapy.* Rockville, MD: Aspen.

Luria, A. R. (1973). *The working brain.* London: Allen Lane, Penguin Press.

Prigatano, G. P., Fordyce, D. J., Zeiner, H. K., Roueche, J. R., Pepping, M., & Wood, B. C. (1986). *Neuropsychological rehabilitation after brain injury.* Baltimore: Johns Hopkins University Press.

Professional Staff Association of the Rancho Los Amigos Hospital. (1980). *Rehabilitation of the head injured adult: Comprehensive management.* Downey, CA: Author.

Rosenthal, M., Griffith, E. R., Bond, M., & Miller, J. D. (Eds.). (1983). *Rehabilitation of the head injured adult.* Philadelphia: F. A. Davis.

Walsh, K. W. (1978). *Neuropsychology.* Edinburgh, Scotland: Churchill Livingstone.

Ylvisaker, M., & Gobble, E. M. (1987). *Community reentry for head injured adults.* Boston: College-Hill.

Assessment

Cicerone, K. D., & Tupper, D. E. (1986). Cognitive assessment in the neuropsychological rehabilitation of head injured adults. In B. P. Uzzell & Y. Gross (Eds.), *Clinical neuropsychology of intervention* (pp. 59–83). Boston: Martinus Nijihoff.

Lezak, M. D. (1983). *Neuropsychological assessment.* New York: Oxford University Press.

Role of Computers

Hooker, C., Lowe, L., Calub, C. D., Todd, M., & Cook C. (1987, September). *Efficacy of computer-assisted cognitive rehabilitation:*

A pilot study. Paper presented at the conference, Cognitive Rehabilitation, Williamsburg, VA.

Katz, R., & Nagy, V. T. (1984). CATS: Computerized aphasia treatment system. *Cognitive Rehabilitation, 2*(4), 8–10.

Kerner, M. J., & Acker, M. (1985). Computer delivery of memory retraining with head injured patients. *Cognitive Rehabilitation, 3*(4), 26–31.

Kreutzer, J. S., & Morrison, C. N. (1986). A guide to cognitive rehabilitation software for the Apple IIe/IIc computer. *Cognitive Rehabilitation, 4*(1), 6–17.

Lynch, W. J. (1983). *The contribution of video games to computer-assisted cognitive training.* Paper presented at the conference, Innovative Rehabilitation Approaches for the Geriatric Patient, Anaheim, CA.

Lynch, W. J. (1986). An update on software in cognitive rehabilitation. *Cognitive Rehabilitation, 4*(2), 14–18.

Malachowski, A. M. (1986). Composing and computing by the writer with head trauma. *Cognitive Rehabilitation, 4*(6), 10–13.

Malec, J., Rao, N., Jones, R., & Stubbs, K. (1984). Video game practice effects on sustained attention in patients with craniocerebral trauma. *Cognitive Rehabilitation, 2*(4), 18–23.

National Head Injury Foundation. (1984). *Computer use in cognitive retraining.* Framingham, MA: Author. (Address: P.O. Box 567, Framingham, MA 01701).

Wilson, P. B. (1983.) Software selection and use in language and cognitive retraining. *Cognitive Rehabilitation, 1*(1), 9–10.

Visual Perception

Abreu, B. C. (1981). Interdisciplinary approach to the adult visual perceptual function-dysfunction continuum. In B. C. Abreu (Ed.), *Physical disabilities manual.* New York: Raven Press.

Potegal, M. (Ed.). (1982). *Spatial abilities.* New York: Academic Press.

Siev, E., Freishtat, B., & Zoltan, B. (1986). *Perceptual and cognitive dysfunction in the adult stroke patient.* Thorofare, NJ: Charles B. Slack.

Language

Adamovich, B., Henderson, J., & Averbach, S. (1985). *Rehabilitation of closed head injury patients.* San Diego, CA: College Hill Press.

Costello, J. M., & Holland, A. L. (Eds.). (1986). *Handbook of speech/language disorders.* San Diego, CA: College Hill Press.

Memory

Cermack, L. S. (Ed.). (1982). *Human memory and amnesia.* Hillsdale, NJ: Lawrence Erlbaum Associates.

Wilson, B. A., & Moffat, N. (Eds.). (1984). *Clinical management of memory problems.* Rockville, MD: Aspen.

8

Prevention

Joy White Danches, MOT, OTR, CIRS

The practice of health promotion and disease or injury prevention has become critically important in health care. Occupational therapists in many kinds of practice are increasingly influencing health behaviors of populations at risk for disease and injury. They also are modifying environmental conditions that affect health. Further, they are screening patients and clients for risk factors and disease, providing early treatment, and advising, counseling, and referring. Other therapists are assuming roles at organizational, community, or government levels and fostering environmental change through advocacy, consultation, or lobbying. However, in the current era of cost-effectiveness and fiscal responsibility, monies allocated to health and prevention services have been closely scrutinized. Only efficient, effective, quality services are surviving in the highly competitive market of health care and prevention.

Definitions of Prevention, Health Promotion, and Wellness

For the sake of clarity it is necessary to define *prevention, health promotion,* and *wellness* at the outset of this chapter. These terms have preconceived meanings to various readers.

Prevention

Prevention refers to services targeted at preventing injury, illness, or disease. It is proactive, taking place before an incident or a health problem occurs. Prevention encourages responsibility for oneself. By contrast, *treatment* refers to services targeted at remediating a health problem that already exists. Treatment is reactive, taking place after an injury or the onset of a disease or an illness.

Prevention can be further described as occurring at three levels: primary, secondary, and tertiary (Jaffe, 1987).
1. *Primary prevention* refers to activities undertaken before the onset of disease. Its goal is to avoid the occurrence of disease or disability and to build resistance in a population potentially at risk. The intent of primary prevention programs is usually to provide a long-term impact.
2. *Secondary prevention* refers to early diagnosis and treatment with the intent of preventing the condition from becoming serious or permanently disabling. Outreach and case finding are examples of secondary prevention.
3. *Tertiary prevention* refers to rehabilitative programs that are aimed at reducing the aftereffects of a presenting problem or illness. It is more remedial in nature than primary or secondary prevention and is directed at preventing further loss or disability.

Prevention services are based on the premise that proper education can reduce medical costs and services. In regard to tertiary prevention Egbert et al. (1964) have demonstrated that preoperative education can decrease postoperative pain and the need for narcotics postoperatively. Healy (1968) has found that preoperative instructions to surgery patients result in earlier discharge from the hospital. Rosenberg (1971) has demonstrated a similar decrease in hospital readmissions because of patient education. Levine and Britten (1973) report decreased hospitalizations, outpatient visits, and costs per patient by educating the hemophilia patient. Kaye and Hammond (1978) have shown lower costs and better health care for rheumatoid arthritis patients by educating them properly.

Occupational Therapy and Primary Prevention

Documentation on occupational therapists' involvement in primary prevention is very limited (Ellexson, 1986; Muffly-Elsey & Flinn-Wagner, 1987). However, presentations on the subject at occupational therapy conferences have increased over the past five years (Dortch & Trombly, 1989; Fisher, 1989; Seaton & Slama, 1989). Because of the lack of literature, a personal base of experience in industrial back injury prevention is emphasized in subsequent sections of this chapter.

Occupational Therapy and Secondary Prevention

Historically, occupational therapists have been significant providers of secondary prevention. Joint protection (Cordery, 1965), energy conservation, positioning techniques, splinting, and other types of education about disease or illness have commonly been included in occupational therapy services. Over the past decade occupational therapists have become more involved in pain management programs (Flower, Naxon, Jones, & Mooney, 1981; Heck, 1988; McCormack, 1988), back schools (Randolph, 1984), and return-to-work services (Bear-Lehman, 1983; Bettencourt, Carlstrom, Brown, Lindau, & Long, 1986; Boyd, Bryan, Hannah, Mangia, & Paul, 1987; Harrand & Hoffman, 1980; Holmes, 1985; Hook, 1986; Howe, Weaver, & Dulay, 1981; Mayer et al., 1985; Mayer et al., 1987; Wilke & Sheldahl, 1985). As these services have evolved, they have begun to to bridge clinically based treatment and the workplace through the provision of on-site job analysis, work-site modifications, and employer education. This shift out of the clinical setting has become the basis for some occupational therapists to venture into primary prevention.

Occupational Therapy and Tertiary Prevention

Traditionally, occupational therapists have been providers of tertiary prevention. Occupational therapy journals and conferences have included documentation and presentations on a wide variety of services for diverse populations since the inception of the profession. Evaluation and treatment techniques for stroke, head injury, and spinal cord injury and for orthopedic, neuromuscular, psychiatric, and other disabling conditions have been and continue to be shared, challenged, and revised among occupational therapists.

Health Promotion and Wellness

Health promotion refers to programs that enhance health or foster wellness. Jaffe (1987) defines it as "systematic efforts by an organization to enhance the wellness of its members through education, behavior change, and cultural support." She writes of *wellness* as a goal or a process rather than as a state or a condition and defines it as "the process of adapting patterns of behavior that lead to improved health and heightened life satisfaction." In 1978 the Representative Assembly of the American Occupational Therapy Association (AOTA) adopted a formal statement on the subject, "The Role of the Occupational Therapist in the Promotion of Health and the Prevention of Disabilities." Occupational therapists' involvement in this area has been reflected in presentations at conferences (Diazio, 1985; Goodro, 1986; Hertfelder & Gwin, 1986; Jaffe & Gray, 1986; Paulson, 1986; Reitz, 1984; Shealy, 1984) and published articles (Allen, 1986; Elias & Murphy, 1986; Jaffe, 1986; Johnson, 1986; Kaplan & Burch-Minakan, 1986; Mann, Edwards, & Baum, 1986; Maynard, 1986; Rider

& White, 1986; White, 1986). A brief overview of health care providers' involvement in health promotion is given in subsequent sections of this chapter; a personal perspective on greater involvement by occupational therapists is offered at the conclusion, in the context of societal trends.

Prevention Providers

A variety of providers compete in the prevention services market. Physicians, historically perceived as the ultimate health care experts, have evolved a specialty in occupational medicine. Many are employed by industry and occupational medicine clinics or serve as consultants. Typically they medically screen job applicants, treat job-related injuries or diseases, and supervise health programs. Some family practitioners and internists have also begun consulting with industries, communities, and governments.

Nurses, traditionally viewed as right-hand people to physicians, have also evolved a specialty in industry. Occupational health nurses are commonly employed by industry to provide first aid, medical screenings, and return-to-work monitoring. In small to medium-sized companies they are often hired as full-time employees to handle the duties previously described for the company physician. In these situations a physician is usually kept on retainer by the company, or a relationship with a local physician or clinic is established. The occupational health nurse can then consult with the physician regarding specific health problems of employees. Occupational health nurses are increasingly becoming involved in ergonomics and prevention modes in addition to health care issues (*Ergonomics and the Changing Role,* 1985; Fitzler, 1982).

In most industries, safety engineers, industrial hygienists, or ergonomists are employed to maintain a safe work environment, manage Occupational Safety and Health Administration (OSHA) requirements and inspections, monitor injured employees, and provide safety programs. They often work with other providers described in this section when providing health-related prevention services.

Psychologists, counselors, physical therapists, and occupational therapists have all begun to provide prevention services as a spin-off of treatment experiences. Psychologists and counselors have generally provided more psychologically oriented services such as programs on stress management, self-image, and motivation (Hodges, Bentley, & Palmer, 1984), whereas physical therapists and occupational therapists have provided more physically oriented services such as programs for fitness or for prevention of back or hand injuries (Huhn & Volski, 1985; Morris, 1984, 1985; Morris & Randolph, 1984).

Finally, trainers are sometimes employed by large corporations to provide a variety of training programs to their employees. Trainers typically have education or social science backgrounds and are skilled at public speaking and media development. They may provide general orientation, specialized job training, or preventive health programs to employees. Some experienced trainers consult with industry.

The aforementioned providers occasionally overlap in their services. What is provided, by whom, depends largely on the structure, the size, the financial status, the insurance losses, and the management philosophy of the contracting company. Most companies with a health promotion emphasis offer programs on smoking cessation, exercise, obesity control, safety, treatment of hypertension, immunization, and breast self-examination (Galvin, 1983). Typically, larger corporations are more involved in health promotion than medium-sized or small firms. For greater detail on work injury and prevention services from a variety of professionals' perspectives, refer to Isernhagen's (1988) book, *Work Injury: Management and Prevention.*

Rationale for the Occupational Therapist as a Prevention Provider

Traditionally, occupational therapists have holistically dealt with health problems or potential problems by evaluating and modifying the patient's or the client's occupation. In 1979 the Representative Assembly of the American Occupational Therapy Association adopted *Occupation as the Common Core of Occupational Therapy,* a policy statement. Evans (1987) defines *occupation* as "the active or 'doing' process of a person engaged in goal-directed, intrinsically gratifying, and culturally appropriate activity" (p. 627). Kielhofner and Burke (1980) propose the concept of human occupation as a framework for the identity and the practice of occupational therapy. According to Evans (1987), "the founders and early pioneers in occupational therapy conceptualized occupation as an essential part of human nature that is manifested by active participation in self-maintenance, work, leisure, play, and rest (Meyer, 1977)" (p. 627). Occupational therapists identify problems in these manifestations of occupation, and they evaluate and treat the problems to minimize disability and to maximize independence. Occupational therapists also screen for an imbalance between leisure activities and those associated with an occupational role (Florey & Michelman, 1982).

Work as a manifestation of occupation has been a focus of occupational therapists since the 1950s. Hightower-Vandamm (1981) has described occupational therapists of that period providing a system to match clients to specific jobs in industry. The client's capabilities for standing, bending, stooping, lifting, climbing, reaching, and writing were profiled and compared with the job requirements. Then the occupational therapist determined whether the client could be returned to his or her former job or should be placed in another position with the same company. Similar services in more recent times have been reported by others (Bettencourt et al., 1986; Boyd et al., 1987; Harrand & Hoffman, 1980; Holmes, 1985; Mayer et al., 1987; Wilke & Sheldahl, 1985). This initially clinically based treatment, bridged to the industrial environment through return-to-work issues, has opened the door of industrial injury prevention to occupational therapists.

Industrial Injury Prevention

Three strategies of primary prevention have been used by industry to reduce and control job injuries: job site redesign, preplacement screening, and employee training. Engineers, ergonomists, physicians, and exercise physiologists have been the dominant providers of research and service in the areas of job site redesign and preplacement screening. Occupational therapists, physical therapists, nurses, physicians, psychologists, counselors, and trainers have been the primary providers of employee training.

Job Site Redesign

Industry often resists proposals for job site redesign for fear of high costs and lower worker productivity. However, these strategies have promised the largest potential savings of injury costs. They target jobs with heavy physical demands and may involve redesign of the work area, the work flow, machines, and tools. Anderson and Catterall (1987b), Ayoub (1973, 1983), Ayoub, Fernandez, and Smith (n.d.), Chaffin (1975), Liles, Deivanayagam, Ayoub, and Mahajan (1984), and Snook (1978, 1983) have contributed research and literature in methods and principles of job site redesign. Most of these researchers have added to the literature some principles for reducing overexertion injuries (e.g., back and knee injuries). Also, Arndt (1987), Armstrong (1983), Armstrong and Chaffin (1979), Armstrong, Fine, Goldstein, Lifshitz, and Silverstein (1987), Bevin (1986), Cannon, Bernaacki, and Walter (1981), Feldman, Goldman, and Keyserling (1983), Hall (1986), Lutz and Hansford (1987), Masear, Hayes, and Hyde (1986), Silverstein, Fine, and Armstrong (1986, 1987), and Smith, Sonstegard, and Anderson (1977) have delineated methods of reducing the likelihood of work-related cumulative trauma (e.g., carpal tunnel syndrome). Carlsoo (1982) provides a review of the literature on the effects of cumulative vibration on the skeleton and the muscles.

Preplacement Screening

Employee selection, preemployment screening, and *preplacement screening* are all terms for a prevention strategy to ensure that workers have the basic physical abilities needed to meet the job requirements. Usually strength and endurance tests are developed and validated in prospective criterion-related studies.

Test design considerations include inexpensive testing equipment, test administration by medical technicians, and a legal framework. The possibility of high employee turnover necessitates keeping test costs to a minimum so that the program is cost-effective. Medical technicians can screen for medical risk factors before the test and can monitor vital signs during test administration, especially during step tests (described in a later section). The test battery should exist within the legal framework created by the Equal Employment Opportunity Commission through Title VII of the Civil Rights Act of 1964, the Rehabilitation Act of 1973, and the Age Discrimination Act of 1975 (Miner & Miner, 1979).

One can expect that women will be denied entry into physically demanding jobs at a rate that will be disproportionate to that for men when both sexes are screened on the basis of strength and endurance at levels required by the jobs in question. *Adverse impact* refers to this disproportionate effect on females, a protected class under the laws just named. An adverse impact due to a screening test battery is acceptable if the battery can be shown to be job related, to achieve the goal of a safe and productive work force, and to have the least adverse impact of the available alternatives.

Overall, tests chosen for screening must meet four criteria: a high degree of similarity to the job, prediction of future risk of injury and future performance, a minimum of gender bias, and reliability from a test-retest standpoint (Miner & Miner, 1979).

Preplacement Isometric Strength Tests

The isometric strength test is the most frequently documented form of a screening test and is recognized by the National Institute of Occupational Safety and Health's (1981) *Work Practices Guide for Manual Lifting.* It is performed by having the candidate pull against a set of handles that will not move. A load cell monitors the force exerted. Chaffin (1985) and Anderson (1988) recommend a 5-second exertion and a recording of the average and maximum force over the last 3 seconds. Up to three trials are usually performed. The handle positions are generally selected to simulate the most difficult tasks on the job in question.

Dynamic strength testing allows the measurement of forces throughout a range of movement. Isokinetic testing and isodynamic testing are two forms of this type of measurement. In an isokinetic test the velocity of movement stays constant at a preset but adjustable rate, and resistance accommodates to match the force applied. With isodynamic testing, the velocity varies and the resistance or the load is preset.

To date, dynamic test equipment, frequently used in the clinic (treatment) setting, has not been documented as a screening tool that predicts risk of injury or performance. By contrast, studies using isometric equipment have shown test results with a predictive value (Anderson & Herrin, 1980; Arnold, Rauschenberger, Soubel, & Guion, 1982; Cady, Bischoff, O'Connell, Thomas, & Allan, 1979; Chaffin, 1981; Chaffin, Herrin, Keyserling, & Foulke, 1977; Herrin, Kochkin, & Scott, 1982; Keyserling, Herrin, & Chaffin, 1980; Keyserling, Herrin, Chaffin, Armstrong, & Foss, 1980; Laughery & Jackson, 1984; Reilly, Zedeck, & Tenopyr, 1979). Studies investigating the predictive value of dynamic test equipment are expected. However, the costs of dynamic equipment remain very high ($40,000+) compared with those of isometric test equipment ($2,000+).

Because the ability to perform a task depends on all links in the body system, most local muscle-testing designs fall short of meeting predictive criteria. The ability to test the whole body strength in the posture from which the physical exertion is initiated is critical when simulating the physical parameters of a job (i.e., the horizontal and vertical locations of the initiation and the destination of movements).

Preplacement Endurance Tests

When endurance is a critical job factor, a test for it should be included in the screening battery. The basic purpose of an endurance test is to subject the job candidate to a graded series of known workloads and to monitor the response of the cardiopulmonary system. The most accurate endurance assessment involves *maximal testing*—testing the individual to his or her maximum (i.e., to exhaustion) and monitoring the oxygen uptake. However, several factors limit the use of maximal testing: Most individuals are reluctant to participate in it; the tests carry the risk of injury if there are preexisting health problems; and because of the risk of injury, a physician should be present during testing.

The most commonly used methods of inducing a graded endurance workload include the bicycle, the treadmill, and the step bench. Again, the goal is to include the whole body in the work as much as possible and to keep the work similar to the job activity. Datta and Ramanthan (1969) and Montgomery (1976) have documented that people are more familiar with a stepping motion than with walking or jogging on a treadmill.

A submaximal step test involves the candidate wearing a heart rate monitor while stepping on and off a 10-inch–high bench at a pace set by a metronome. Usually the test consists of up to three stages of stepping for 3 minutes each. A faster stepping pace is required at each successive stage. The candidate only progresses to the next stage if the heart rate is below 65 percent of the maximum. The literature reflects studies that show a very high correlation between predicted maximum oxygen uptake using submaximal step tests and direct measurements of oxygen uptake with maximal treadmill tests (Kasch, Phillips, Ross, Carter, & Boyer, 1972; McArdle, Katch, Pechar, Jacobson, & Ruck, 1972).

A number of studies reflect the use of the step test for preplacement testing of physical ability (Anderson & Catterall, 1987a; Arnold et al., 1982; Ayoub, 1983; Reilly et al., 1979). Reilly et al. (1979) and Anderson and Catterall (1987b) have also indicated that the step test adds significantly to the ability of the strength testing to predict injury rate and performance.

Preplacement Screening Validation

Retrospective validations are typically used to evaluate the effectiveness of a screening battery. A representative sample of incumbents are given the test battery. Then first reports of injury, records of lost time, and costs incurred for workers' compensation are usually collected for the sample for the period from when they started their current job through the date on which they were tested. Some studies also include productivity for the week during which workers were tested, when available.

Training Programs for Industrial Injury Prevention

The following overview of training programs for industrial injury prevention is limited to the author's experiences. A back school for outpatients at the clinic where the author was employed became the basis for venturing into the industrial market. Many back school outpatients commented that they wished they had known how to take care of their back before their injury and that they wished their employer had offered back school information to them earlier.

Concurrently a small company of approximately 200 employees inquired about the clinic's back information program. Through continuing dialogue with the company's occupational health nurse and personnel manager, the clinic entered into a contract for a customized program of direct employee training.

Direct Employee Training

The initial development of the training program was based on back injury statistics. The personnel manager and the occupational health nurse elaborated on the company's injuries and decided upon a slide format with a script, to be developed by the author and a physical therapist. The personnel manager guided the two therapists on a tour of the plant, explained the processes and the flow of materials, and pointed out areas of concern as well as areas that could not be altered. The therapists took slides during the tour to capture the essence of the plant's operations and to have as a reference when problem-solving back injury risks. The therapists also took notes during the tour and secured brochures on the company's operations, which helped to clarify terms, manufacturing processes, etc.

Back at the clinic the therapists highlighted the high-risk jobs, tasks, and postures to be included in the script. A script outline became the basis for a script, which in turn led to a storyboard. The personnel manager and the occupational health nurse reviewed the script and the storyboard and edited them for phrasing about which management, the employees, or the industry might be sensitive.

Next, the nurse took the therapists through the plant again to secure the slides necessary to finish the storyboard. Then the therapists completed the slide program. The personnel manager and the nurse reviewed the slides and the script for accuracy of work descriptions and safety procedures and for preferred areas of inclusion or deletion.

After changes were made in the script and the slides, the therapists developed handouts for the employees that highlighted some of the script's main points. The program was named "The Backbone of Capitol Wire and Cable," the same theme being used later for other training programs to prevent back injury developed by the two therapists.

When all of the materials had been approved by the personnel manager and the nurse, a schedule was set up for the therapists to present the program. Because the plant operated around the clock, several 1-hour sessions were scheduled. At the beginning of each training session, the personnel manager or the nurse made opening remarks about the importance of back injury prevention and introduced the therapists. The slide presentation came next, followed by employee participation in exercises and proper lifting techniques.

The nurse showed the slide program to all new employees at orientation and to all incumbents who hurt their back. She

Figure 8-1
Capital Wire
Man Hours Worked Per Year vs. Dollar Cost of Low Back Injuries
(training program implemented first quarter 1982)

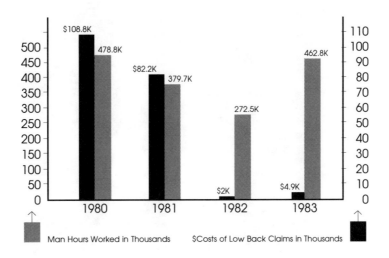

Man Hours Worked in Thousands $Costs of Low Back Claims in Thousands

Note. From "Program Compliance Key to Injury Prevention" by A. Morris, 1984, *Occupational Health and Safety,* 53(3), 45. © 1984 by A. Morris. Reprinted by permission.

also reviewed back care principles at the job site with injured employees returning to work.

A significant reduction in injuries and costs occurred over a three-year period (see Figure 8-1). Because a controlled study was not performed, the training program could not definitively be given credit for the reduction. However, the personnel manager and the nurse felt that the program had provided the impetus for the reduction. The therapists believed that the persistent follow-through by the nurse had also been a significant factor in keeping the information and the importance of back care fresh in the minds of the employees. Later, many other companies contracted for similar training.

Train-the-Trainers Approach

A two-tiered train-the-trainers approach was taken with a program on back injury prevention in order to reach over 700 city employees in diverse job tasks and geographical areas. The safety director and the therapists realized that many different functions existed within city government under one management umbrella. Physical stress factors and program needs varied across departments. A flexible approach that would be sensitive to specific departments was necessary.

The safety director and the insurance carrier confirmed the high incidence and the high costs of low back pain among city

Figure 8-2
Logo Used by Back Systems, Inc., for Back Injury Prevention Program

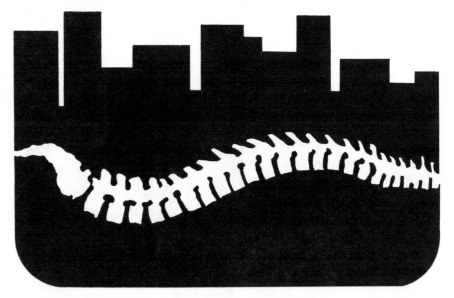

THE BACKBONE OF THE CITY

Note. © 1989 by Back Systems, Inc. Reprinted by permission.

workers. This information established the statistical justification and identified the eight city departments of highest need: Building Services; Parks and Recreation; Police and Fire; Solid Waste; Streets and Traffic; Utilities Maintenance; Vehicle Maintenance; and Warehouse.

The safety director introduced the therapists to the department heads. The therapists interviewed the department heads to learn the mission of the department, the division and the distribution of work, the work functions, and the physical stress factors. The therapists observed work in progress for each department, interviewed workers, photographed work functions, and developed guidelines to address the specific needs of each department.

Using the theme, "The Backbone of the City" (see Figure 8-2), the therapists developed a *basic synchronized slide-tape program* to be used with all city workers. It included an overview of city workers on the job; the reasons for city workers to be concerned about back care; the workings of the back; postures that abuse or wear out the back; and tips for posture correction, effective spinal rest, low-stress body mechanics, and exercise and fitness.

The synchronized slide-tape program included 35 mm slides, sequenced and numbered; a programmed audiocassette cued with audible and inaudible (1000 Hz) tones; and the written script with slide cues indicated for manual delivery. This format allowed for delivery in three possible ways: by using equipment that automatically synchronized the slide with the tape; by using a tape player with a slide projector; or by reading the script and manually advancing a slide projector. The intended uses of this comprehensive slide-tape package were for basic, continuing back safety programs for city employees, for new employee orientation, and for retraining of injured employees returning to work.

The therapists also developed short departmentalized slide programs with written scripts that covered back care, safety, and body mechanics for each of the eight previously identified departments. The slides for the departments' programs were sequenced and numbered, and the scripts included written cues for slide advance during manual delivery.

The train-the-trainer approach included a two-day *instructor training course*. Department heads and supervisors were selected to attend as representatives of their respective departments. The goal of the course was to train the trainers so that they would be able to explain basic spinal anatomy, mechanics, and degeneration; to describe the causes of spinal stress associated with work postures and movements; to identify stressful postures and work habits among employees; to teach the principles of spinal care and low-stress body mechanics; and to conduct training sessions in practical body mechanics with their employees' participation. Trainers completed a questionnaire at the end of the course (see Appendix 8-A).

The therapists developed a 300-page *trainers' manual* for use as a reference during the training session. It was also designed to be used afterward by the trainers as a resource on back care and back injuries. It included the following:

1. A pretest and a posttest
2. The background and the rationale for development of the program
3. An overview of all materials available for program delivery
4. All program scripts
5. A sample format for a program
6. Spinal anatomy and mechanics
7. An overview of treatments used in the management of back pain
8. Principles of rest, posture, and body mechanics
9. Principles of exercise and fitness
10. Simple exercises for back care, stretching, and warm-up
11. Principles of job analysis
12. Teaching concepts and guidelines

13. Analyses of jobs in all departments covered
14. Guidelines for data collection, implementation, and follow-up.

The posttest is reproduced in Appendix 8-B.

The city for which the program was developed agreed to the program's being reproduced by the company employing the therapists so that other cities across the United States could benefit. This decision was made before program development. Consequently representatives from more than 50 cities participated in the instructor training courses conducted by the therapists, and most purchased the materials. Also the train-the-trainers approach was used with numerous industries.

The posttest scores were significantly better than the pretest scores in all instructor training courses, and the vast majority of participants' surveys were very positive. Because of the nature of city government, the statistical impact in terms of incidence and costs was very difficult to secure.

Three-Tiered Training

The therapists used a three-tiered training approach with GTE Domestic Telcos to reach 100,000 employees. The therapists and the corporate director of employee safety orchestrated the development of this program. The safety directors from Telcos divisions across the continental United States and Hawaii were involved in editing the scripts and the other materials at various stages. The therapists used local GTE facilities for observing work, interviewing employees, and photographing activity. A GTE training center housed geographically close to the therapists was used for developing the basic video and support materials. Slides were taken for specific department programs, and scripts were written for the basic and department programs by the therapists. GTE trainers nationwide participated in the instructor training course. These trainers then trained "leaders," who were supervisors from the field, and the leaders in turn trained employees.

The corporate director of employee safety reported a 22 percent reduction in total claims and a 25 percent reduction ($600,000) in direct medical and indemnity expenses for workers' compensation. He stated that he felt the program was at least partially responsible for the reductions.

Safety journals and books have published articles on other injury prevention programs (Fitzler, 1982; Isernhagen, 1988; Morris, 1984). Only one study has included control groups; it demonstrated back school effectiveness (Bergquist-Ullman, 1977).

Health Promotion

The author found limited documentation of occupational therapists providing health promotion services. Kirchman, Reichenbach, and Giambalvo (1982) have described preventive activities and services for the well elderly. Lindsay (1983) has documented the occupational therapist's role in the treatment of alcoholism. The treatment was provided in a clinical setting; however, in the author's opinion this type of service could be used as health promotion when set up as an employee assistance program. Johnson has written a book on her concepts of wellness (1986a) and has summarized her beliefs on the implications of wellness for occupational therapists (1986b). Elias and Murphy (1986) suggest ways for researchers more confidently to attribute cost reductions to health promotion activities. Allen (1986) describes consulting in an office environment to provide work-site health programs. Maynard (1986) outlines a role for occupational therapists in an employee assistance program aimed at health promotion and disease prevention. Kaplan and Burch-Minakan (1986) write about a promotion program at New England Telephone called Reach Out for Health. Rider (1986) reviews health promotion activities and assesses the degree to which health promotion concepts have been integrated into educational curricula.

Mann, Edwards, and Baum (1986) describe the potential for involvement of occupational therapists in a program for promoting the quality of life of older adults. The Older Adult Service and Information System (OASIS) offers people choices after retirement. The program is based on the theory that actively involved older adults are less likely than inactive ones to succumb to many of the chronic infirmities of old age.

Other health care providers have documented more diverse health promotion programs. Tate (1987) has reported practices at the Food and Machinery Corporation (FMC) and at American Telephone & Telegraph (AT&T). They are briefly described in the following sections, along with two other health promotion programs.

FMC Health Promotion

At FMC a Well Aware program was used. It focused on developing baseline information on the health status of FMC workers and their families. It was also designed to identify risk factors, to promote wellness programs that would reduce the risk factors and injuries, to increase the level of consumer information, and to enhance employees' consumer skills.

The data collection phase included detailed surveys completed by workers, which focused on their health habits and interest levels; a health risk assessment; and analysis of long-term disability disease categories and medical claims data. Participation was voluntary. Each location determined the incentives to offer employees participating in the program, the smoking policy, the types of food to be available as an alternative to the normal fare, and the types of exercise programs to be offered.

The core program included topics such as wellness standards for nutrition, stress management, smoking cessation, and exercise. It also addressed problem areas such as digestive diseases and arthritis. Prevention of cancer and cardiovascular diseases was included. The employees were taught how to talk with physicians about treatment and medications and how to arrange for second opinions when appropriate.

The corporate staff established targets for employee participation to be achieved by 1988. The goals were that 60 percent of the work force would participate in some type of motivational program or lecture and 30 percent would engage in specific behavioral change programs. Results are being accumulated.

AT&T Health Promotion

AT&T introduced a program of wellness and health promotion called the Total Life Concept. The program included health-risk appraisals and evaluations and a variety of interventions such as stress management, weight control, and smoking cessation.

AT&T also established an Employee Assistance Program (EAP) in 1981 to deal with all debilitating problems that affected workers' well-being, alcohol and drug abuse among them. The EAP staff included recovering alcoholics, social workers, a priest, a minister, and a lawyer who also had a degree in counseling. The impact of the two programs had not been evaluated at the time this chapter was written.

Health and Religion Project

The Health and Religion Project in Rhode Island demonstrated creativity in employing a credible, accessible source. It used 20 churches (Roman Catholic, Baptist, and Episcopal) to deliver behavior change programming on major cardiovascular risk factors. Smoking, elevated blood pressure, elevated serum cholesterol, excess weight, and physical inactivity were addressed (Lasater, Wells, Carleton, & Elder, 1986).

Massachusetts Department of Public Health

The Massachusetts Department of Public Health began an aggressive statewide program to prevent deaths from heart disease, cancer, and cerebrovascular disease through a reduction in their underlying risk factors. The following facts prompted the program:

1. Heart disease, cancer, and cerebrovascular disease together cause more than two out of three deaths in the United States annually.
2. These three diseases are largely a result of widespread risk factors such as smoking, unhealthy diet, high blood pressure, physical inactivity, and environmental toxic exposure.
3. The prevalence of these risk factors can be significantly lowered, resulting in major reductions in mortality rates for the three diseases.

In five years the program is estimated to have saved at least 2,000 lives annually (Havas & Walker, 1986).

Design of Injury Prevention and Health Promotion Programs

Program design depends on the company's and the provider's objectives. Some health promotion or injury prevention programs may be offered through government grants, through research, or as a free service, whereas others may be conducted for profit. Occasionally feasibility studies are marketed at no charge or for a nominal fee before contracts are issued for more costly programs. Drawing on computerized reports of medical claims data generally collected by risk managers, benefit directors, and insurance carriers, the feasibility study can identify and prioritize the diseases and the injuries that can be affected and can discover program options. Additionally the feasibility study serves as a basis against which the proposed program outcomes can be measured.

Health-Risk Appraisals

Available surveys or health-risk appraisals can also serve as a basis for program design. Health-risk appraisals are self-scored questionnaires or computer programs that use demographic and risk-factor data to estimate the most likely causes of death and to provide guidance on how to reduce the risk of death. They also serve to motivate employees to modify negative habits and life-styles (Fletcher & Smith, 1986).

National Health Surveys

On a more global basis the Health Promotion and Disease Prevention component of the 1985 National Health Interview Survey can serve as a basis for designing health promotion programs. For example, this survey measured the nation's progress in achieving its 1990 objectives concerning cigarette

Table 8-1
Part of Body Injured in 1986 Work Accidents

Eyes	90,000
Head (except eyes)	110,000
Arms	160,000
Trunk	580,000
Hands	90,000
Fingers	250,000
Legs	230,000
Feet	70,000
Toes	40,000
General	180,000

Note. From *Accident Facts* (1987 ed.) (p. 33) by National Safety Council, 1987, Chicago: Author. © 1987 by National Safety Council. Reprinted by permission.

smoking. The survey indicated that the first smoking-related objective, to reduce to below 25 percent the proportion of the U.S. population who smoke, has not been achieved. Thirty-one percent of the U.S. population smoke. Greater than 85 percent are aware of the special risk to smokers of developing or making worse chronic obstructive lung disease, chronic bronchitis, and emphysema. Greater than 90 percent are aware that smoking is a major cause of lung cancer; however, awareness of the risk of laryngeal, esophageal, bladder, and other kinds of cancer from smoking is not as high. Finally, greater than 85 percent are aware that cigarette smoking is one of the major risk factors for heart disease (Shopland & Brown, 1987). Many companies now provide smoking cessation classes for their employees.

As a second example, a nutrition objective for the United States is that by 1990, 50 percent of the overweight population will have adopted weight regimens, balancing diet and physical activity. In the 1985 National Health Interview Survey, more than half of the overweight respondents were trying to lose weight, and almost half of this group reported both increasing their physical activity and decreasing their intake of calories. The next most common weight-loss regimen was dietary restriction without exercise. This finding suggests that educational efforts should emphasize the need to increase physical activity as part of appropriate weight-loss regimens (Stephenson, Levy, Sass, & McGarvey, 1987).

Injury Statistics

Regarding accidents, injuries, and occupational disease, National Safety Council (1987) data (see Table 8-1) can serve as a basis for development of general prevention programs.

Some state safety associations and workers' compensation commissions also keep injury statistics. In most cases this information is available for a fee. The Worker's Compensation Research Institute in Boston, Massachusetts, is another source. Its membership consists of representatives from insurance companies and corporations.

Socioeconomic Considerations Relating to Employees

Socioeconomic and educational levels of the consumer are critical variables to consider in designing a program. As an example, younger adults and the more highly educated have been found to be more knowledgeable about appropriate weight-loss regimens (Stephenson et al., 1987). On the basis of the author's experience, the following factors are also recommended for consideration in designing programs:

1. Various languages may be spoken by employees within an organization. Employees who speak a language other than English may not be able to read English or their own language.
2. Written materials used alone are rarely read. Visuals are much more effective: "A picture is worth a thousand words."
3. Too much detail crowds out the main message. Remember the KISS ("Keep it short and simple") principle when speaking or developing handouts.
5. Bear in mind cultural values when attempting to establish credibility with audiences. Some conservative American males and some foreign-born males may not be very receptive to female presenters.
6. A program design that allows audiences to remain passive stands little chance of creating an impact. Include a session in which participants can apply what they have learned (e.g., exercises or lifting) and allow some time afterward to check their understanding (e.g., with a posttest).

Marketing

Developing credibility is the first step in building referral sources. For most therapists this initially occurs with such successful client outcomes that expert status in a certain injury or disease area is established. However, many experts fall to novice status when approaching businesses or the community with programs. The most successful programs include experts in the subject disease or injury, in marketing and sales, and in program design and implementation (including public relations and presentations).

Marketing Plan

According to Barnett (1984), a good marketing plan consists of four steps: developing a good product or service; pricing it fairly; making it readily available to the consumer; and communicating and promoting it effectively. The basic purpose of promotion is to facilitate the movement of information through the marketing network. Communicating and promoting has four (potential) aspects: advertising; personal selling; sales promotion; and publicity.

Business cards, brochures, advertisements, and trade shows are excellent marketing tools. All too often, through an unplanned conversation therapists find a potential consumer and secure his or her business card, but have no business card to give in return. As for brochures, none at all is better than a sloppy or unprofessional one. Typographical errors and inaccurate information immediately dispel professional credibility. Advertisements placed in media commonly read or viewed by the consumer can over time create name recognition for the service provider. Identifying the appropriate radio or television station and time spot or identifying the trade journal or magazine most commonly read by the consumer requires research. Press releases to media sources can lead to free publicity by prompting interviews and articles on programs. Speaking, exhibiting, and mingling at trade shows or professional conferences allow for excellent exposure to the consumer if the events are properly selected.

The real test of the service is the program outcome or benefit perceived by the consumer. Documented outcomes then become valuable marketing tools and references for future consumers. Quotes from previous consumers in brochures, copies of letters from consumers documenting program outcomes, and a list of references with addresses and phone numbers reinforce program credibility. No one should be listed as a reference who has not specifically given consent.

Future Work Force Trends and Opportunities

According to *Workforce 2000,* a publication by the Hudson Institute (1987), four key trends will shape the last years of the 20th century:[1]

1. *The American economy should grow at a relatively healthy pace,* boosted by a rebound in U.S. exports, renewed productivity growth, and a strong world economy.

---

[1]From *Workforce 2000* (p. xiii) by the Hudson Institute, 1987, Indianapolis: Author. © 1987 by Hudson Institute. Reprinted by permission.

2. Despite its international comeback, *U.S. manufacturing will be a much smaller share of the economy in the year 2000* than it is today. Service industries will create all of the new jobs, and most of the new wealth . . .
3. *The workforce will grow slowly, becoming older, more female, and more disadvantaged.* Only 15 percent of the new entrants to the labor force . . . will be native white males, compared to 47 percent in that category today.
4. *The new jobs in service industries will demand much higher skill levels* than the jobs of today. Very few new jobs will be created for those who cannot read, follow directions, and use mathematics. Ironically, the demographic trends in the workforce, coupled with the higher skill requirements of the economy, will lead to both higher and lower unemployment: more joblessness among the least-skilled and less among the most educationally advantaged.

Workforce 2000 also identifies important policy issues: Those who determine policy must find ways to—[2]

- *Stimulate Balanced World Growth:* To grow rapidly, the U.S. must pay less attention to its share of world trade and more to the growth of the economies of the other nations of the world, including those nations in Europe, Latin America, and Asia with whom the U.S. competes.
- *Accelerate Productivity Increases in Service Industries:* Prosperity will depend much more on how fast output per worker increases in health care, education, retailing, government, and other services than on gains in manufacturing.
- *Maintain the Dynamism of an Aging Workforce:* As the average age of American workers climbs toward 40, the nation must insure that its workforce and its institutions do not lose their adaptability and willingness to learn.
- *Reconcile the Conflicting Needs of Women, Work, and Families:* Three-fifths of all women over age 16 will be at work in the year 2000. Yet most current policies and institutions covering pay, fringe benefits, time away from work, pensions, welfare, and other issues were designed for a society in which men worked and women stayed home.

---

[2]From *Workforce 2000* (p. xiv) by the Hudson Institute, 1987, Indianapolis: Author. © 1987 by Hudson Institute. Reprinted by permission.

- *Integrate Black and Hispanic Workers Fully into the Economy:* The shrinking numbers of young people, the rapid pace of industrial change, and the ever-rising skill requirements of the emerging economy make the task of fully utilizing minority workers particularly urgent between now and 2000. Both cultural changes and education and training investments will be needed to create real equal employment opportunity.
- *Improve the Educational Preparation of All Workers:* As the economy grows more complex and more dependent on human capital, the standards set by the American education system must be raised.

Occupational therapists can directly influence (2) through (4) by providing injury prevention and health promotion services. Appropriate preplacement screening can favorably affect productivity. Various health promotion services can directly fortify the dynamism of an aging work force. Creative health promotion strategies can assist in reconciling the conflicting needs of women, work, and families. Relationships established with benefit directors for the usual health promotion services can be a foundation for exploring options for resolving the conflicting needs.

The market exists for occupational therapists to explore. However, only cost-effective, well-marketed services will survive. Television, radio, and printed materials have educated the public on health costs and benefits. Physical fitness programs have been made widely available through health spas, community centers, and home videos. The high cost of medical care in an aging society has convinced many to take their health seriously. Additionally HMOs (health maintenance organizations), DRGs (diagnosis-related groups), mandatory second opinions, preadmission screenings, and medical bill audits have coerced the medical community and the patient into accountability. Risk managers have broadened the scope of their jobs from ascertaining the amount of necessary insurance coverage to constructing creative insurance packages, self-insurance, and health promotion.

Awareness of the need for injury prevention and health promotion has been heightened in corporations, communities, and individuals. The challenge is to convince a company or other consumer that one's service can meet its needs cost-effectively.

Summary

The practice of health promotion and disease or injury prevention has become critically important in health care. Traditionally, occupational therapists have been providers of tertiary prevention, that is, rehabilitative programs aimed at reducing the aftereffects of a presenting problem or illness. Recently, occupational therapists, along with psychologists, counselors, and physical therapists, have begun to provide prevention services as a spin-off of treatment experiences. These services have mainly taken the form of employee training. However, opportunities exist in job-site redesign and preplacement screening. They also have emerged in the realm of health promotion and wellness. Increasing the productivity of workers, maintaining the dynamism of an aging work force, and reconciling the conflicting needs of women, work, and families are compelling policy issues of the 1990s that occupational therapists can directly address through prevention and health promotion services.

Glossary

Adverse impact—the disproportionate exclusionary effect of a policy or a practice on a class (women and minorities) protected by legislation.

Dynamic strength test—a screening test for jobs, performed by having the candidate pull against a handle that moves at a set rate. A load cell monitors the force exerted.

Health promotion—programs that enhance health or foster wellness; "systematic efforts by an organization to enhance the wellness of its members through education, behavior change, and cultural support" (Jaffe, 1987).

Isometric strength test—the most frequently documented form of a screening test for jobs, performed by having the candidate pull against a handle that will not move. A load cell or a strain gauge monitors the force exerted.

Maximal testing—testing the individual to his or her maximum (i.e., to exhaustion) and monitoring the oxygen uptake.

Occupation—"the active or 'doing' process of a person engaged in goal-directed, intrinsically gratifying, and culturally appropriate activity" (Evans, 1987, p. 627).

Preplacement screening—a prevention strategy to ensure that workers have the basic physical abilities needed to meet the job requirements. *Employee selection* and *preemployment screening* are synonymous terms.

Prevention—services targeted at preventing injury, illness, or disease.

Primary prevention—activities undertaken before the onset of disease. The goal is to avoid the occurrence of disease or disability and to build resistance in a population potentially at risk.

Secondary prevention—early diagnosis and treatment with the intent of preventing the condition from becoming serious or permanently disabling.

Tertiary prevention—rehabilitative programs that are aimed at reducing the aftereffects of a presenting problem or illness. Tertiary prevention is more remedial than primary or secondary prevention and is directed at preventing further loss or disability.

Submaximal step testing—testing in which the candidate wears a heart rate monitor while stepping on and off a bench 10 inches high at a pace set by a metronome. Usually the test consists of up to three stages of stepping for 3 minutes each. A faster stepping pace is required at each successive stage. The candidate only progresses to the next stage if the heart rate is below 65 percent of the maximum.

Treatment—services targeted at remediating a health problem that already exists.

Wellness—"the process of adapting patterns of behavior that lead to improved health and heightened life satisfaction" (Jaffe, 1987).

References

Age Discrimination Act of 1975, Pub. L. No. 94-135, 42 U.S.C. 6101 (1982 and Supp. V 1987).

Allen, V. R. (1986). Health promotion in the office. *American Journal of Occupational Therapy, 40,* 764–769.

American Occupational Therapy Association. (1979, April). *Occupation as the common core of occupational therapy* (Policy 1.12). Rockville, MD: Author.

American Occupational Therapy Association. (1979). The role of the occupational therapist in the promotion of health and prevention of disabilities [Position paper]. *American Journal of Occupational Therapy, 33,* 50–51.

Anderson, C. K. (1988). *Strength and endurance testing for preemployment placement.* Unpublished paper, Back Systems, Dallas, TX.

Anderson, C. K., & Catterall, M. J. (1987a). The impact of physical ability testing on incidence rate, severity rate, and productivity. In S. S. Asfour (Ed.), *Trends in ergonomics/human factors* (Vol. 4, pp. 577–584). Amsterdam, Netherlands: Elsevier Science Publishers.

Anderson, C. K., & Catterall, M. J. (1987b). A simple redesign strategy for storage of heavy objects. *Professional Safety, 32*(11), 35–38.

Anderson, C. K., & Herrin, G. D. (1980). *Validation study of preplacement strength testing at Dayton Tire and Rubber Company* (Technical Report). Ann Arbor, MI: University of Michigan, Center for Ergonomics.

Armstrong, T. J. (1983). *An ergonomics guide to carpal tunnel syndrome* (Ergonomics Guides). Akron, OH: American Industrial Hygiene Association.

Armstrong, T. J., & Chaffin, D. B. (1979). Some biomechanical aspects of the carpal tunnel. *Journal of Biomechanics, 12,* 567–570.

Armstrong, T. J, Fine, L. J., Goldstein, S. A., Lifshitz, Y. R., & Silverstein, B. A. (1987). Ergonomics considerations in hand and wrist tendinitis. *Journal of Hand Surgery, 12A*(5, Pt. 2), 830–837.

Arndt, R. (1987). Work pace, stress, and cumulative trauma disorders. *Journal of Hand Surgery 12A*(5, Pt. 2), 866–869.

Arnold, J. D., Rauschenberger, J. M., Soubel, W. G., & Guion, R. M. (1982). Validation and utility of a strength test for selecting steelworkers. *Journal of Applied Psychology, 67,* 588–604.

Ayoub, M. (1973). Work place design and posture. *Human Factors, 15,* 265–268.

Ayoub, M. M. (1983). Design of a preplacement screening program. In T. O. Kvalseth (Ed.), *Ergonomics of workstation design* (pp. 152–185). London: Butterworths.

Ayoub, M. M., Fernandez, J. E., & Smith, J. L. (n.d.). *Design of workplace.* Lubbock, TX: Texas Tech University, Institute for Ergonomics Research.

Barnett, J. (1984). *Promotion management.* St. Paul, MN: West Publishing.

Bear-Lehman, J. (1983). Factors affecting return to work after hand injury. *American Journal of Occupational Therapy, 37,* 189–194.

Bergquist-Ullman, M. (1977). Acute low back pain in industry. *Acta Orthopaedica Scandinavica, 170,* 9–103.

Bettencourt, C. M., Carlstrom, P., Brown, S. H., Lindau, K., & Long, C. M. (1986). Using work simulation to treat adults with back injuries. *American Journal of Occupational Therapy, 40,* 12–18.

Bevin, A. G. (1986). The carpal tunnel syndrome. *Seminars in Occupational Medicine, 1,* 131–139.

Boyd, M. M., Bryan, T., Hannah, J., Mangia, M., & Paul, B. (1987, December 24). Work simulation keeps industrial workers on the road to recovering from injury. *O.T. Week, 1*(49), 4–5.

Cady, L. D., Bischoff, D. P., O'Connell, E. R., Thomas, P. C., & Allan, J. H. (1979). Strength and fitness and subsequent back injuries in firefighters. *Journal of Occupational Medicine, 21,* 269–272.

Cannon, L., Bernaacki, E., & Walter, S. (1981). Personal and occupational factors associated with carpal tunnel syndrome. *Journal of Occupational Medicine, 23,* 255–258.

Carlsoo, S. (1982). The effect of vibration on the skeleton, joints, and muscles: A review of the literature. *Applied Ergonomics, 13,* 251–258.

Chaffin, D. B. (1975). Ergonomics guide for the assessment of human static strength. *American Industrial Hygiene Association Journal, 36,* 505–511.

Chaffin, D. B. (1981). Functional assessment for heavy physical labor. *Occupational Health and Safety, 50*(1), 24–64.

Chaffin, D. B., Herrin, G. D., Keyserling, W. M., & Foulke, J. A. (1977). *Pre-employment strength testing in selecting workers for materials handling jobs* (NIOSH Contract No. CDC 99-74-62). Cincinnati, OH: National Institute for Occupational Safety and Health, Physiology and Ergonomics Branch.

Civil Rights Act of 1964, Title VII, Pub. L. No. 88-352, 42 U.S.C. 2000e (1982).

Cordery, J. (1965). Joint protection: A responsibility of the occupational therapist. *American Journal of Occupational Therapy, 19,* 285–293.

Datta, S. R., & Ramanthan, N. L. (1969). Energy expenditure in work predicted from heart rate and pulmonary ventilation. *Journal of Applied Physiology, 26,* 297–302.

Dortch, H. L., & Trombly, C. A. (1989, April). *Prevention of cumulative trauma disorders through education.* Paper presented at the annual conference of the American Occupational Therapy Association, Baltimore.

Egbert, L. D., Battit, G. E., Welch, C. E., et al. (1964). Reduction of postoperative pain by encouragement and instruction of patients: A study of doctor-patient rapport. *New England Journal of Medicine, 270,* 825–827.

Elias, W. S., & Murphy, R. J. (1986). The case for health promotion programs containing health care costs: A review of the literature. *American Journal of Occupational Therapy, 40,* 759–763.

Ellexson, M. T. (1986). The unique role of OT in industry. *Occupational Therapy in Health Care, 2*(4), 35–46.

Ergonomics and the changing role of the occupational health nurse. (1985). Sponsored by the Dallas and Fort Worth Area Association of Occupational Health Nurses and the University of Texas at Arlington, School of Nursing, Arlington, Texas.

Evans, K. A. (1987). Definition of occupation as the core concept of occupational therapy [Nationally Speaking]. *American Journal of Occupational Therapy, 41,* 627–628.

Feldman, R. G., Goldman, R., & Keyserling, W. M. (1983). Peripheral nerve entrapment syndromes and ergonomic factors. *American Journal of Industrial Medicine, 4,* 661–681.

Fisher, G. (1989, April). *A winning combination: Occupational therapists and occupational health services.* Paper presented at the annual conference of the American Occupational Therapy Association, Baltimore.

Fitzler, S. (1982, February). Attitudinal change: The Chelsea back program. *Occupational Health and Safety,* pp. 24–27.

Fletcher, D. J., & Smith, G. L. (1986). Health-risk appraisal: Helping patients predict and prevent health problems. *Postgraduate Medicine, 80,* 69–71, 74–76, 81–82.

Florey, L. L., & Michelman, S. M. (1982). Occupational role history: A screening tool for psychiatric occupational therapy. *American Journal of Occupational Therapy, 36,* 301–308.

Flower, A., Naxon, E., Jones, R. E., & Mooney, V. (1981). An occupational therapy program for chronic back pain. *American Journal of Occupational Therapy, 35,* 243–248.

Galvin, D. (1983). Health promotion and disability management and rehabilitation at the workplace. *Internnector* (newsletter of the University Center for International Rehabilitation, Michigan State University, East Lansing, MI), *4*(2), 1–6.

Goodro, S. (1986, April). *Cardiovascular wellness: An approach to preventive health care.* Paper presented at the annual conference of the American Occupational Therapy Association, Minneapolis.

Hall, C. D. (1986). *The carpal tunnel syndrome: Occupational problems in medical practice.* Wilmington, DE: Medical Publications.

Harrand, G. M., & Hoffman, P. R. (1980, Spring/Summer). The physical capacity evaluation. *National Reporter* (published by Stout Vocational Rehabilitation Institute, School of Education and Human Services, University of Wisconsin).

Havas, S., & Walker, B. (1986). Massachusetts' approach to the prevention of heart disease, cancer, and stroke. *Public Health Report, 101,* 29–39.

Healy, K. (1968). Does preoperative instruction really make a difference? *American Journal of Nursing, 68,* 62–67.

Heck, S. A. (1988). The effect of purposeful activity on pain tolerance. *American Journal of Occupational Therapy, 42,* 577–581.

Herrin, G. D., Kochkin, S., & Scott, V. (1982). *Development of an employee strength assessment program for United Airlines* (Technical Report). Ann Arbor, MI: University of Michigan, Center for Ergonomics.

Hertfelder, S., & Gwin, C. (1986, April). *HMOs: A new practice arena.* Paper presented at the annual conference of the American Occupational Therapy Association, Minneapolis.

Hightower-Vandamm, M. D. (1981). The role of occupational therapy in vocational evaluation, Part 1. *American Journal of Occupational Therapy, 35,* 563–565.

Hodges, J., Bentley, K., & Palmer, T. (1984, October 11–12). *Private sector job safety programs: H.C.B. Contractors.* Testimony presented at a joint meeting of the Texas Job Injury Interagency Council and the Texas Job Injury Advisory Committee, Austin, TX.

Holmes, D. (1985). The role of the occupational therapist—Work evaluator. *American Journal of Occupational Therapy, 39,* 308–313.

Hook, T. W. (1986). A private practice work evaluation unit. *Occupational Therapy in Health Care, 2*(4), 59–65.

Howe, M. C., Weaver, C. T., & Dulay, J. (1981). The development of a work-oriented day center program. *American Journal of Occupational Therapy, 35,* 711–718.

Huhn, R. R., & Volski, R. V. (1985). Primary prevention programs for business and industry: Role of physical therapists. *Physical Therapy, 65,* 1840–1844.

Isernhagen, S. (1988). Back schools. In S. Isernhagen (Ed.), *Work injury: Management and prevention* (pp. 19–28). Rockville, MD: Aspen.

Isernhagen, S. (Ed.). (1988). *Work injury: Management and prevention.* Rockville, MD: Aspen.

Jaffe, E. (1986). The role of occupational therapy in disease prevention and health promotion [Nationally Speaking]. *American Journal of Occupational Therapy, 40,* 749–752.

Jaffe, E. (1987, October 22–25). *Occupational therapy's role in health promotion and wellness: The right to health.* Paper presented at the 53rd Annual Conference and Institutes of the Texas Occupational Therapy Association, Austin, Texas.

Jaffe, E., & Gray, M. (1986, April). *Occupational therapy's role in health promotion and wellness.* Paper presented at the annual conference of the American Occupational Therapy Association, Minneapolis.

Johnson, J. A. (1986a). *Wellness: A context for living.* Thorofare, NJ: Slack.

Johnson, J. A. (1986b). Wellness and occupational therapy. *American Journal of Occupational Therapy, 40,* 753–758.

Kaplan, L. H., & Burch-Minakan, L. (1986). Reach Out for Health: A corporation's approach to health promotion. *American Journal of Occupational Therapy, 40,* 777–780.

Kasch, F. W., Phillips, W. H., Ross, W. D., Carter, J. E., & Boyer, J. L. (1972). A comparison of maximal oxygen uptake by treadmill and step-test procedures. *Journal of Applied Physiology, 21,* 1387–1388.

Kaye, R. L., & Hammond, A. H. (1978). Understanding rheumatoid arthritis: Evaluation of a patient education program. *JAMA, 239,* 2466–2467.

Keyserling, W. M., Herrin, G. D., & Chaffin, D. B. (1980). Isometric strength testing as a means of controlling medical incidents on strenuous jobs. *Journal of Occupational Medicine, 22,* 332–336.

Keyserling, W. M., Herrin, D. B., Chaffin, D. B., Armstrong, T. A., & Foss, M. L. (1980). Establishing an industrial strength testing program. *American Industrial Hygiene Association Journal, 41,* 730–736.

Kielhofner, G., & Burke, J. P. (1980). A model of human occupation, Part 1: Conceptual framework and content. *American Journal of Occupational Therapy, 34,* 572–581.

Kirchman, M. M., Reichenbach, V., & Giambalvo, B. (1982). Preventive activities and services for the well elderly. *American Journal of Occupational Therapy, 36,* 236–242.

Lasater, T. M., Wells, B. L., Carleton, R. A., & Elder, J. P. (1986). The role of churches in disease prevention research studies. *Public Health Report, 101,* 125–131.

Laughery, K. R., & Jackson, A. S. (1984). *Pre-employment physical test development for roustabout jobs on offshore platforms* (Technical Report). Oklahoma City, OK: Kerr Mcgee.

Levine, P. H., & Britten, A. F. (1973). Supervised patient-management of hemophilia: A study of 45 patients with hemophilia A and B. *Annals of Internal Medicine, 78,* 195–201.

Liles, D. H., Deivanayagam, S., Ayoub, M. M., & Mahajan, P. (1984). A job severity index for the evaluation and control of lifting injury. *Human Factors, 26,* 683–693.

Lindsay, W. P. (1983). The role of the occupational therapist—Treatment of alcoholism. *American Journal of Occupational Therapy, 37,* 36–43.

Lutz, G., & Hansford, T. (1987). Cumulative trauma disorder controls: The ergonomics program at Ethicon, Inc. *Journal of Hand Surgery, 12A*(2, Pt. 2), 863–866.

Mann, M., Edwards, D., & Baum, C. M. (1986). OASIS: A new concept for promoting the quality of life for older adults. *American Journal of Occupational Therapy, 40,* 784–786.

Masear, V. R., Hayes, J. M., & Hyde, A. G. (1986) An industrial cause of carpal tunnel syndrome. *Journal of Hand Surgery, 11A,* 222–227.

Mayer, T. G., Gatchel, R. J., Kishino, N., Kelley, J., Capra, P., Mayer, H., Barnett, J., & Mooney, V. (1985). Objective assessment of spine function following industrial injury: A prospective study with comparison group and one-year follow-up (1985 Volvo Award in Clinical Sciences). *Spine, 10,* 482–493.

Mayer, T. G., Gatchel, R. J., Mayer, H., Kishino, N. D., Keeley, J., & Mooney, V. (1987). A prospective two-year study of functional restoration in industrial low back injury. *JAMA, 258,* 1763–1767.

Maynard, M. (1986). Health promotion through employee assistance programs: A role for occupational therapists. *American Journal of Occupational Therapy, 40,* 771–776.

McArdle, W. D., Katch, F. I., Pechar, G. S., Jacobson, L., & Ruck, S. (1972). Reliability and interrelationships between maximal oxygen intake, physical work capacity and step-test scores in college women. *Medicine and Science in Sports, 4,* 182–186.

McCormack, G. L. (1988). Pain management by occupational therapists. *American Journal of Occupational Therapy, 42,* 582–590.

Meyer, A. (1977). The philosophy of occupational therapy. *American Journal of Occupational Therapy, 31,* 639–642.

Miner, M. G., & Miner, J. B. (1979). *Employee selection within the law*. Washington, DC: Bureau of National Affairs.

Montgomery, C. (1976). Pre-employment back x-rays. *Journal of Occupational Medicine, 18,* 495–498.

Morris, A. (1984). Program compliance key to injury prevention. *Occupational Health and Safety, 53*(3), 44–48.

Morris, A. (1985). Identifying workers at risk to back injury is not guesswork. *Occupational Health and Safety, 55*(12), 16–20.

Morris, A., & Randolph, J. (1984). Back rehabilitation programs speed recovery of injured workers. *Occupational Health and Safety, 53*(7), 53–55, 64, 66, 68.

Muffly-Elsey, D., & Flinn-Wagner, S. (1987). Proposed screening tool for the detection of cumulative trauma disorders of the upper extremity. *Journal of Hand Surgery, 12A*(5, Pt. 2), 931–935.

National Institute of Occupational Safety and Health. (1981). *Work practices guide for manual lifting* (Technical Report No. 81-122). Cincinnati, OH: U.S. Department of Health and Human Services.

National Safety Council. (1987). *Accident facts* (1987 ed.). Chicago: Author.

Paulson, K. (1986, April). *Health promotion as purposeful activity*. Paper presented at the annual conference of the American Occupational Therapy Association, Minneapolis.

Randolph, J. W. (1984). The role of occupational therapy in back school. *Occupational Therapy in Health Care, 1*(3), 93–102.

Rehabilitation Act of 1973, Pub. L. No. 93-112, 29 U.S.C. 701 (1982).

Reilly, R. R., Zedeck, S., & Tenopyr, M. L. (1979). Validity and fairness of physical ability tests for predicting performance in craft jobs. *Journal of Applied Psychology, 64,* 262–274.

Reitz, S. (1984, April). *Preventive health: Essential component for occupational therapy*. Paper presented at the annual conference of the American Occupational Therapy Association, Kansas City, MO.

Rider, B. A., & White, V. K. (1986). Occupational therapy education in health promotion and disease prevention. *American Journal of Occupational Therapy, 40,* 781–783.

Rosenberg, S. G. (1971). Patient education leads to better care for heart patients. *HSMHA Health Report, 86,* 793–802.

Seaton, M. K., & Slama, P. B. (1989, April). *Evaluating interrelationships between worker traits and job tasks*. Paper presented at the annual conference of the American Occupational Therapy Association, Baltimore.

Shealy, N. (1984, April). *The caring relationship*. Speech delivered at the annual conference of the American Occupational Therapy Association, Kansas City, MO.

Shopland, D. R., & Brown, C. (1987). Toward the 1990 objectives for smoking: Measuring the progress with 1985 NHIS data. *Public Health Report, 102,* 68–73.

Silverstein, B. A., Fine, L. J., & Armstrong, T. J. (1986). Carpal tunnel syndrome: Causes and a preventive strategy. *Seminars in Occupational Medicine, 1*(3), 213–221.

Silverstein, B. A., Fine, L. J., & Armstrong, T. J. (1987). Occupational factors and carpal tunnel syndrone. *American Journal of Industrial Medicine, 11,* 343–358.

Smith, E., Sonstegard, D. A., & Anderson, W. H., Jr. (1977). Contribution of flexor tendons to carpal tunnel syndrome. *Archives of Physical Medicine and Rehabilitation, 58,* 379–385.

Snook, S. (1978). The design of manual material handling tasks. *Ergonomics, 21,* 963–985.

Snook, S. (1983). The perspective of industry. In *Proceedings on industrial low back pain* (conference sponsored by the University of Vermont, Rehabilitation Engineering Center, and the University of Iowa, Department of Orthopedic Surgery). Burlington, VT.

Stephenson, M. G., Levy, A. S., Sass, N. L., & McGarvey, W. E. (1987). 1985 NHIS findings: Nutrition knowledge and baseline data for the weight-loss objectives. *Public Health Report, 102,* 61–67.

Tate, D. G. (1987). The healthy organization: Disability management and health promotion practices at the workplace. *Journal of Rehabilitation, 53,* 63–66.

White, V. K. (1986). Promoting health and wellness: A theme for the eighties [Guest editorial]. *American Journal of Occupational Therapy, 40,* 743–748.

Wilke, N. A., & Sheldahl, L. M. (1985). Use of simulated work testing in cardiac rehabilitation: A case report. *American Journal of Occupational Therapy, 39,* 327–330.

Chapter 8, Appendix A

TML
Instructor Course
February 27–28, 1985

Participant Survey

1. The areas of the presentation from which I received the most useful information were: (Why?)

2. I would like to see the program put more emphasis on the following areas: (Why?)

3. Because of my experience and background, the following information was repetitious and unnecessary for me:

4. Did the program meet the stated goals?

    Comments:

5. Please rate the audiovisuals used.

    Excellent _____ Good _____ Fair _____ Poor _____

    Comments:

6. Please rate the manuals and handout materials.

    Excellent _____ Good _____ Fair _____ Poor _____

    Comments:

From Back Systems, Inc., Dallas, TX.

7. What are your impressions of the instructors?

8. Do you feel prepared to train employees in the use of this program?

9. How do you think this program will be received by employees?

10. Would you be willing to serve as a reference regarding this course? If yes, please write your name on this survey.

Chapter 8, Appendix B

**TML
Trainer's Posttest**

True/False

_____ 1. Holding an object at arm's length is better for your back than holding an object close to your body.

_____ 2. Only 5 percent of the people diagnosed with back pain have disk-related problems.

_____ 3. A myelogram is a surgical procedure for reducing back pain.

_____ 4. Data collection is vital for targeting back safety efforts for your high-risk jobs.

_____ 5. First aid for back pain includes ice massage, aspirin, rest, and stretching.

_____ 6. Your "target heart rate" for exercise is the same as the maximum number of heart beats per minute considered to be safe for your age.

_____ 7. Most back pain is caused by one specific injury.

_____ 8. Ninety percent of the population will respond negatively to conservative care.

_____ 9. The training package can be used for back safety programs, during new employee orientation sessions, and with employees returning to work after a back injury.

_____ 10. The concept of "rest" while at work requires 30 minutes of time.

Multiple Choice

_____ 1. Comprehensive job analysis should include analysis of
   a. productivity standards.
   b. endurance, mental stress, and environmental stress.
   c. strength, movement patterns, and postures.
   d. both *b* and *c*.

_____ 2. Pivoting the body means
   a. dancing.
   b. taking a step and turning your body in the direction of your work.
   c. twisting and bending.

_____ 3. The goals of a back training program are
   a. to decrease the cost of accidents and compensable claims.
   b. to prevent injury and disability of employees.
   c. to decrease lost productivity due to accident/injury.
   d. all of the above.

From Back Systems, Inc., Dallas, TX.

_____ 4. When sitting for intensive work
   a. sit back in the chair and stretch your neck forward toward your work.
   b. sit on the front half of the chair with the back arched and elbows braced on the desk.
   c. adjust the chair back support for contact with the low back and bring the work toward you.
   d. both *b* and *c*.

Fill in the Blanks

1. An excessive low back arch can be controlled by _____ _____ .

2. Proper lifting of heavy objects includes holding the object _____ and planting the feet _____ .

3. Pivoting helps to prevent stressful _____ of the spine.

4. Excessive arching of the low back is commonly called _____ .

5. The structures that hold the spine together and give it posture, movement, and support are the _____ and the _____ .

6. Sitting properly includes keeping the natural curves particularly _____ and _____ level.

7. Nationally the average cost of all workers' compensation low back injuries is $_____ .

8. _____ out of five Americans will someday have back pain that will affect their ability to work.

9. The natural spinal curves are _____ , but these curves may change depending on the activity a person pursues.

10. The ideal lifting height for an individual is between his or her _____ and _____ level.

9

The Occupational Therapist as an Expert Witness

Doris J. Shriver, OTR, CVE

The occupational therapist has unique skills and may possess the expertise to testify in the litigation of such matters as personal injury, workers' compensation, and Social Security disability disputes. Although the legal preparation and presentation of evidence in any litigation is clearly the purview of the attorney, an understanding of the basic rules that govern litigation permits the occupational therapist, before the fact, to prepare testimony that is qualified and properly stated. Ideally therapists will prepare themselves with the attorney presenting them as an expert witness. However, in some cases they may be called and offered little or no assistance before testimony.

This chapter presents selected legal descriptions that generally govern the course of litigation and their potential applications to the occupational therapist as an expert witness. The language tends to be technical and requires close reading for full comprehension. The expert witness role is difficult and warrants careful study.

Rules Governing Evidence

The Federal Rules of Evidence (established by a congressional act effective July 1, 1973) generally govern the rulings on evidence in criminal and civil litigation. To achieve consistency between the Federal Rules of Evidence and uniform rules of evidence proposed by the states, the National Conference of Commissioners on Uniform State Laws, 1974, adopted new Uniform Rules of Evidence for state procedures in which the federal rules do not apply.

The laws that govern legal proceedings depend on the type of litigation. Personal injury, which includes accidents, malpractice, and product liability, is tried under civil and criminal law. Workers' compensation and Social Security proceedings are heard before administrative officers or bodies to whom or which investigatory, regulatory, and administrative functions have been delegated. Quasi-judicial powers are exercised in these hearings. The objective in both a judicial proceeding and a quasi-judicial proceeding is the same—the resolution of factual disputes. The administrative officers or bodies may have rules that allow evidence, testimony, or technical procedures to be more relaxed, but the gap between judicial and quasi-judicial proceedings is narrow.

For example, in most states the statutes for workers' compensation apply the Federal Rules of Evidence except to medical records, hospital and physician records, rehabilitation reports, and employer reports, which are admissible without foundation if they are "relative" to a case. In civil and criminal law these are subject to hearsay rules. Under the federal Employers' Liability Act (workers' compensation for railroad workers), cases may be filed in either federal or state civil courts; proceedings are administrative, but subject to judicial review; and the same rules of procedure as those followed by the courts are applied, although they are somewhat relaxed.

Another example is the Social Security Administration (SSA), whose rules require the expert witness to conduct himself or herself according to civil and criminal court procedures. Witnesses may be appointed by an administrative law judge as independent experts and be required to answer hypothetical questions that are asked by the judge. These experts are prequalified according to SSA guidelines at the national level, and a list of their names is made available to the judge. A claimant may nonetheless request the presence of an expert witness who has to be qualified by the judge at the time of the hearing. This expert would also conduct himself or herself according to civil and criminal court procedures.

States generally rely upon the Federal Rules of Evidence. However, state statutes and administrative regulations may vary slightly and should be referred to in specific matters. The following descriptions regarding evidence and the expert witness have been taken from Volumes 1 through 4 of *Jones on Evidence* by Spencer A. Gard, 1972, and the *Cumulative Supplements,* issued July 1987. This reference incorporates definitions from the Federal Rules of Evidence, the Uniform Rules of Evidence, and state rulings.

Qualifications of an Expert Witness
General Application

An expert witness may be called to testify by either a plaintiff (an injured party) or a defendant. The same expert may be called by both parties (the plaintiff and the defendant) when it appears that equally competent experts are not available to the two sides. The fruits of the expert's talents may be used by either side unless access is denied to one party on the broad ground of unfairness, such as when that party has been unwilling to locate, prepare, and pay for similar expertise. Experts may be inherited along with a lawsuit as a result of relationships established before litigation (e.g., the client-therapist relationship). Also, experts who have no previous connection with a matter are often sought by attorneys to supplement the testimony of others or to supply an exclusive expert opinion.

The qualifications of an ordinary or lay witness to give testimony as to the inferences that he or she has drawn from the facts he or she has perceived are tested by the capacity of people generally to draw reliable conclusions from given facts. If the conclusions to be drawn are beyond this capacity and dependent on specialized knowledge, education, experience, or training, a witness who has such special qualifications testifies as an expert and not as an ordinary witness. The controlling rule of evidence in the federal jurisdiction speaks in terms of scientific, technical, or other specialized knowledge. When it appears that testimony as to such things will assist the trier of fact (the court) in understanding the evidence or in determining a fact in issue, an expert may testify if he or she is qualified by "knowledge, skill, experience, training or education" in the subject.

It is recognized that qualifications may be attained by both study and practice of a particular subject, science, or art and also that an expert witness may become qualified by actual experience or long observation. The testimony of an expert in a particular field is limited to that special field. The occupational therapy expert may not testify about matters unrelated to occupational therapy.

One who purports to possess the requisite special knowledge, skill, or experience must first qualify himself or herself to testify. The qualification process takes place before any testimony can be given. The witness is asked questions regarding his or her training, knowledge, skills, and experience. Initial questions are presented by the party requesting the witness's presence. The opposing party and in some cases the judge may then ask the witness about his or her qualifications. The opposing party may attempt to limit or discredit the witness or otherwise to prove that the witness is not an expert. Documents such as a curriculum vitae and professional literature may be submitted to support or discredit a witness.

An expert witness may state facts about, but may not give an opinion as to, his or her own qualifications. An expert who has not yet been qualified by the court may be called, and another expert who has been qualified may give an opinion as to the qualifications of the first expert. Once the testimony of an expert has been found to be qualified and has been received, the other expert may not question his or her qualifications. An expert may, however, question an opinion stated by another expert. For example, a plaintiff's occupational therapy expert may question an opinion of a defendant's occupational therapy expert.

The outcome of the litigation may, and often does, turn on the qualifications of an expert and his or her ability to present conclusions clearly and persuasively so that the judge or the jury will respect them.

Qualifying the Occupational Therapist as an Expert

The definition of occupational therapy, the educational background of an occupational therapist, and the personal expertise of a particular occupational therapist as an expert witness represent to the court the parameters of his or her testimony and provide information that the judge uses to determine if the therapist will be accepted as an expert. Because many courts do not have readily accessible data to determine the necessary qualifications of occupational therapists, an occupational therapist who is attempting to qualify may need to offer relevant information in some detail. The following definitions may be helpful.

The *education* of the occupational therapist is guided by the "Essentials and Guidelines of an Accredited Educational Program for the Occupational Therapist" as established and adopted by the American Occupational Therapy Association (AOTA) (1983/1989) in collaboration with the Council on Medical Education of the American Medical Association (AMA). The entry-level curriculum includes basic human sciences, the human development process, specific life tasks and skills, and occupational therapy principles and applications. Course work may include, but is not limited to, anatomy, neurophysiology, psychology, psychiatry, pediatrics, gerontology, orthopedics, home economics, industrial and manual arts, self-care activities, kinesiology, vocational rehabilitation, economics, public health, principles of research, management systems, general medicine and surgery, human diseases and injuries, and community resources.

Certification of an occupational therapist indicates that he or she has earned a bachelor's or a master's degree in a curriculum accredited by AOTA and AMA; has successfully completed six months of supervised clinical training; and has passed a certification examination. A license to practice in a particular state may be required by state law.

The *definition* of occupational therapy is evaluation of, treatment of, and consultation to people of all ages whose abilities are threatened or impaired by developmental deficits, aging, poverty and cultural differences, physical injury or illness, or psychological and social disability. The primary focus of occupational therapy is to assist people in achieving a purposeful life in the most independent manner possible in the areas of self-care, work, play, and leisure. [The reader should refer to AOTA's "Definition of Occupational Therapy for Licensure" (1981) and "Occupational Therapy Product Output Reporting System and Uniform Terminology for Reporting Occupational Therapy Services" (1981/1989) to develop a definition that can be related with clarity and comfort.]

The *experience* and the *specialty* of the individual occupational therapist should be related in terms of advanced education, continuing education, special certifications, publications, professional organization memberships and offices, lectureships, and awards and honors. Education, certification, and licensure do not themselves qualify one as an expert in anything more than the general practice or principles of occupational therapy. In most cases this would not be useful information. Some degree of specialization and experience must be presented. If, for example, the ultimate issue to be decided requires facts about the ability of a burn victim to function, the occupational therapist would need to demonstrate an expertise in this area and may need to identify the actual number of burn cases in which he or she has provided evaluation, treatment, or consultation services. The therapist may also be required to demonstrate expertise in certain treatment and evaluation procedures.

General definitions of occupational therapy and the therapist's qualifications are helpful to the court and the jury. However, the main focus should be to qualify the occupational therapist as an expert for the case at hand. Pediatric experience should be expanded upon for a pediatric case, mental health experience for a mental health case, and so on in relation to any disability that would be of concern in a particular case.

Evidence
General Application

Evidence is weighed in value and admissibility according to the qualifications of the witness offering the evidence and the relevance and the materiality of the evidence. *Relevant* describes evidence that logically tends to prove or disprove any fact or proposition, material or not. *Material* characterizes evidence that tends to link up other evidence, supply a relevant circumstance, or otherwise prove an ultimate fact in issue.

An opinion is no stronger than the facts that support it and the explanation of its basis. Factual information is supplied to the expert in a number of ways. One way is through firsthand knowledge gained from an examination of a client, from an interview with a client, or by performance of tests. The admissibility of hearsay and the opinion of others is limited. Obviously experts become experts by relying on hearsay (lectures) in the course of their training and experience. However, with few exceptions the hearsay rule does not allow evidence from hearsay sources when such evidence pertains to the acquisition of factual knowledge in a particular case. An expert may not give an opinion based on the statements of co-workers or others made out of court. However, statements made by a client to a service provider that have been used to diagnose and treat a condition are admissible hearsay knowledge and may be referred to during the service provider's testimony. Under exceptional circumstances medical experts have been allowed to rely on information regarding a client furnished by relatives. Evidence obtained according to standardized testing or treatment procedures that are supervised and interpreted by the expert is usually acceptable. However, the expert may need to describe in detail the standardization process and the qualifications of the therapist who gathers the data and provides it to the expert for final analysis.

A second way in which an expert receives factual information is by listening to the testimony of other witnesses in court who testify to the facts, or by reading the record of their testimony. Questions calling upon an expert to form an opinion based on the evidence he or she has heard are often rejected because they are thought to usurp the province of the jury or the judge. However, if an expert has heard a deposition read or has heard the testimony of a witness or several witnesses in which no conflict appears, he or she may be allowed to give an opinion based on the assumption that such evidence is true.

A third way in which an expert is supplied with factual information is by being presented on the witness stand with questions that state the facts hypothetically or that assume facts supported by some evidence to be true. This is done if the expert does not have sufficient factual knowledge from his or her own perception, from acceptable extensive sources of information, or from hearing or reading testimony in evidence. The hypothetical question combines a statement of some assumed facts with a request to the witness to state an opinion based on the assumption that the facts presented are true. For example: "Based on the assumption that disabled workers tend to earn lower wages than able workers, what would your opinion be regarding this particular client's ability to earn wages?" The court uses its discretion as to the form that the interrogation of an expert witness may take.

An occupational therapy expert whose employment has not been for the purpose of treatment, but for the purpose of testifying, may express an opinion of reasonable occupational therapy probability as to the nature and the extent of a client's injuries, based on the client's narration of history and complaints and on subjective as well as objective symptoms and findings. Testimony to facts that are not contemporary to the matter of controversy or not subsequent to a material change is insufficient. The facts on which the expert relies should have a logical connection to the facts under inquiry.

The general experience and the reliability of an expert in distinguishing between acceptable and unacceptable information upon which to draw is considered an adequate safeguard. An example is when an expert in medical science relies on extracts from treatises in that science that he or she states are recognized by the medical profession as authoritative and that have influenced or tended to confirm his or her opinion.

Most courts allow specialists from anywhere in the United States to testify. This is based on the theory that most of the knowledge of specialists should be substantially equivalent because of uniform requirements for certification and continuing education.

The value of an expert's testimony depends on a number of considerations: the comprehensiveness of the factual information used by him or her, the extent to which the facts are believed by the trier of fact, and the reasonableness of the conclusions. An expert must be able to give persuasive reasons for his or her conclusions.

Evidence Provided by the Occupational Therapist

An occupational therapist provides evidence as a result of evaluation of, treatment of, or consultation to a patient or a client. Fact-gathering methods include, but are not limited to, record review, interview, checklists, standardized and nonstandardized tests, clinical evaluation, clinical observations, and disability-specific treatment strategies and activities.

The AOTA has adopted "Standards of Practice for Occupational Therapy" (1983/1989), "Occupational Therapy Product Output Reporting System and Uniform Terminology for Reporting Occupational Therapy Services" (1981/1989), a "Uniform Occupational Therapy Evaluation Checklist" (1981), "Occupational Therapy Code of Ethics" (1988), and numerous role-and-function documents, position papers, and position statements to guide the therapist in the application of occupational therapy principles. These professional standards describe the assessment process, which includes evaluation of medical, educational, social, and vocational histories; activities of daily living; and sensorimotor, cognitive-perceptual, and behavioral components of performance. Standardized tests used in assessment should be reliable and valid, with norms that are not discriminatory according to age, culture, or ability to function. Some standardized evaluation tools require that the therapist possess additional certification in order to administer and interpret results.

To ensure the reliability and the validity of results, nonstandardized tests, interviews, clinical evaluation, and observations should be performed according to professional protocol. Reports should clearly state which measures are subjective and which, objective. For example, an evaluation of joint range of motion has standard ranges, norms, and positions that are to be observed and measured objectively. A client may demonstrate subjectively his or her range of motion for measurement by an occupational therapist. The therapist observes for consistency of performance in relationship to a diagnosis, reported activities of daily living, measured muscle strength, sensory evaluations, and behaviors. The therapist interprets the data from such an evaluation and applies the findings to performance in the areas of self-care, work, play, and leisure.

Once the basis, the relevance, and the materiality of the evidence addressed by an occupational therapist have been established, he or she may provide such evidence in the form of testimony. Admissibility of expert testimony is subject to the same tests of relevance and materiality as are applied to evidence generally and subject to the same limitations arising from its being unduly prejudicial, cumulative, too remote, or within the realm of common knowledge.

Testimony

An expert is called only as a witness and has no authority or standing in court different from that of an ordinary witness. It is clearly not within an expert's province to act as the judge or the jury. An expert may, however, arrive at a reasonable factual conclusion from the evidence. In technical matters requiring special knowledge, skill, experience, and the like, the judge and the jury may be quite lost without the aid of those who understand the problem better than they do. An expert's testimony should be intended to assist rather than impede the final decision of the judge or the jury.

An expert witness may not give an opinion that represents a mere guess or that is nothing more than speculation or conjecture. There are also rules about how certain an expert may be in terms of an opinion. Generally the rule is that an expert may use such language as expresses his or her actual state of mind on the matter in terms of *possibility, probability,* or *actuality.* This is commonly described as testimony that a result might, could, or would follow from a state of given facts.

Answering questions in terms of possibility, probability, and actuality is a critical point of understanding for a therapist. It is possible, for example, that a client who demonstrates uncooperative behaviors may be displaying symptoms of depression. This, however, must be corroborated by a substantial accounting of observed behaviors in the performance areas of activities of daily living, self-care, and psychosocial and cognitive skills. A probability of dysfunctional performance would be reflected in impaired sensation, poor muscle strength, and decreased range of motion when measured according to standardized procedures and when correlated with the expected symptoms of a diagnosis. An actual fact would be the loss of an extremity or a spinal cord lesion.

The therapist, in making statements of possibility and probability, must be prepared to convince the court or the jury that his or her findings were gathered and analyzed in such a fashion that little or no element of doubt exists. Statements of actuality do not require much explanation.

The range of matters that may properly be subjects of expert occupational therapy testimony is limited only by occupational therapy science, knowledge, and experience. Experts are generally expected, however, to testify in a specific area of expertise and to provide an opinion that shows the physical condition of a person, the temporary and permanent effects, the existence of pain, and the probable effects of an injury or a mental state. An occupational therapy expert may also state an opinion as to whether or not certain symptoms of disease or injury that are manifested by a party are real, imaginary, or feigned. However, he or she cannot testify directly as to the veracity of a party as a witness; that is, the therapist cannot call the party a malingerer.

There is no fixed pattern or method for asking questions of a witness. The courts give considerable latitude to counsel in following a plan for trial technique and the dictates of common sense for effective presentation of the evidence, but that latitude is always subject to the power of the judge to keep the trial orderly and fair. During direct examination, leading questions are not permitted. In other words, questions that suggest to the witness the answer that he or she is to make are objectionable. For example, the question from counsel to witness, "As a result of your evaluation, do you believe this client has suffered a total and permanent disability?", would be leading and objectionable.

The relevance and the materiality of testimony need not always appear at the time it is offered. The usual course is to receive at any proper and convenient stage of the trial, in the discretion of the judge, any evidence that counsel shows will be rendered material and relevant by other evidence that he or she undertakes to produce. If the evidence is not subsequently connected with the issue, it is to be withdrawn from the case.

Power to control and regulate the taking of oral testimony is vested in the trial court (the judge, the hearing officer, etc.). Although counsel is ordinarily allowed to manage and conduct the examination of witnesses, the court may propound questions to a witness, suggest the form of a question, ask leading questions, or call and examine a witness and permit counsel to cross-examine him or her. Jurors also may be permitted to examine witnesses if this is necessary to draw out or clear up some uncertain point. The court may of its own motion check and silence a witness who volunteers unsolicited testimony or whose answers are unresponsive or irrelevant to the questions asked. The court may also permit a witness to narrate the relevant facts on direct examination in his or her own way and without being questioned.

Although power to regulate and control the order of the introduction of evidence is vested in the trial judge, the customary procedure requires the injured party (the affirmative) to introduce all evidence that is necessary to support the substance of his or her claim; then the party denying the affirmative allegations produces his or her proof; and finally the proof in rebuttal is received. This is the primary rule of the courts.

Cross-Examination

Although the rules governing the cross-examination of witnesses generally apply to expert witnesses, great latitude is allowed in the cross-examination of an expert witness. The party cross-examining an expert is not confined to the theory on which the adversary has conducted his or her examination; rather the cross-examiner may go into detail and may put the case before the expert in all its phases.

The expert may be asked to answer questions that present hypothetically the facts claimed to constitute the case or the defense of the cross-examining party, or the expert may be interrogated as to pertinent hypothetical cases if no evidence has been given. In ascertaining the grounds or the reasons for such opinions, the cross-examiner is not confined to the scope of the evidence already given in the case; he or she is allowed to ask questions that would be wholly irrelevant except for the purpose of ascertaining the value of the expert's opinion or the degree of credibility to be attached to the expert's testimony.

Like other witnesses, an expert may be subjected on cross-examination to such tests as may be necessary to ascertain whether his or her testimony is accurate, impartial, and credible. Questions may be asked about his or her previous opinions that may differ from his or her opinions on the stand and the reasons for the change. The expert may also be asked about the number of cases in which he or she has testified and the fees for the services. It is not objectionable for the cross-examiner to ask leading questions.

An expert witness may be cross-examined with reference to the statements in a recognized textbook, even though the testimony of the expert has in no part been based on such authority. Learned treatises may be used by incorporating them in questions to the expert to test his or her qualifications and to impeach his or her testimony.

It would be difficult for any registered occupational therapist being presented as an expert in the field of occupational therapy to be impeached based on his or her qualifications. Education and certification alone indicate a measure of expertise. The therapist's testimony may be limited, however, according to his or her experience or knowledge of the facts in a particular case. Impeachment tends to occur when an expert makes conflicting statements, misrepresents the facts, has no knowledge of the facts, or presents himself or herself as biased toward one party. The expert, in any case, has the right to an opinion (although impeachable) and cannot be sued for having one.

An expert appointed by the court is considered an officer of the court and not a witness for either party, but such an expert may be called as a witness by either party and cross-examined with respect to his or her findings and report to the court. The courts have inherent power to appoint impartial expert witnesses when occasion demands, either with or without a request from a party or parties. In some jurisdictions, statutes or court rules provide for the appointment of expert witnesses.

Depositions and Interrogatories

The term *deposition* describes the written testimony of a witness that has been formally produced by either oral or written interrogation (which may include videotaping), with opportunity for cross-examination. It is given in advance of the trial at which it is intended to be available for use as evidence, the trial in connection with which it is to be used for discovery purposes, or both. The word *discovery* signifies the process of compelling a party, in connection with preparation for trial, to disclose to the adversary information that may be in his or her possession.

Interrogatories are written responses to written questions and are subject to cross-interrogatories. The expert may need to provide (a) the subject matter or the area in which he or she is to testify, (b) the substance of the facts and the opinions to which he or she is to testify, and (c) a summary of the grounds for each opinion. The deposition of a witness is taken either by oral examination or by the submission of interrogatories and cross-interrogatories, as may be provided by the procedure of a particular jurisdiction.

Statutes providing for and regulating the use of depositions have been enacted in all of the states. In jurisdictions that have adopted the federal procedures or similar ones, a distinction is made, at least in name, between discovery depositions and those taken for use as evidence. In most of those jurisdictions, as in the federal one, this distinction is meaningless, except as indicating the broad scope of inquiry when the deposition is taken. But in a few states the right to use a discovery deposition as evidence may depend on the designation in the notice of the purpose in taking the deposition, whether as evidence or for discovery. Many of the statutes provide that depositions may be taken for use in one specific proceeding. Under such statutes a deposition may not ordinarily be used in another proceeding.

A formal notice in writing for the taking of depositions is generally prescribed to advise the other party or parties of the time and the place of the taking and of the witnesses to be interrogated. When no notice is given in a pending action, the deposition or the statement thus procured is subject to rejection for any evidentiary purpose. When the deposition of a party to the action is to be taken, it is generally held that the notice itself is sufficient to require the presence of the party without the necessity for issuing a subpoena, and failure to appear subjects the defaulting party to appropriate sanctions. A witness who has been properly notified and who refuses or neglects to attend at the time and the place specified is punishable as for contempt.

Ordinarily the examination of the deponent—that is, the person giving the deposition—is conducted as if he or she were being examined as a witness in court. Depositions are generally taken in the presence of a court-commissioned officer and a stenographer, the latter afterward reducing testimony to typewriting. It is generally stipulated that this course may be followed and that the signature of the witness is waived. The taking of a deposition, even though pursued before or on the authority of a judge, is not a judicial proceeding.

Objections to the form of a deposition or to the competency of a witness must be taken before a case is called to trial. Objections to form—for example, objections to leading questions—should be made at the time of the taking of the deposition. If a party permits depositions to be read at the trial without objection, it is then too late to object. Once the proper objections have been made, depositions or portions of depositions may be suppressed by the court and never heard at the trial. Objections to a deposition for any reason after it has been heard at the trial are generally not granted.

Because there is no immediate ruling on objectionable questions, an expert witness must answer all questions asked. Objections are merely recorded for future judicial review. It is therefore often difficult to maintain a logical flow in testimony. Depositions for the purpose of discovery can require an exhaustive presentation of even the most minute details.

The use of depositions at a trial is justified on the grounds that the witness cannot be produced in person. However, the procedure in most jurisdictions bars the use of a deposition as evidence in lieu of testimony if a witness is available to give firsthand oral testimony in court. A witness may be allowed to correct his or her testimony appearing in a deposition by oral testimony given at the trial. An accurate reproduction of deposition statements—or on the other hand, inconsistencies in them—will have an important bearing on the weight of the testimony.

Testimony from the Occupational Therapist

An occupational therapist serving as an expert witness should prepare for testimony with the party requesting his or her expertise, or if the therapist is a court-appointed expert, he or she should prepare by reviewing the guidelines to be followed for that judicial or administrative body. There is no substitute for a thorough preparation and understanding of the material to be presented, which may include reviewing an entire medical record and supporting documents. A clear understanding of the issues and the direction that one intends to take will minimize a potentially confusing cross-examination or thwart impeachment.

In the course of testimony the therapist should respond to questions as directly and clearly as possible, addressing answers to the court or the jury. Witnesses have been historically appraised according to their demeanor, confidence, and ability to present the truth. Psychological messages conveyed by such means as tone of voice, posture, and body language are interpreted by the court or the jury and may add to or detract from the weight of the testimony. The therapist should be thoroughly prepared as well as relaxed, confident, and well rested.

Most questions presented to the expert occupational therapist are direct and require direct answers. However, if a question is multifaceted, confusing, or in the therapist's opinion not answerable with a yes or a no, then it is appropriate to ask that the question be restated, or to state that the answer requires clarification in order to be accurate. The business of evaluating and treating the whole person tends to go beyond black-and-white issues, and in the interest of fairness the therapist as an expert witness should offer detailed explanations.

Do's and Don'ts of Expert Testimony

The following excerpt from the *Expert Witness Checklists* should be reviewed before testimony is given:[1]

> You, as an expert, will be asked to render opinions using your special training and experience. These opinions must be based on the facts of this case. Your opinions and interpretations of the facts will help the judge and jury decide this case. Your qualifications, your testimony, and the way in which you deliver your testimony must persuade the judge and jury to agree that your opinions are correct and that my client, therefore, should prevail in this suit.
>
> Your opinions are your own and you must tell the truth. As counsel for my client, I will provide you with the information you need to draw your conclusions. But the

---

[1] From *Expert Witness Checklists* (pp. 140–149) by D. Danner, 1983, Rochester, NY: Lawyers Co-operative; San Francisco, CA: Bancroft-Whitney. © 1983 by The Lawyers Co-operative Publishing Company, Rochester, New York. Reprinted by permission.

effect your opinions will have on the jury may be affected, in turn, by the way in which you deliver your testimony in court. The following checklist is designed to help you understand some ground rules and pointers to enhance the persuasive impact of your testimony. Please study my suggestions and feel free to ask me any questions you may have. We will discuss your testimony in greater detail before you testify.

1. You may be asked whether you have talked with an attorney about the case. The answer, of course, is that you did speak with an attorney and that is how you came to be called as a witness. It is perfectly proper for you to have consulted with me.

2. The cross-examiner may know as much about you and your field as your counsel does and the opponent may have retained an expert to assist him. During pretrial preparation, you should reveal to your counsel all derogatory material regarding your background, qualifications, preparation, opinions, or interest in the case so that counsel can limit its damaging effect during direct examination.

3. You should insist on sufficient preparation for your testimony, in consultation with your counsel, so that you feel comfortable on the witness stand. The attorney should advise you of what to expect on direct and cross-examination and describe trial procedure.

4. You should be as thorough as is necessary under the circumstances in preparing your opinions for trial. Exhaustion of all possible tests and procedures may not be required but be prepared to justify any omissions. You should inform your attorney of all unfavorable information developed by your analysis as well as all favorable information.

5. You can expect to be challenged in these areas: your qualifications, your bias or interest in the case, your reasons for testifying, your fees, your familiarity with the case, your disagreement with conflicting expert authority, your communication with your lawyer, your prior testimonial experience on [sic] your publications.

6. The most effective cross-examination often is confined to developing points which were omitted on direct examination because they were unfavorable to the party calling the witness. You can slip favorable information into your cross-examination testimony but be reasonable and careful.

7. Prepare a description of your qualifications and their significance. Explain the various levels of certifica-

tions or honors available, e.g., whether you are board certified. Do not exaggerate your expertise; at the same time, do not understate it out of modesty. On cross-examination, do not express opinions that you are not qualified to express. Keep your answers within your area of expertise. Acknowledge the limits of your expertise and admit what you don't know without embarrassment.

8. What is your bias or interest? Have you testified for plaintiffs as well as defendants in previous cases? Do you have any relationship with any party or attorney or the judge?

9. What are your reasons for testifying on this occasion—are there any particular axes being ground?

10. Prepare to discuss your fees. State the fee without equivocation. State that you are being paid for your time and effort at normal rates a professional would charge, and you are not paid to say whatever you are told to say. Repudiate any suggestion that the fee is dependent on the outcome of this case.

11. a. Do not guess an answer. Qualify it as necessary; and if you can't give an answer, don't. Don't be afraid to admit that you don't know an answer. Don't exaggerate your answer or the extent of your analysis.

    b. You can expect to be asked to state each step of your analysis and how long each took. If you failed to perform tests or analyses that may or should have been done, you should be prepared to explain why such tests were not used. If you are asked to assume hypothetical facts different from those in issue, you may explain that the facts assumed are different from the case here—or you may ask for more time to render a considered opinion.

12. a. If your opinions are inconsistent with those of other authorities, be prepared to explain why you disagree and to list consistent authorities.

    b. Your first-hand, individual diagnostic and analytical ability should be given more credence than a more general medical textbook or periodical.

    c. In most cases you can be challenged with "authoritative writings" only if you state that you relied on them as authoritative in your field. You may avoid referring to any source as authoritative so the opponent may not then use other parts from the "authority" to impeach you. As an alternative, you could acknowledge that a source

is helpful in some areas but not the final word and not necessarily accurate in all circumstances.
   d. You may deny that the material is authoritative.
   e. You may distinguish this case from the situation the authority considered.
   f. You should be willing to express your honest disagreement with authorities. Having other authorities on your side certainly would help.
   g. You should ask to examine any source offered to you as authoritative.
13. Create a list of your publications and of your prior testimonial experiences. Let your attorney know whether you recall taking any position inconsistent with your current testimony.
14. The expert must communicate effectively with the judge and jury:
   a. Do not patronize the judge or jury—enhancing their self-esteem will encourage them to decide in your favor.
   b. Speak in an understandable manner using clear and simple terms the judge and jury can understand.
   c. Technical jargon must be explained and used sparingly.
   d. Although the jury may appear uninformed or bored, they will ultimately decide the case and it is the expert's job to convince them. Be attentive to them and mold your testimony to keep their attention.
   e. Be positive and assertive, but not arrogant. Modest yet firm confidence should be most persuasive.
   f. Speak up so that all can hear you. The reporter cannot record inaudible gestures, nods, or shrugs—each response must be audible.
   g. Above all, you should take your role as expert witness seriously—an expert has been invited to render opinions which are crucial to the case and your testimony may affect your professional reputation.
15. The expert should remember that appearances are important:
   a. Demonstrations of relief, defeat, or triumph may detract from your performance.
   b. Take the stand and leave the courtroom deliberately and confidently.
   c. Avoid pins or insignias identifying you with any group.

d. Your posture should be correct. Maintain a professional demeanor. Sit upright, hold your head erect, and try to avoid nervous mannerisms.
e. Dress neatly and in accordance with the importance of the occasion.
f. You should be respectful and courteous towards the opponents as well as towards the judge and jury.
g. Don't be pompous.
h. Do not communicate with the opponent or his counsel. Do not discuss the case in the hallway or talk with jurors. If a juror attempts to talk to you refuse and report it to your attorney.
i. Speak directly to the judge and jury and look them in the eye.
j. Control your temper. Anger and hostility towards the opponent—or arguing with the opponent—will jeopardize your testimony. If a cross-examining attorney can provoke you to a display of anger or sarcasm, he will succeed in discrediting your testimony. Be patient. Try to keep the same tone of voice or answering style during direct and cross-examination.
k. Do not show exasperation, boredom, or fatigue, even though the questioning may be very extensive.
l. Avoid revealing surprise or displeasure at evidence developed during cross-examination.
m. The object is for you to project an air of professionalism and reasonable confidence which will persuade the jury that you know what you are speaking about and that you are correct.

16. There are several things for the expert to consider as he answers each question:
    a. You need not answer every question—be able to admit you don't know without speculation, embarrassment or apology.
    b. Listen carefully to the entire question. Don't begin to answer until you are sure you understand the question. If the question is unclear, ask examining counsel to state it more clearly. This should avoid the occasional trick question.
    c. If your attorney objects to a question, do not answer until you have heard the judge's ruling. If the judge overrules the objection, you may ask the examining attorney to repeat the question. You generally will not be allowed to ask questions of your attorney during your examination.

If the judge sustains the objection, do not answer the previous question.

d. Prepare your answer before beginning. Be thoughtful and careful—quick answers suggest either that you are not a careful person or that you have rehearsed or memorized your answers. Once a question is asked, make it a practice to double check your answer against any records you may have with you, even if you are sure of the answer. At the same time, it is important not to hesitate too long because this may suggest that you are unprepared, uncertain, or threatened. At the very least, however, pause briefly before answering an opponent's question to give your attorney an opportunity to object to the question.

e. Answer the question as asked, without elaborating, and be concise and accurate. Don't volunteer information not specifically asked for by the opponent, but don't be too abrupt or hostile.

f. Qualify your answer if that is necessary for you to give an accurate and truthful answer. Qualify your answers only as necessary. Don't allow yourself to be forced into a flat "yes" or "no" answer if a qualified answer is required. You have a right to explain or qualify your answer if that is necessary to make it truthful. Even if you are required to give a simple yes or no answer to a question you will have an opportunity to explain your answer at some point, if it needs explanation. If opposing counsel cuts you off in the middle of an important explanation, you should state that you have not finished your answer so your counsel can ask you to amplify your answer during his examination.

g. Give factual information in answer to a question only if you have knowledge of the facts; otherwise, identify any assumptions you have to make. Do not hide any facts you know and which you are specifically asked about.

h. The law requires only that you testify to your best recollection. If you are uncertain about an answer to a question, indicate this uncertainty in your response.

i. Answer all questions truthfully. Any display of embarrassment or reluctance to answer will tend to discredit your testimony. If you have to make admissions you think are damaging, do so with-

out embarrassment or fuss, and qualify them as necessary.
   j. Don't exaggerate. Any attempt to puff up your qualifications or to elaborate the extent of the examination you have made may be exposed.
   k. Be objective and impartial. Avoid all actions which might suggest that you are partisan. Don't be afraid, however, to take issue with opposing counsel to correct him but do so only if necessary and then without belligerence.
   l. Don't try to bluff. If you don't know the answer to a question, don't guess.
   m. Don't be smug. A jury is quite likely to react adversely to an attitude of superiority—a modest attitude should elicit a more favorable response.
   n. Be reasonable and fair. Be able to concede gracefully that, with different facts, you might reach a different opinion.
   o. Never mention the words "insurance" or "insurance company." This could result in a costly mistrial since the judge or jury is to make a decision based solely on the merits of the case and not whether there are funds available. This rule is particular to personal injury litigation.
17. Don't take notes, documents, or reports to the witness stand unless your counsel approves because opposing counsel will be entitled to examine them.
18. The expert can expect that various trick or confusing questions may be asked:
   a. Compound questions—if one question is buried in another, ask the opposing lawyer to separate them before you answer.
   b. Double negatives—the potential for confusion is obvious.
   c. Misquotations or mischaracterizations of your prior testimony or publication. Correct even minor deviations.
   d. Attempts to introduce intervening or independently sufficient causes within a hypothetical question. If some of the conditions posed deviate significantly from the facts, bring this to counsel's attention.
   e. Hypothetical questions which do not contain enough information or the right information to support a conclusion. State what is missing or that you cannot answer the question as asked.

f. Catch-all, general, broad questions. Keep your answer accurate and truthful, and as brief as possible. (i.e., Tell me all you know about . . .)
19. The expert can expect some cross-examiners to exhibit the following styles:
   a. An ingratiating cross-examiner who befriends the expert and tries to get him to agree to apparently innocuous statements. Be vigilant and circumspect about your answers, but you must agree with correct statements.
   b. A cross-examiner who threatens silently, often with a stack of ostensibly authoritative papers or books.
   c. An over-dramatic actor—your confident responses should show the jury who to trust.
   d. A cross-examiner who pauses after each answer. Once you are finished, do not feel compelled to fill the silence by volunteering information.

This list may seem long and complicated, but you need not memorize it. When we go over your testimony in detail, I will remind you of some points when necessary. Most of all, however, you should use this list to remind yourself that your testimony will be crucial to my client's case. My client will best be served if you use your best professional efforts and convey your knowledge to the jury in a natural but sincere and serious manner.

Summary

The occupational therapist is uniquely qualified to present testimony in disability evaluations as either the treating therapist or as a hired expert witness. The therapist develops pretrial evidence in the form of evaluation, treatment, or consultation data. These data are gathered according to professional protocol. Testimony during depositions or from the stand is based on this evidence. The role of the occupational therapist is to present logical and persuasive reasons to support his or her qualifications as an expert and to lend a measure of understanding to a client's ability or inability to perform activities in the areas of self-care, work, play, and leisure. Therapists who are qualified with enough education and experience and who have a basis on which to form an opinion should consider giving expert testimony as a professional obligation.

Glossary[2]

Claimant—"one who claims or asserts a right, demand or claim. See . . . **Plaintiff**" (p. 225).

Corroborating evidence—"evidence supplementary to that already given and tending to strengthen or confirm it. Additional evidence of a different character to the same point" (p. 311).

Court—"an organ of the government, belonging to the judicial department, whose function is the application of the laws to controversies brought before it and the public administration of justice. . . . [The term includes] both judge and jury. . . . An organized body with defined powers, meeting at certain times and places for the hearing and decision of causes and other matters brought before it . . . .

"The words "court" and "judge," or "judges," are frequently used in statutes as synonymous" (p. 318).

Cumulative evidence—"additional or corroborative evidence to the same point. That which goes to prove what has already been established by other evidence. See also **Corroborating evidence**" (p. 343).

Deposition—"the testimony of a witness taken upon interrogatories, not in open court, but in pursuance of a commission to take testimony issued by a court, or under a general law or court rule on the subject, and reduced to writing and duly authenticated, and intended to be used upon the trial of a civil action or criminal prosecution. A discovery device by which one party asks oral questions of the other party or of a witness for the other party. The person who is deposed is called the deponent. The deposition is conducted under oath outside of the courtroom, usually in one of the lawyer's offices. A transcript—word for word account—is made of the deposition. Testimony of witness, taken in writing, under oath or affirmation, before some judicial officer in answer to questions or interrogatories. . . . See also **Discovery; Interrogatories**. . . .

"*Oral deposition.* Form of discovery by addressing questions orally to person interrogated. . . .

"*Written questions.* Form of discovery in which written questions are addressed to person interrogated" (p. 396).

Discovery—"in a general sense, the ascertainment of that which was previously unknown; the disclosure or coming to light of what was previously hidden . . . .

"*Trial practice.* The pre-trial devices that can be used by one party to obtain facts and information about the case from the other party in order to assist the party's preparation for trial.

---

[2]Quotations are from *Black's Law Dictionary* (5th ed.) by H. C. Black, 1979, St. Paul, MN: West Publishing Co. © 1979 by West Publishing Co. Reprinted by permission.

Under Federal Rules of Civil Procedure (and in states which have adopted rules patterned on such), tools of discovery include: . . . interrogatories, production of documents or things, . . . physical and mental examinations and requests for admission" (p. 419).

Foundation—"preliminary questions to witness to establish admissibility of evidence, *i.e.*, 'laying foundation' for admissibility" (p. 591).

Hearsay—"a statement, other than one made by the declarant while testifying at the trial or hearing offered in evidence to prove the truth of the matter asserted. . . .

". . . Evidence not proceeding from the personal knowledge of the witness, but from the mere repetition of what he has heard others say. That which does not derive its value solely from the credit of the witness, but rests mainly on the veracity and competency of other persons. The very nature of the evidence shows its weakness, and it is admitted only in specified cases from necessity" (p. 649).

Impeachment of a witness—"to call in question the veracity of a witness, by means of evidence adduced for such purpose, or the adducing of proof that a witness is unworthy of belief. . . . In general, . . . a witness may be impeached with respect to prior inconsistent statements, contradiction of facts, bias, or character. A witness, once impeached, may be rehabilitated with evidence supporting credibility.

". . . [Federal rules permit] the use at trial of a witness's prior deposition to discredit or impeach testimony of the deponent as a witness" (p. 678).

Interrogatories—"a set or series of written questions drawn up for the purpose of being propounded to a party, witness, or other person having information of interest in the case.

"A discovery device consisting of written questions about the case submitted by one party to the other party or witness. The answers to the interrogatories are usually given under oath, *i.e.*, the person answering the questions signs a sworn statement that the answers are true" (p. 735).

Material evidence—"that quality of evidence which tends to influence the trier of fact because of its logical connection with the issue. Evidence which has an effective influence or bearing on question in issue is 'material.' . . .

. . . .

"See also **Relevant evidence**" (p. 881).

Plaintiff—"a person who brings an action; the party who complains or sues in a civil action and is so named on the record. A person who seeks remedial relief for an injury to rights; it designates a complainant" (p. 1035).

Quasi judicial—"a term applied to the action, discretion, etc., of public administrative officers or bodies, who are required to investigate facts, or ascertain the existence of facts, hold hearings, and draw conclusions from them, as a basis for their official action, and to exercise discretion of a judicial nature" (p. 1121).

Relevant evidence—"evidence having any tendency to make the existence of any fact that is of consequence to the determination of the action more probable or less probable than it would be without the evidence. . . .

"Basic test for admissibility of evidence is relevancy, and testimony is 'relevant' if reasonable inferences can be drawn therefrom regarding or if any light is shed upon, a contested matter" (p. 1160).

Remoteness of evidence—"when the fact or facts proposed to be established as a foundation from which indirect evidence may be drawn, by way of inference, have not a visible, plain, or necessary connection with the proposition eventually to be proved, such evidence is rejected for 'remoteness'" (p. 1164).

Trier of fact—the court.

References

American Occupational Therapy Association. (1981). Definition of occupational therapy for licensure. In *Policy manual of the American Occupational Therapy Association, Inc.* (Policy #5.3.1). Rockville, MD: Author.

American Occupational Therapy Association. (1981). Uniform occupational therapy evaluation checklist. *American Journal of Occupational Therapy, 35,* 817–818.

American Occupational Therapy Association. (1988). Occupational therapy code of ethics. *American Journal of Occupational Therapy, 42,* 795–796.

American Occupational Therapy Association. (1989). Essentials and guidelines of an accredited educational program for the occupational therapist. In *Reference manual of the official documents of the American Occupational Therapy Association* (pp. II.1–5). Rockville, MD: Author. (Original work published 1983).

American Occupational Therapy Association. (1989). Occupational therapy product output reporting system and uniform terminology for reporting occupational therapy services. In *Reference manual of the official documents of the American Occupational Therapy Association* (pp. VII.19–29). Rockville, MD: Author. (Original work published 1981).

American Occupational Therapy Association. (1989). Standards of practice for occupational therapy. In *Reference manual of the official documents of the American Occupational Therapy Association* (pp. IV.1–3). Rockville, MD: Author. (Original work published 1983).

Employers' Liability Act (as amended), 45 U.S.C. § 51 (1982).

Gard, S. A. (1972, 1987). *Jones on evidence* (6th ed.) and *Cumulative supplements*. Rochester, NY: Lawyers Co-operative; San Francisco, CA: Bancroft-Whitney.

Related Reading

Danner, D. (1985). *Pattern interrogatories, cumulative supplement*. Rochester, NY: Lawyers Co-operative.

Denkensohn, B., & Fliss, A. (Eds.). (1987). *Personal injury review—1987*. New York: Matthew Bender.

Kornblau, B. L. (1988, September). The role of the occupational therapist in the medicolegal arena. *Work Programs Special Interest Section Newsletter, 2*(3), 1–2.

Poynter, D. (1987). *The expert witness handbook: Tips and techniques for the litigation consultant*. Santa Barbara, CA: Para Publishing.

Smith, S. L. (1984, November). The forensic model of occupational therapy. *Occupational Therapy in Health Care, 1,* 17-22.

Steich, T. J. (1985, May). So you want to be an expert witness. *Federal Report,* No. 85-3, pp. 6–11.

Wyrick, J., & Wyrick, A. (1988, September). The process of personal injury evaluation. *Work Programs Special Interest Section Newsletter, 2*(3), 3–4.

Appendix A
Resources

AOTA Products

Relevant Information Packets
Accessibility and Architectural Modifications
Adaptive Equipment/Rehabilitation Technology
Developmental Disabilities
Health Promotion/Wellness Programs
Mental Health
Occupational Therapy for the Injured Worker
Pain Management
Seating and Positioning
Stress Management

Publications
Bair, J., & Gray, M. (Eds.). (1985). *The occupational therapy manager.* Rockville, MD: American Occupational Therapy Association.
Kirkland, M., & Robertson, S. C. (Eds.). (1985). *Planning and implementing vocational readiness in occupational therapy* (PIVOT). Rockville, MD: American Occupational Therapy Association.
Kuntavanish, A. A. (1987). *Occupational therapy documentation: A system to capture outcome data for quality assurance and program promotion.* Rockville, MD: American Occupational Therapy Association.
Scott, S. J. (Ed.). (1988). *Payment for occupational therapy services.* Rockville, MD: American Occupational Therapy Association.

Official Documents (available from the Practice Division)
Generic Standards of Practice for Occupational Therapy Services. (1983).
Guide to Classification of Occupational Therapy Personnel. (1985, 1987).
Guide to Supervision of Occupational Therapy Personnel. (1981).
Hierarchy of Competencies Relating to the Use of Standardized Instruments and Evaluation Techniques by Occupational Therapists. (1984).
Occupational Therapy Product Output Reporting System and Uniform Terminology for Reporting Occupational Therapy Services. (1989).
Standards of Practice for Occupational Therapy Services for Clients with Physical Disabilities. (1979).
Standards of Practice for Occupational Therapy Services for the Developmentally Disabled. (1979).
Standards of Practice for Occupational Therapy Services in Mental Health Programs. (1979).

Organizations

Commission on Accreditation of Rehabilitation Facilities (CARF)
101 North Wilmot Road, Suite 500
Tucson, AZ 85711
(602) 748-1212

Joint Commission on Accreditation of Healthcare Organizations (JCAHO)
875 North Michigan Avenue
Chicago, IL 60611
(312) 642-6061

Vocational Evaluation and Work Adjustment Association (VEWAA)
c/o National Rehabilitation Association
633 South Washington Street
Alexandria, VA 22314
(703) 836-0850

Appendix B

Work Hardening Guidelines

Preface

A work hardening program conducted by occupational therapy personnel is an individualized, work-oriented activity process that involves a client in simulated or actual work tasks. These tasks are structured and graded progressively to increase psychological, physical, and emotional tolerance and improve endurance, general productivity, and work feasibility. The eventual goal of work hardening services is to improve the client's occupational performance skills to allow effective functioning in homebound, sheltered, modified, or competitive work. Consideration is given to actual capabilities, as well as to the needs for practicing preventive care measures, avoiding abnormal stress patterns, being aware of and reducing environmental hazards, increasing safety in performing work-related tasks, and effecting a positive psychological adjustment to work (1, 2).

Work hardening services in an occupational therapy setting are offered by occupational therapy personnel with knowledge and skills related to work processes and an understanding of work roles. Therapists interpret work-related information and design work activities that improve behavioral, physical, and emotional functioning. In addition, the therapist may assess environmental limitations and suggest adaptations leading to viable work-related outcomes. Work hardening addresses the whole person with respect to physical, physiological, psychosocial, cognitive, developmental, and interpersonal skills.

Occupational therapists assess people according to standards adopted by the American Occupational Therapy Association and applicable licensing statutes. Procedures are structured according to the client's needs and the goals of service.

Historical Perspective

Work hardening is a work-oriented treatment program designed to improve the client's productivity. Although "work hardening" may be a relatively new term, the perception of the value of work and its therapeutic properties for the injured or psychiatric client has long-standing roots in the practice of occupational therapy. As early as 1900, work was viewed as an alternative to the custodial care of the disabled. Likewise, industrial therapy was implemented in psychiatric hospitals, where jobs were analyzed according to skill level, physical and mental demands, and potential benefits. World War I increased awareness that disabled veterans with training could return to the workplace. World War II set the stage for expanded opportunities for the development of vocational rehabilitation, curative workshops, work evaluation programs, and, more recently, prevocational programs (2).

Work hardening requires the ability to synthesize three major bodies of knowledge. These are (a) knowledge of neuromuscular characteristics of clients, including their limitations in strength, range of motion, and endurance; (b) the knowledge and skill to perform a complex task analysis on the job (for example, analyzing whether the job to be performed by the client is repetitious, bilateral or unilateral, or requires constant or intermittent concentration); and (c) knowledge of the psychosocial aspects of work, including the need for productivity, recognition, self-confidence, and achievement, and in psychopathological work disturbances. Occupational therapists are uniquely qualified to synthesize this knowledge for the design and implementation of work hardening programs.

Screening

Occupational therapists have the responsibility to perform an initial screening to determine appropriateness for assessment.

Screening methods include the following:
- review of pertinent records, which may include educational, legal, employment, medical, and other related records;
- intake interview identifying life-style, work history, and educational background;
- observation of motor, sensorimotor, visual perceptual, interpersonal, and cognitive skills;
- communication of the findings to the appropriate source with recommendations for services and/or referral to other more appropriate programs.

Referral

Typical referral sources for work hardening may include:
- physicians
- attorneys
- rehabilitation personnel
- employers
- educational personnel
- human service agency personnel
- insurance representatives
- self-referrals

Under federal, state, or private workers' compensation systems and/or professional licensing requirements, the following may be required:
- the physician's referral;
- the physician's written consent and statement of medical restrictions;
- the physician's final report with permanent medical contraindications and the extent of disability identified;
- written authorization from the referral source if other than a physician;
- a statement of referral questions to be answered and/or anticipated goals.

Assessment

Components of the occupational therapy work hardening assessment often include the following:
- physical evaluation that is related to work with baseline measurement of the client's current or demonstrated physical abilities including mobility, strength, endurance, sensation, hand function, and gross and fine motor coordination;
- evaluation procedures that include measures of sensorimotor, cognitive, and psychosocial skills with respect to the client's interests, motivation, age, education, culture, and ethnic background;
- evaluation of work behaviors, including the client's response to supervision, attendance, punctuality, initiative, and interpersonal relations, and the ability to follow policies and procedures;
- functional evaluation of the client's body mechanics and ability to work under pressure and over time;
- evaluation of the client's cardiopulmonary responses to work and ability to work under stress, including analysis of the client's knowledge of appropriate body mechanics, work simplification techniques, and methods of symptom control;
- evaluation of the client's knowledge and use of common and specific tools, if required for job performance;
- job analysis, including an on-site evaluation when necessary to develop a step-by-step breakdown of specific job tasks and critical job demands to identify program areas as they relate to the client's condition;
- analysis of the need for modification of the equipment or workplace that would help the client perform with greater efficiency, effectiveness, and safety.

Program Planning

Occupational therapists use the results of the assessment to develop an individualized work hardening program that involves selection of the media, methods, environment, and personnel needed to accomplish goals and objectives that are:

(a) stated in measurable terms appropriate to the client's level of functioning, limitations, referral restrictions, and expected prognosis for program results or competitive employment; and

(b) consistent with current principles, practices, and concepts of occupational therapy considering ethical practices and legal requirements.

The planning process includes collaborating with the client, the referral source, and other related personnel to determine short- and long-term goals that often include:

- establishing an appropriate productivity level for homebound, sheltered, modified, or competitive work;
- increasing physical and psychological tolerances, such as cardiopulmonary endurance and stress tolerance;
- improving functional ability to perform self-care and self-paced work-related tasks;
- facilitating interpersonal communication in employer/employee relations;
- developing work behavior traits and attitudes, such as attention to task, punctuality, response to supervision, and self-confidence;
- minimizing or controlling pain or the effects of pain;
- determining the frequency and duration of work hardening services;
- participating in a case conference to discuss assessment findings, to review goals and objectives, to formulate recommendations, and to coordinate program implementation.

Program Implementation

- Work hardening services are implemented according to the program plan.
- Occupational therapists formulate modifications in the work hardening program when changes occur in the client's performance that are consistent with program goals.
- Occupational therapy personnel document the results of the program and the frequency of the services provided according to regulations and procedures established by facilities, government agencies, and accrediting bodies.
- Case conferences are conducted to report the client's status and change. Written reports are regularly submitted to the referral source and other professionals related to the case.

Discontinuation of Services

- Occupational therapists discontinue services when the client has achieved the goals or has demonstrated an inability to benefit from work hardening services.
- Occupational therapists prepare written reports that include
  - results and an interpretation of standardized and nonstandardized tests administered;
  - statements of program goals and objectives;
  - comparisons between initial assessment and discharge status;
  - recommendations and effect on performance of adaptive devices/modifications;
  - client behaviors and attitudes applicable to the work environment; and
  - recommendations and conclusions.
- Occupational therapy personnel participate in case conferences to outline progress, modifications or adaptations, physical and psychological tolerances, recommendations, and any other information pertinent to the referral source for work-related planning.

Quality Assurance

Occupational therapy personnel conducting work hardening programs shall periodically and systematically review all aspects of individual programs provided and total services offered for effectiveness, efficiency, and quality by using predetermined criteria that reflect professional consensus, research, and theory.

References
1. Holmes D: The role of occupational therapy—Work evaluator. *Am J Occup Ther* 39 (5): 308-312, 1985
2. Matheson LN, Ogden LD, Violette K, Schultz K: Work hardening: Occupational therapy in industrial rehabilitation. *Am J Occup Ther* 39 (5): 314-321, 1985

Bibliography
Marshall EM (guest editor): Work evaluation (special issue). *Am J Occup Ther* 39 (5), 1985

AUTHORS:
   Commission on Practice
   Esther Bell, MA, OTR, FAOTA, Chairperson
   Lana Ford, MS, OTR, Coordinator

CONTRIBUTORS:
   Colorado Network of Occupational Therapy Work Evaluators
   Betty Wild Frazian, MA, OTR
   Kris Violette, OTR
   Susan Smith, MS, OTR/L, FAOTA

Approved by the Representative Assembly 4/86

Appendix C

The Role of Occupational Therapy in the Vocational Rehabilitation Process

The American Occupational Therapy Association (AOTA) submits this paper to reaffirm the profession's continuing commitment to Man in his pursuit of physical, social, vocational, and economic independence. Specifically, this paper identifies the role and responsibilities of occupational therapy to individuals involved in the vocational rehabilitation process. Occupational therapy reached its greatest prominence in vocational rehabilitation following the 1954 amendments to the Vocational Rehabilitation Act. This enabling legislation led to the establishment of pre-vocational units within rehabilitation facilities where occupational therapists assumed a major responsibility in developing the principles of pre-vocational exploration. The role of occupational therapy has been further expanded by the 1978 amendments to the Rehabilitation Act that expanded the rehabilitation services for all ages as well as creating centers that provide independent living services to the handicapped.

Occupational therapy, as a medically oriented rehabilitation profession, has extensive and well-documented experience in developing the components of an effective rehabilitation program. The occupational therapy educational process includes course work and supervised field experiences in such areas as human development; task and activity analyses needed to promote physical and mental restoration; basic work-related skills, including work simplification techniques and activities of daily living and adaptive equipment. With this background, occupational therapists are broadening the scope of knowledge and practice in the rehabilitation process to ensure the successful transition from the evaluatory phase to the work environment for workers and potential workers. Occupational therapy is based upon the fundamental belief that engagement in purposeful activity (occupation), including both the interpersonal and environmental dimensions, may prevent or remediate dysfunction and elicit maximum performance in the work role adaptation.

The principles of occupational therapy practice, as they relate to the vocational process, are applied through the provision of a planned and orderly sequence of services designed to prepare the individual for vocational evaluation, training, and eventual employment or the highest degree of independent function.

Screening

The occupational therapist conducts an initial screening interview to obtain a history of occupational performance related to work, self-maintenance, leisure, and social roles. This preliminary assessment will guide further evaluations needed to determine the nature of the client's functional capacities, performance skills, and future vocational goals.

Evaluation

Evaluative methods are employed to identify the individual's capacities and deficits in the motor, sensory integrative, cognitive, psychological, and social components of performance. The assessment of the client's ability to perform specific tasks, as required in self-maintenance, leisure, and work-related goals, is undertaken. A summary of the client's capacities, goals, and task performance is prepared, and a statement of short- and long-term goals of occupational therapy intervention is recorded.

Treatment

The treatment process involves the use of selected activities, assistive devices, and educational techniques to restore the client to the highest level of independent function. The application of activity to treatment is directed toward improving muscle strength, range of motion, coordination, endurance, and sensory function. Activities are also used to improve working capacity, cognitive functions, social relatedness, personal habits, time management, and role function. The specific aims of the occupational therapy treatment are to assist the individual to recover or to develop competence in the physical, psychological, social, and economic aspects of daily living and to provide opportunities to learn those skills needed for adaptation in educational, work, home, and community environments. Once the restorative phase of treatment has been completed, the need for pre-vocational assessment of clients with residual disabilities is considered. Preparation for the pre-vocational phase of rehabilitation involves a determination of whether the client can return to a previous occupation or whether vocational evaluation and training will be required to achieve gainful employment.

Pre-Vocational Interest Assessment and Counseling

The occupational therapist initiates the pre-vocational process by obtaining and interpreting all vocationally significant data relevant to the client's treatment. The therapist forms an initial impression of the client's readiness and potential for the pre-vocational process and prepares a tentative pre-vocational plan. During this preliminary stage it is the responsibility of the therapist to identify the client's vocational interests and goals, and to obtain appropriate vocational interest tests if they are indicated. Together, the therapist and the client may explore those job opportunities and occupational requirements that best suit the client's interests and capabilities.

Pre-Vocational Evaluation

The goal of pre-vocational evaluation is to assess and predict work behavior and vocational potential through the application of practical, reality-based assessment techniques. The objectives include: testing and evaluating work abilities related to a specific job task; assessing the client's learning abilities and retention of skills; evaluating physical, psychological, and social factors such as work tolerance, habits, and interpersonal qualities. Testing objectives are met through the use of carefully selected media that simulate or closely resemble actual job-related requirements. The therapist, in selecting job-sampling techniques, must ensure that the evaluation program provides a realistic measure of abilities and an accurate prediction of work potential. Before the tests are given, the client receives an orientation to the purpose of the evaluation and to the specific tests being used. Throughout the period of test administration, the therapist adheres to standard evaluation procedures and closely observes, scores, and records the client's performance in each job sample.

A detailed report of evaluation results is prepared and includes the identification of work samples used; a summary of the client's physical and emotional capacity; a statement reflecting the client's interest and aptitude to engage in the jobs related to the work samples used; and a recommendation for further work adjustment services, formal vocational training or termination from the program.

Pre-vocational evaluation is a highly specialized field and those occupational therapists with proper qualifications and preparation may perform test administration.

Work Adjustment Services

Work adjustment services are offered to those clients who have not acquired the work habits and skills needed to function adequately in formal vocational training or actual employment. Work adjustment involves a variety of tasks related to personal, social, daily living requirements, as well as educational preparation and job readiness. Although these tasks are a part of normal development, many clients coming from disadvantaged environments may have experienced delays in skill development and may thus require special remedial services. The occupational therapist provides the client with a series of learning experiences that will enable the client to make appropriate vocational decisions and develop work habits necessary for eventual employment.

Work Activity Services

For many of the more severely or multiply-handicapped clients, competitive employment may be unrealistic or only possible in the distant future. Placement in a work activity program provides these clients with a purposeful and functional vocational or supportive (long-term training) program.

As part of the vocational rehabilitation team, the occupational therapist may develop adaptive or assistive devices, may assist in designing more effective work stations, or provide other services to improve functional performance. The occupational therapist may also serve as a general consultant to other members of the rehabilitation team.

Vocational Evaluation, Training, and Placement

The formal vocational rehabilitation process commences at the termination of the pre-vocational period. The pre-vocational process may be viewed as an intermediary step between the functional assessment of the client's physical and mental capacities and the specific recommendations for further vocational rehabilitation.

The formal vocational rehabilitation period includes additional work evaluations, specific training for employment, the preparation of the client and employer for job placement, and follow-up care.

Following job placement, the occupational therapist may be called upon to perform task analysis, provide work simplification training, or needed assistive devices required for effective job performance.

These services provided by occupational therapists may occur in various settings, including rehabilitation centers, schools, sheltered workshops, work activity centers, community agencies, general hospitals, correctional institutions, and industry. Occupational therapists are sometimes employed by vocational rehabilitation centers; others provide their services on a consultation basis.

It is the responsibility of the occupational therapist to maintain an ongoing relationship with the referral source throughout the pre-vocational period and to provide the referral source with an accurate report of the client's pre-vocational experience and recommendations for continued vocational rehabilitation.

In summary, occupational therapy has had a history of active involvement in the vocational rehabilitation process and will continue to strive to ensure Man's right to a productive and purposeful life.

References

1. Gronofsky J: *A Manual for Occupational Therapists on Pre-Vocational Exploration.* Dubuque, IA: Wm. Brown Book Co., 1959
2. Malikin D, Rusalem H (Editors): *Vocational Rehabilitation of the Disabled.* London: University of London Press, Ltd., 1969
3. Nadolsky JM: Vocational evaluation theory in perspective. *Rehab Lit* 32 (8): August 1971
4. Wegg L: The essentials of work evaluation. *Am J Occup Ther* 14: 65-69, 1960
5. Cromwell F: *The Occupational Therapist's Manual for Basic Skills Assessment—Primary Pre-Vocational Evaluation.* Pasadena, CA: Fair Oaks Printing Co., September 1960
6. Rosenberg B, Wellerson T: A structured pre-vocational program. *Am J Occup Ther* 14: 57-60, 1960
7. Llorens L, Levy R, Rubin E: Work adjustment program. *Am J Occup Ther* 18: 15-18, 1964
8. Overs R: Writing work evaluation reports: Chore or challenge? *Am J Occup Ther* 18: 63-65, 1964
9. Ethridge D: Pre-vocational assessment of rehabilitation potential of psychiatric patients. *Am J Occup Ther* 22: 161-167, 1968
10. Clark B, Lerner G: Occupational therapists participants in pre-vocational screening. *Am J Occup Ther* 20: 91-92, 1966
11. Deacon S, Dunning R, Dease R: A job clinic for psychiatric clinics. *Am J Occup Ther* 28: 3, 1974
12. Solberg NA, Chueh W: Performance in occupational therapy as a predictor of successful pre-vocational training. *Am J Occup Ther* 30 (8): 481, 1976
13. Conine TA, Hopper DL: Work sampling: A tool in management. *Am J Occup Ther* 32 (5): 301-304, 1978

Prepared by an Ad Hoc Committee of the Commission on Practice: Paul Ellsworth, Jane Davy, Maralynne Mitcham, Jeanette Parkin, Stephanie Presseller
October 1979

Adopted by the AOTA Representative Assembly, April, 1980

Appendix D

Occupational Therapy Services in Work Programs

Occupational Therapy uses work-related activities in the evaluation and treatment of persons whose ability to function in a competitive work environment has been impaired by developmental disability, illness or injury. Treatment goals include the promotion of effective work-related behaviors, skills and physical capabilities.

Work-related evaluations use standardized tests, and activities and tasks designed to evaluate specific work-related skills, physical abilities and behaviors. Performance checklists and questionnaires may also be employed.

Examples of evaluations include:
- Physical capacity testing
- Job site evaluation
- Vocational interest and aptitude testing
- Endurance and tolerance testing
- Work tolerance screening
- Work simulation activities
- Range of motion evaluation
- Muscle strength evaluation
- Ergonomic evaluation

Therapeutic activity is then provided to assist the individual in adapting and/or returning to productive work. Services provided by occupational therapists in work programs include:
- Work hardening through job simulation
- Body mechanics and joint protection
- Prevention programming/injury reduction
- Stress management/pain management
- Work readiness
- Vocational exploration
- Ergonomic/biomechanic evaluation to eliminate architectural barriers
- Work site/station and tool modification
- Job acquisition/supported employment
- Education and retraining in home management
- Identification of symptom magnification or malingering
- Retirement planning
- Driver re-training
- Case management
- Expert witness testimony
- Utilization of assistive therapeutic devices

Occupational therapy personnel provide work program services through:
Hospitals
Sheltered workshops
Industry
Schools
Insurance companies
Outpatient rehabilitation facilities
Correctional institutions
Long term care facilities
Community based health care centers
Mental health facilities
Private practice

Payment for occupational therapy services in work programs is available through:
- Worker's Compensation insurance plans
- Self-insured employers
- Individual insurance plans
- State agencies

The Occupational Therapist is a health care professional who has a bachelor's or master's degree in occupational therapy and has completed a clinical internship. The **Occupational Therapy Assistant** has an associate degree in occupational therapy and has also completed a clinical internship.

Occupational therapy personnel use their knowledge of the structure and function of the human body, the effects of illness and injury, and the components of activity to increase the client's involvement in productive activity and safe practices.

Information developed by: Melanie T. Ellexson, Chair; Karen Jacobs; Linda Ogden-Niemeyer; Sallie Taylor; Joane Wyrick
Work Programs Special Interest Section Standing Committee

Appendix E

Occupational Therapy Services in Work Hardening

Work hardening is a structured, productivity oriented program using real or simulated activities as its principal means of treatment.

Who will benefit from work hardening?

Injured workers return more quickly and safely to employment with a clear knowledge of their capabilities for the job.

Employers receive assurance that the employee is physically competent to perform on the job and ready to return to work. The employer will also realize a decrease in lost work days, lost productivity and worker's compensation costs.

Insurance carriers receive rapid case resolution and a decrease in the administrative costs of case management.

Rehabilitation counselors gain a clear picture of the worker's physical capacities which aids in focused program planning and expanded job options.

What are the goals of work hardening?

To insure a smooth, rapid and safe transition into the work force by addressing problems such as low self-esteem, severe deconditioning, disabling pain, fear of injury and symptom magnification.

To develop physical tolerances for work, including flexibility, strength and stamina.

To develop safe worker habits such as correct sitting and standing postures and safe lifting practices.

To develop and reinforce appropriate worker behaviors.

To provide data concerning a worker's physical tolerances which are essential to the vocational planning process.

To provide a testing ground to determine if tool or job site modification will remove barriers to work return.

Who should be referred for work hardening?
- Individuals whose physical tolerances do not allow return to a former position at full work performance.
- Individuals whose physical limitations require modification and/or accommodation to return to the same job class or industry.
- Individuals who seek to re-enter the job market but require assistance in overcoming physical or behavioral barriers.
- Individuals who need to document their physical capabilities to perform specific job demands.

Where is work hardening provided?
- At free standing facilities
- Affiliated with outpatient service departments of rehabilitation centers or hospitals
- As part of a comprehensive rehabilitation facility program
- At work site programs provided by a company to serve the needs of a specific business or industry

Who pays for work hardening?
- Worker's Compensation insurance plans
- Self-insured employers

From Public Affairs Division, American Occupational Therapy Association, Rockville, MD.

- Individual insurance plans
- State agencies

What specialized education and experience do occupational therapy practitioners bring to work hardening?

Occupational therapists hold bachelor's or master's degrees, and occupational therapy assistants, associate degrees. Occupational therapy education includes the study of human growth and development with specific emphasis on the social, emotional and physiological implications of illness and injury.

Occupational therapy personnel are also skilled in **developing and guiding a job-specific program of graded activity for the worker, job task analysis, job station and tool modification, and identifying and remediating behaviors inappropriate to the work environment.**

Occupational therapy practitioners must complete supervised clinical internships in a variety of health care settings and are required to pass a national certification examination. Many states require licenses of occupational therapy practitioners.

Information developed by: Melanie T. Ellexson, Chair; Karen Jacobs; Linda Ogden-Niemeyer; Sallie Taylor; Joane Wyrick
AOTA Work Programs Special Interest Section

Appendix F
Significant Legislation Related to Work

Year   **Description of Legislation**

1916   National Defense Act
Improved military efficiency and enabled soldiers to become more competitive in civilian life. The focus was educational, but no agency was established to carry out the directives.

1917   PL 64-347: Smith-Hughes Act (Vocational Education Act)
Created the Federal Board for Vocational Education (FBVE).

1918   PL 65-178: Smith-Sears Act (Soldiers Rehabilitation Act)
Enlarged the role of FBVE to provide programs for disabled veterans who were unable to succeed at gainful employment.

1920   PL 66-236: Smith-Fess Act (Civilian Rehabilitation Act)
Initiated rehabilitation for the general public. Provided funds for vocational guidance and training, occupational adjustment, prostheses, and placement services. Occupational therapy was reimbursed if it was part of medical treatment. No reimbursement was included for psychiatrically or developmentally disabled people.

1921   PL 67-47: Veterans Bureau Act
Established the Veterans Bureau as an independent agency with a director responsible to the President.

1933   PL 73-2: Veterans Administration Act
Recognized the Veterans Bureau and designated this federal agency as the Veterans Administration.

1935   PL 74-271: Social Security Act
Established unemployment compensation, old-age insurance, child health and welfare services, crippled children services, and public assistance for the aged, the blind, and dependent children.

1943   PL 78-16: Welsh-Clark Act (World War II Disabled Veterans Rehabilitation Act)
Provided vocational rehabilitation for disabled veterans of World War II.

1943   PL 78-113: Barden-LaFollette Act (Vocational Rehabilitation Act)
Changed the original provisions of PL 66-236. Added physically disabled, blind, developmentally delayed, and psychiatrically disabled to those served. Established the Office of Vocational Rehabilitation (OVR). Put a new emphasis on activities of daily living (ADL) and adaptation. Removed ceiling on appropriation.

1944   PL 78-346: Servicemen's Readjustment Act (GI Bill)
Provided for the education and training (tuition and subsistence) of individuals whose education or career had been interrupted by military service.

1945   PL 79-176: Joint Congressional Resolution for a National Employ the Physically Handicapped (NEPH) Week
Established an annually observed NEPH week. In 1954, Truman changed it to President's Committee on Employment of the Physically Handicapped; in 1962, Kennedy changed it to President's Committee on Employment of the Handicapped.

1954   PL 83-565: Hill-Burton Act (Vocational Rehabilitation Act Amendments)
Authorized greater financial support, research and demonstration grants, professional preparation grants, state agency expansion and improvement grants, and grants to expand rehabilitation facilities. Many occupational therapists received this money for training and education.

Information on 1916–1986 legislation adapted from "Work Assessments and Programming" by K. Jacobs, 1988, in H. L. Hopkins and H. D. Smith (Eds.), *Willard and Spackman's Occupational Therapy* (7th ed.)(pp. 273-274), Philadelphia: J. B. Lippincott. © 1988 by J. B. Lippincott Company. Reprinted by permission. Information on 1986-1988 legislation from *Summary of Existing Legislation Affecting Persons With Disabilities* (Publication No. E88-22014) by Office of Special Education and Rehabilitative Services, Clearinghouse on the Handicapped, 1988, August, Washington, DC: Author.

Year	Description of Legislation
1965	**Vocational Rehabilitation Act Amendments of 1965** Increased services for several types of disabled and socially handicapped people. Made construction money available for rehabilitation centers and workshops.
1968	**PL 90-480: Architectural Barriers Act** Led the way to changes in access for disabled people.
1970	**PL 91-517: Developmental Disabilities Services and Facilities Construction Act** Gave states broad responsibility for planning and implementing a comprehensive program of services to developmentally delayed, epileptic, cerebral palsied, and other neurologically impaired individuals.
1973	**PL 93-112: Rehabilitation Act** Expanded services to the more severely disabled. Provided for affirmative action in employment (Section 503) and nondiscrimination in facilities (Section 504) by federal contractors and grantees.
1975	**PL 94-142: Education For All Handicapped Children Act** Provided educational assistance to all handicapped children in the "least restrictive environment." Occupational therapists were included as "related personnel."
1978	**PL 95-602: Amendments to the Rehabilitation Act of 1973** Expanded rehabilitation to include independent living. Established the National Institute of Handicapped Research. Provided employer incentives for training and hiring disabled individuals.
1983	**PL 98-199: Education of the Handicapped Act Amendments of 1983** Established a better transition from school to work.
1984	**PL 98-210: Carl D. Perkins Vocational Act** Authorized federal grants to states to assist them in (1) extending, improving, and maintaining existing programs of vocational education; (2) developing new programs; (3) providing part-time employment for youths who need earnings to continue their vocational training on a full-time basis; and (4) assisting persons of all ages (secondary, postsecondary, and adult levels) in entering the labor market, upgrading their skills, or learning new ones. Provided funding for the following grant programs: Adult Training and Retraining, Career Guidance and Counseling, High Technology Training, Title II Basic Grants, Consumer and Homemaking Education, and Community-Based Organizations (CBO) programs.
1986	**PL 99-357: Carl D. Perkins Vocational Education Act Amendment** Rectified a problem with state allocation of funds, particularly for the Consumer and Homemaking Education program.
1986	**PL 99-457: Education of the Handicapped Act Amendments** Provided a significant increase in federal funds to encourage states to provide special education and related services to preschoolers ages 3 through 5 years. Specified that federal funds for this age group would be terminated if this were not initiated by school year 1990–91. Included a mandate for a new comprehensive, interagency program to provide early intervention to infants and toddlers with handicaps, ages birth through 2 years.
1986	**PL 99-506: Rehabilitation Act Amendments of 1986** Clarified that in evaluating rehabilitation potential, one must consider recreation, employability, and rehabilitation engineering needs. Clarified *employability* to include part-time work as a viable outcome of rehabilitation services. Defined *rehabilitation engineering* as a systematic application of technologies to help people with disabilities overcome barriers in education, rehabilitation, employment, and independent living. Also, further defined *supported employment* as "competitive employment" in an "integrated setting" that includes ongoing support services and transitional employment for the chronically mentally

Year	Description of Legislation

ill (see Chapter 6 on supported employment). Authorized a grant program for special projects and demonstrations in supported employment.

1986 PL 99-371: Education of the Deaf Act of 1986

In Title II, extended statutory authority of the National Technical Institute of the Deaf to provide technical training and education to prepare deaf people for employment.

1986 PL 99-496: Job Training Partnership Act

Amended the 1982 legislation (PL 97-300) to include special consideration for people with handicaps in the awarding of discretionary grants. Funds have been used since 1982 to place people with mild and moderate handicaps in community jobs.

1987 PL 100-203: Omnibus Budget Reconciliation Act of 1987

Permitted states to offer prevocational, educational, and supported employment services to people deinstitutionalized at any time before the waiver program.

1987 PL 100-146: Amendments to the Developmental Disabilities Assistance and Bill of Rights Act

Reauthorized the programs in this act with one additional area, family support service. The purpose of the act is to assist people with developmental disabilities to achieve their maximum potential through increased independence, productivity, and integration into the community. (Definitions of *employment-related activities* and *supported employment* were in the 1984 Amendments, PL 98-527.)

1988 PL 100-407: Technology-Related Assistance for Individuals with Disabilities Act of 1988

Authorized funds to assist states in developing technology-related assistance programs for individuals of all ages with disabilities. Insofar as it assists in employability, technology can be a part of the grant applications by the states.